P9-EDZ-913

COLONIALISM ON TRIAL

Indigenous Land Rights and the Gitksan and Wet'suwet'en Sovereignty Case

Don Monet

and

Skanu'u (Ardythe Wilson)

NEW SOCIETY PUBLISHERS
Philadelphia, PA   Gabriola Island, BC

Canadian Cataloguing in Publication Data

Monet, Don.
    Colonialism On Trial

    ISBN 1-55092-160-6 (bound). - - ISBN 1-55092-161-4 (pbk.)

    1. Gitksan Indians—Land tenure. 2. Wet'suwet'en Indians—Land tenure.* 3. Indians of North America—
British Columbia—Land tenure. 4. Gitksan Indians—Claims. 5. Wet'suwet'en Indians—Claims.*
    I. Skanu'u.   II. Title.
    KEB529.5.L3M65 1991   346.71104'32'089972   C91-091830-9

Copyright © 1992:   text—Skanu'u and the Gitksan & Wet'suwet'en people;
                     artwork—Donald Harrington Monet (Niis Biins).
All rights reserved.

**Fifty percent of the royalties made on this book will be directed into a Trust Fund for the
Office of the Hereditary Chiefs, to contribute toward the costs of the Appeal.**

Inquiries regarding requests to reprint all or part of *Colonialism On Trial* should be addressed to:
  New Society Publishers,
  4527 Springfield Avenue, Philadelphia PA, USA 19143
or
  P.O. Box 189, Gabriola Island BC, Canada V0R 1X0.

U.S.A.: ISBN 0-86571-218-2 Hardback
U.S.A.: ISBN 0-86571-219-0 Paperback
Canada: ISBN 1-55092-160-6 Hardback
Canada: ISBN 1-55092-161-4 Paperback

Cover graphic by Art Wilson; cover design by Barbara Hirshkowitz and Martin Kelley.

Book design by Don Monet; typesetting by New Society Publishers, Canada.

Printed in the United States of America on partially recycled paper by
Capital City Press, Montpelier, Vermont.

To order directly from the publishers, add $2.00 to the price for the first copy, 75 cents each additional.
Send check or money order to:
  New Society Publishers,
  4527, Springfield Avenue, Philadelphia PA, USA 95061
or
  P.O. Box 189, Gabriola Island BC, Canada V0R 1X0.

New Society Publishers is a project of the New Society Educational Foundation, a non-profit, tax-exempt
public foundation in the U.S.A., and of the Catalyst Education Society, a non-profit society in Canada.
Opinions expressed in this book do not necessarily represent positions of the New Society Educational
Foundation, nor the Catalyst Education Society.

Table of Contents

AUGUSTANA UNIVERSITY COLLEGE
LIBRARY

Acknowledgments

Many people—both Native and non-Native—have helped me shape this book. For their generosity, wisdom and support, I am grateful. They include: Gaxsgabaxs (Gertie Watson), and Gwaans (Olive Ryan), for their warm encouragement, sound advice and many ideas for illustrations; Yaga'lahl (Dora Wilson) and Gisdaywa (Alfred Joseph) for their support, Michael Jackson for his introduction, and Maas Gaak (Don Ryan), for his epilogue and support; and, especially, Skanu'u (Ardythe Wilson).

Thanks go to the people at the Office of the Chiefs, who were always ready to rib me, and go out of their way to help: Vicki Russell, Marvin George, Herb George, Gene Joseph, Lorna Simms, Veronica Greene, and Linda Mathews. I thank Elaine Green, Geneva Hagen, Sue Kay; Lynda O'Hara for her friendship and humor; Paula Pryce, Geoff Watling, Caril Chasens, Art Wilson, and Luu Goomxw (Eric Macpherson). I thank 'Maat (Bev) and Ian Anderson, my neighbors, advisors and friends, who provided me with water, fish and moose meat, through the worst part of the process. I thank the Canada Council Explorations Program, for a seven month stipend during part of the three year process; and Richard Daly, Sheila Ryan, Alfy Bolster, Suzanne Roy, Zoe Lambert, Charlie and Margaret Austin, Brad Reddekopp, Alexandria Patience, Leslie Cerny, Danny and Homer Muldoe, Rosalie Tizya, Bev Clifton, Andy Clifton, Art Wilson, Kay and J.P. Monette, Peter Monet, and Ron George. I thank the many Chiefs and their families who accepted me as part of this process, especially Gwaans, Elijah and Hanamuxw for honoring me with a place at their table.

Thank you all.

—Don Monet

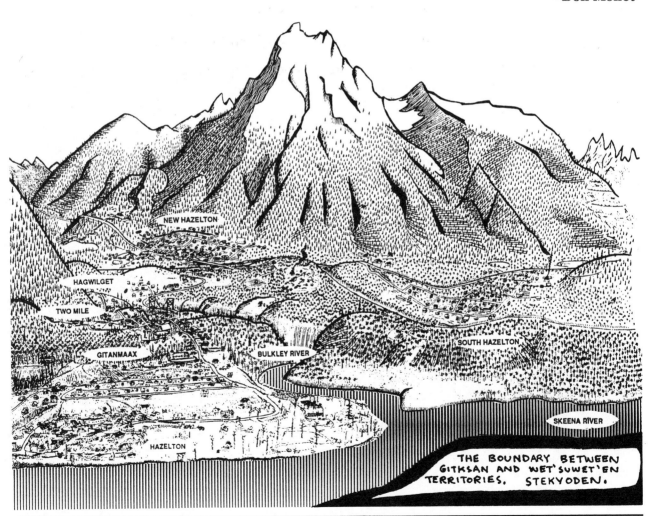

Preface

Don Monet

This project has been a great challenge for me; my first attempt at serious portraits—all the more difficult as I meet people daily who know my subjects intimately.

I had never intended to become a portrait artist but, since they don't allow cameras in court, my drawings became the only visual record of the three and a half years of the daily courtroom drama. This was a sensitive role to play.

The first witness—Gyolugyet (Mary McKenzie)—took me aside at a convention in Gitanmaax and said, "I'm glad you told me beforehand that you can't draw very well, or I might have been insulted.... I just tell people that I was born ugly!"

Antgulilbix (Mary Johnson), thought she'd get a hair-do, because she said she knew "that guy" would be drawing her! "Maybe he won't make *me* look ugly, too," she hoped. But afterwards she concluded, "It didn't work!" Then she added, "But you are getting better; we are all starting new adventures, all trying new things and learning, too."

During the time of the trial, I became somewhat educated, not only in portraiture, but in law, culture, politics and, of course, legal theatrics. I kept a sketchbook and, in the end, filled ten of them. I used pen and ink, some half-tones, and experimented a lot with the photocopy machine. Since I chose to sit in the gallery with other observers, rather than in the main courtroom with the press, close to the witnesses and lawyers, I missed the little asides and antics the lawyers engaged in—gladly—and, rather, got to pass cartoons around, and get the feedback of the community. I ate lunch daily at the office the Chiefs set up next to court, and it was on their wall that I taped the photostats of my daily work. The people began to recognize and critique my work.

I freely admit that I am not an unbiased, dispassionate reporter. Quite the opposite—I am an engaged, political cartoonist, supporting the cause of justice for the Gitksan and Wet'suwet'en people. As the judge for this trial, Allan McEachern, told lawyer, Louise Mandell, "He's not a bad cartoonist, but I perceive a certain bias toward the plaintiffs...."

But my individual politics is just a sidenote. This book is about the Gitksan and Wet'suwet'en people's search for justice. Against the wholesale attacks on their culture and resources, their laws, their languages, and their children, their communities are impoverished, but their spirit remains strong. Contrary to what the dominant society would like to believe, the First Nations peoples are not a "dying race." They are here. And they will continue.

Since much of this book is written through the eyes of a cartoonist, the reader will glimpse a tiny bit of each piece of evidence—enough to get a sense, a flavor, of each part of the trial. I thought, as I pored over the 369 days of transcript at the library of the Chiefs in Hazelton—a veritable "paper giant"—about the even larger "giant," the *real* civilization behind this un-reasonable facsimile brought to court. The people went to a foreign court and showed the judge and the world bits and pieces of their ancient histories, each one of which would in reality take years to learn. This is part of the context.

If it were the job of this book to introduce you to the complexity of a brave but economically poor nation fighting for truth and justice, then it must fail. For, to be properly introduced, you must come here to visit; and, to be truly introduced, you must stay. Look at this work rather as a grab-bag, a cross section, of information about an historical trial for justice, an evidentiary collection of facts and faces and words from one of the most important land title actions of the century.

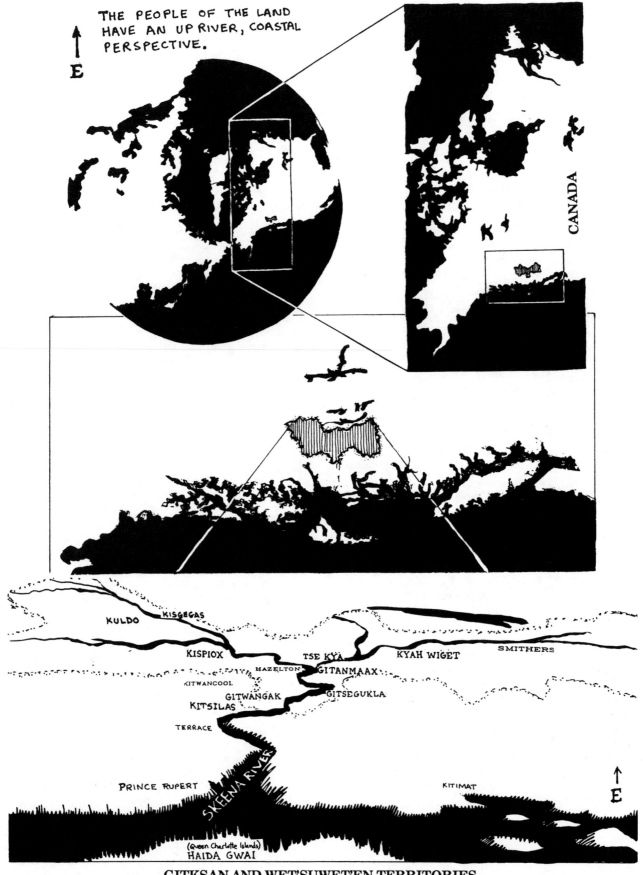

THE PEOPLE OF THE LAND HAVE AN UP RIVER, COASTAL PERSPECTIVE.

E

CANADA

KULDO
KISGEGAS
KISPIOX
TSE KYA
KYAH WIGET
SMITHERS
HAZELTON
GITANMAAX
KITWANCOOL
GITWANGAK
GITSEGUKLA
KITSILAS
TERRACE
PRINCE RUPERT
SKEENA RIVER
KITIMAT
E

(Queen Charlotte Islands)
HAIDA GWAI

GITKSAN AND WET'SUWET'EN TERRITORIES

Preface

Skanu'u (Ardythe Wilson)

At the time the court case began, I was working for Northern Native Broadcasting, and I had done some coverage of the court case. I had seen some drawings by a cartoonist, Don Monet, who was fairly new to the area. He was still very raw at that time, but his heart was in the right place. He saw that there was a great deal of injustice taking place, so he started educating himself about what was going on.

People would notice his cartoons, and they'd say, well, this isn't quite right, or they would start adding to them, and making suggestions and comments. Sometimes, it was so terrible in the court and, in the darkest times, the humor of a people always emerges, so it was a way to release the tension. The government lawyers would treat our Chiefs and Elders with a great deal of disrespect. They would offend and anger our people in the gallery, although our Chiefs and Elders didn't react. They were so well-contained and disciplined because they understood so well what they had to do and why they were doing it. Don would get very angry, and he would depict our anger in a cartoon, and we would get some kind of release—even though the situation was horrendous, we could still laugh at it. It was wonderful how that happened. Don's small notebooks became stuffed with the wonderful ideas coming out from the people in the galleries.

Our life was not "nasty, brutish and short," as Judge McEachern suggested it was; nor was it the idyllic life that some people tend to romanticise it as. At the time of European contact we had a very complex, structured, organized society. We had laws that governed our lives, based not on enforcement, but on consensus and social understanding and the desire for credibility in the eyes of our community. We clearly understood how our survival depended on the maintenance of our territories and organization of our people.

When the traders came into our territory, they understood that they had to deal with us on our terms if they wanted to carry on their business. They knew that there were key people in our community whom they had to approach, and they had to respect our ways. The changes came fast and furious when the European settlers came and actually built their homesteads in our valleys. The two conflicting systems collided, and that's when the problems began. At that earliest time, a record of our resistance to the arbitrary stealing of our land started. Over the decades, there have always been certain people who led the resistance in a number of different ways and on a number of different fronts. By the 1920s, we had people who had become well acquainted with the system we had to fight.

In 1977, the federal government accepted our comprehensive claim, as they termed it, for negotiation. However, the federal government refused to negotiate without the provincial government, and the provincial government refused to recognize the existence of aboriginal title and rights. In the meantime, the tremendous clearcutting and other logging practices of the province and the companies were being accelerated, and a lot of destruction was taking place. So the Chiefs decided to force the province to the table with us. That's why we took this case to court.

There was great reluctance when we saw the history of the courts in our territories—we were always on the losing end. But in considering this situation, the Chiefs said, what other choice do we have? Even though they realized that this was a course of action that had to be taken, there was great uncertainty. We knew that in order for the courts to understand what it was we were talking about, it was necesary for us to show them our histories, our laws, our practices, our customs, our obligations, our responsibilities. And in order for that to happen, we had to open up our Houses and our families to people who had no understanding or respect for who we are. I think what we dreaded most was exactly what McEachern did.

I've heard a lot of older people say, "No more! We're closing up our treasure boxes of histories, and that's that." We will no longer bare ourselves to people such as we did in the court case. We've given them an opportunity to take an honest look at who we are, and what has taken place in our histories before European contact, and they have despoiled it. Then, in the same breath, they say, "We have come this far, we have sacrificed much, and we have to continue the fight." Our people are very resilient. Once they had gotten over the shock and anger and the pain that McEachern's decision caused, what he did and said about our people, there was a lot more commitment and dedication to seeing this thing through—that it won't be for naught.

One day, we saw all those lawyers swaggering around in the courtroom, and one of the older ladies said, "Don't they just look like a bunch of crows flocking around a piece of carrion?" And

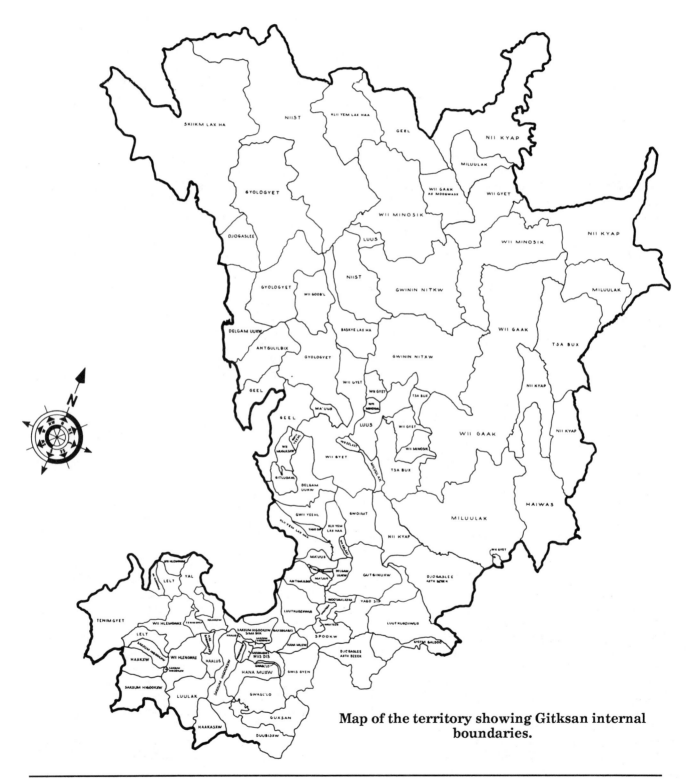

Map of the territory showing Gitksan internal boundaries.

everybody got a good chuckle. Later, one of those ladies said something about Wyget being at work. Now, Wyget is a trickster figure whose stories are used to teach lessons to children; if they don't do things the way they're expected to, then certain consequences will befall them. Don made the connection between the lawyers' appearing like crows and "Wyget's" mischief-making in the courtroom. And every time something went wrong, we'd say, "Well, Wyget's at his tricks again...."

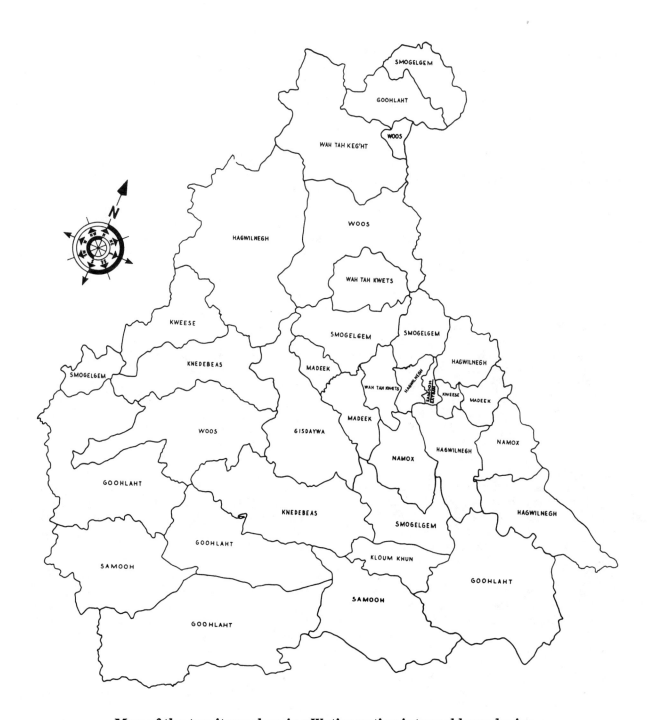

Map of the territory showing Wet'suwet'en internal boundaries.

A Legal Overview

The Case In Context

For many people in North America, the phenomenon of indigenous peoples going to the court to assert their legal rights to their traditional homelands seems a recent one, part of what has been referred to as the "judicialization of society." In actual fact, indigenous rights litigation has been part of the legal landscape of the United States, Canada and other Commonwealth jurisdictions for almost three centuries.

While indigenous rights litigation has a long history, the case brought by the Gitksan and Wet'suwet'en has a number of distinctive features. In the first place, the Gitksan and Wet'suwet'en, in characterizing their case as "a search for the legal pathways to justice," were convinced that for a foreign court to embrace the full dimension of their legal rights it was necessary for a western-trained legal mind to understand and respect their world view. This world view included the oral record of their history; the nature of their kinship society in which reciprocity rather than profit underlay the social and economic fabric; their relationship to their territory which encompassed the responsibilities of stewardship; and the framework of their laws and institutions which maintained peace without courts, police officers and prisons.

In previous cases, this world view had been filtered through the eyes of anthropologists and other non-Native "experts." The Gitksan and Wet'suwet'en in this case also retained anthropologists to conduct research and to give evidence before the court, but that evidence was supplementary to the primary evidence of the people themselves. Thus, in this case, many of the hereditary chiefs of the Gitksan and Wet'suwet'en testified in their own language, providing a Canadian court with a firsthand sense of the cultural and spiritual distinctiveness of what it is to be Gitksan and Wet'suwet'en.

Many of Don Monet's cartoons portray the hereditary Chiefs who testified and reflect the distinctive contribution each one of them has made. Other cartoons have vividly captured important moments in the trial; for example, a legal argument regarding the admissibility, as an exception to the hearsay rule, of ancient songs and events charged with spiritual significance as evidence of the "facts of history." Still others provide visual reference points for the difference between Gitksan and Wet'suwet'en concepts of law remembered and validated in the Indian way and those remembered and validated in the "pen and ink work" of the western tradition.

It is not, however, only the nature and scope of the Indian evidence which makes the Gitksan and Wet'suwet'en trial unique. The legal argument presented to the court was also the most extensive ever mounted in an indigenous rights case. In a search for first principles governing the legal relationship between the First Nations of North America and the European colonizing nations, the Gitksan and Wet'suwet'en lawyers went back to the pivotal events in the late 15th century in the establishment of the Spanish colonial empire in the Americas. The legal argument traced how the barbarity of the Spanish regime led to a remarkable legal debate before the Court of Spain at Valladolid in 1550 in which jurists debated the legality and justice of waging war on the Indians. This debate is raised whenever the issue of indigenous rights and the interests of European colonial governments are joined. For the Spanish jurist, Juan Supulveda, the argument against recognizing the rights of indigenous peoples was based on their alleged inferiority compared to European civilizations. The defamation of the cultures and societies of First Nations was reflected in the denial of their rights to their territories. On the other hand, people like Bartolome de la Casas who asserted that the Indians did have rights to their territories, this proposition was supported by a conception of indigenous peoples as having their own distinct cultures and societies which, while different, were the equals and contemporaries of European civilizations.

This debate in Spain was related to a central part of the Gitksan and Wet'suwet'en legal argument; a failure to understand the nature of first Nations societies and to treat them with respect, inevitably and inexorably led, not only before the Court of Spain but also in court cases in the United States, in Canada, in Australia and New Zealand, to a denial of their legal rights.

In the search for first principles, the Gitksan and Wet'suwet'en provided the court with a review of the history of treaty-making between the First Nations peoples and the Dutch, French, and English. The court was provided with details of treaties made in the Puritan colonies of New England and in Quaker Pennsylvania which recognized Indian nations as the original proprietors of the soil and acknowledged their rights to self-government. The court was exposed to the historical evidence of the manner in which the Six Nations of the Iroquois Confederacy constructed their famous Covenant Chain which linked them to their Indian allies and to the British over a period of 150 years. This treaty-making was characterized by one of mutual respect in which the British came to learn the diplomatic language of the Iroquois and the distinctive metaphorical imagery which characterized Covenant Chain diplomacy. The central features of North American Indian policy, later reflected in the famous Royal Proclamation of 1763, which sought to provide a guarantee of Indian rights, was in fact the outcome of a long history of treaty-making designed to ensure the accommodation of European and Indian interests.

Other evidence was also introduced to illustrate how at the other end of the colonial world, in New Zealand, the British and the Maori, in the Treaty of Waitangi in 1840, sought to arrive at an accommodation which also reflected a recognition of the pre-existing rights of the Maori to govern themselves and to maintain their traditional lands within a framework which permitted European settlement.

The legal argument also showed how, while the North American courts initially developed a legal code which acknowledged the rights of indigenous peoples, later in the 19th century, those rights were reinterpreted, sometimes out of existence, as colonial governments developed policies to assimilate Native peoples. In Canada, this policy criminalized some of the most important Indian political institutions and ceremonies and, in 1927, prohibited raising monies to pursue Indian land claims.

The Gitksan and Wet'suwet'en lawyers showed how legal decisions of the 19th century and early twentieth century in both Canada and the U.S. were heavily influenced by assumptions about First Nations peoples which originated in the Court of Spain. It was argued, in the words of the former Chief Justice of Canada, that these assumptions reflected the biases of another era and ought not to be endorsed by contemporary Canadian courts in the adjudication of indigenous rights.

The Gitksan and Wet'suwet'en argued that justice for First Nations peoples both required and permitted, based upon common law principles, a recognition of their proprietary relationship to their territory (their ownership) and their continuing right to govern themselves within that territory (their jurisdiction).

In the course of this legal review of the historical relationship between indigenous peoples and European governments, the Gitksan and Wet'suwet'en pointed to some of the great struggles of the past. In particular, they asked the court to regard the fate of the Cherokee Nation in the 19th century who, notwithstanding the vindication of their rights by the U.S. Supreme Court in the landmark case of Worcester vs. Georgia (1832), were subsequently force-marched from their homelands east of the Mississippi to Oklahoma in the infamous Trail of Tears in which some 4,000 perished. The Gitksan and Wet'suwet'en pointed to their own dispossession and urged the court to protect against further dispossession through clearcut logging by acknowledging their rights to their homelands within the four corners of the common law and the Canadian Constitution.

Viewed against this background, the judgment of Chief Justice McEachern in March of 1991 was a bitter disappointment. The judgment fails to see the Gitksan and Wet'suwet'en as equals and contemporaries. It is no surprise, then, that the judgment fails to recognize that they have any continuing indigenous rights to their homeland, those rights having been legally extinguished by the acts of colonial governments in the 19th century in enacting land legislation and opening up the territory for settlement. In this way the economic imperatives of European colonization give rise to legal imperatives in which Indian rights are extinguished without Indian consent and without compensation. Whereas the Gitksan and Wet'suwet'en sought to place their court case in the larger context of history, the judgment of the Chief Justice dissociates itself from that history, asserting that events and treaties made elsewhere with other First Nations peoples bear no relationship to what happened "on the ground" in British Columbia.

Because so much of the Gitksan and Wet'suwet'en's evidence and legal argument is not even mentioned in Chief Justice McEachern's judgment, it is difficult to get a measure of what was placed before the court simply by reading the judgment. Don Monet's remarkable collection of illustrations bears testament to evidence and arguments which find no official reflection in the judgment in *Delgamuukw vs. Her Majesty the Queen.*

—**Michael Jackson**

Delgam Uukw (Albert Tait)

Photo: by Stephen Bosch

The Legal Process

In Canadian Commonwealth law, there is a choice of either one judge or six jurists for an action of this type. The Chiefs decided to forego the jury trial considering its expense and complexity. The plaintiffs present an opening statement, the defendants a statement of defence. The trial begins with the presentation of a witness, and a series of questions about the witness' "qualifications." The plaintiffs then ask questions of the witness, if accepted, called "Evidence in Chief or Direct." In turn, the defendant asks questions called "Cross Examination." The last word comes from questions by the plaintiffs called "Re-Direct," following which we move on to the next witnesses.

At many times during the trial, the "Evidence in Chief" is interrupted by "Submissions and Proce-dures"—submissions being given by the lawyers on questions of *argument, legal precedence* or special requests about *procedure*. Finally, the trial moves to the legal "Argument" stage where the lawyers summarize the basis of the evidence they have submitted. Each then gives a "Closing Statement," and the judge decides, giving his "Reasons for Judgment." This book is a chronology of those events.

The next stage is for one or both of the parties to bring the decision to Appeal Court of the Province where three judges listen to argument, with no new witnesses or evidence, and reconsider the decision. After this, the case can be brought to the highest court in Canada, the Supreme Court, and then the World Court.

—Don Monet

Introduction

The Best Of All Titles

We would liken this district to an animal, and our village, which is situated in it, to its heart. Lorne Creek, which is almost at one end of it, may be likened to one of the animal's feet.

We feel that the whitemen, by occupying this creek, are, as it were, cutting off a foot. We know that an animal may live without one foot, or even without both feet; but we also know that every such loss renders him more helpless, and we have no wish to remain inactive until we are almost or quite helpless.

We have carefully abstained from molesting the whiteman during the past summer. We felt that, though we were being wronged and robbed, as we had not given you the time nor opportunity to help us, it would not be right for us to take the matter into our own hands. Now we bring the matter before you, and respectfully call upon you to prevent the inroads of any whiteman upon the land within the fore-named district.

In making this claim, we would appeal to your sense of justice and right. We would remind you that is the duty of the Government to uphold the just claims of all peaceable and law-abiding persons such as we have proved ourselves to be. We hold these lands by the best of all titles. We have received them as the gift of the Creator to our Grandmothers and Grandfathers, and we believe that we cannot be deprived of them by anything short of direct injustice.

In conclusion, we would ask you, would it be right for our Chiefs to give licenses to members of the tribe to go to the district of Victoria to measure out, occupy, and build upon lands in that district now held by whitemen as grazing or pasture land? Would the whitemen now in possession permit it, even if we told them that, as we were going to make a more profitable use of the land, they had no right to interfere? Would the Government permit it? Would they not at once interfere and drive us out? If it would not be right for us so to act, how can it be right for the whiteman to act so to us?

—Gitwangak Chiefs, 1884

Indians meet Colonel Henry Bouquet in 1754, nine years before the Royal Proclamation which established the principle of indigenous rights now contained in Canadian law.

Courtesy: Public Archives, Canada.

Chapter 1

Invisible People?
The Hidden History Of Canada

Written accounts of exploration and colonization by white people are almost always scattered with phrases "vast and empty wilderness," "untouched," or "no sign of human existence."

In their hunger to claim "new found land" for their country and trading house, they easily dismiss the notion that "humans" have walked and lived on the very ground upon which they now stand. Coming face-to-face with the original inhabitants of the land blows their "vast and empty wilderness" myth to bits, but the firm belief of their superiority dictates that these peoples were merely "savages," "heathens" or "uncivilized facsimiles of modern man" who wandered aimlessly about the country.

Therefore, wasn't it their duty, as modern men with advanced technology, to pluck these heathens out of their primitive state and set them sternly on the road to civilization? Was it not most practical to herd them together and limit their movement to ensure their speedy civilization? It was incomprehensible that the "uncivilized savages" would have any notion of land ownership and social systems to govern that ownership. This tendency of the European explorers, colonists and settlers to view First Nations peoples at the lower end of their evolutionary ladder made it easy for them to dismiss us as being of little consequence to the greater victory of opening new frontiers for settlement. The indigenous peoples of what is now known as Canada were well on the way to becoming invisible to European eyes.

For the first 400 years of European invasion from the eastern shores of North America, the Gitksan and We'suwet'en lived within their own system and territories. We were secure in the knowledge of our origins; secure in the knowledge of our matrilineal descendency; and we were secure in the knowledge of our systems and laws. We had as yet to be subjected to the jaundiced eye of the European.

Long before Columbus stepped ashore on the soils of North America, my ancestors were recounting the history of my House dating back to the last Ice Age and beyond. These histories are still being recounted, becoming lengthier with each new generation. A mere six generations ago, the first white man stumbled into our territories. Little did our ancestors know, while healing, feeding and clothing that poor, starving and diseased man with the white skin, that many more would follow to repeat the injustices spreading across the land.

The history books of Canada, especially those used to educate young minds, made little or no reference to the realities of its interaction with the First Nations. One vivid memory I carry to this day is a depiction of an Iroquois "Chief," an ally of the British in their war against the French, who was described as "a splendid savage who ripped the heart out of his enemy and gobbled it up as blood streamed down his naked chest." I remember clearly the sidelong glances I received from my classmates in a senior secondary school in British Columbia's Lower Mainland where I was only one of a few Native students in a school population of over 1,300. I knew, then, that their vision of me was colored by that stark misrepresentation and romantic image of what it was to be "Indian."

Coloring and elaborating this view which perpetuates the attitude of racial, cultural and technological superiority has been the single most successful strategy of colonialists throughout the world. Stream the thinking of the public to coincide with the manipulations of the rulers, and anything is possible. How easy it is to compartmentalize the original inhabitants of this country as just one of many "ethnic groups" or "visible minorities." How easy to gain understanding of the "problem " by grouping all the First Nations under one general and mistaken heading—"Indians." And now, as we march steadily into the 21st century, we have mastered the systems and technology of the European to address the injustices. We are no longer "invisible." We are now "militant and radical."

A true understanding of an issue requires a

person to be fully cognizant of the facts, context and history of that issue. Half-truths, omissions and misrepresentations do not make a true picture. Just as there is a written history for the Europeans, so there is an oral history for indigenous societies the world over. A meshing of the two will provide an immediate and accurate reality.

This chapter of our history shows both the written milestones of colonialism and its impacts as it winds its way sinuously toward the Gitksan and Wet'suwet'en, and the oral chronology of our people which parallels the movement of the Europeans. It is by no means exhaustive, but provides perhaps the basis for an introductory understanding of the major developments in Gitksan and Wet'suwet'en territories, and in the course of doing so, enriches the history of North America.

—Skanu'u, (Ardythe Wilson)
House of Gutginuxs

**Hanamuux, Fireweed Clan, Gitseguecla.
From a painting by W. Langdon Kihn,
1924.**
Photo courtesy of National Museums of Canada.

**Chief Medeek, Wolf Clan, Moricetown.
From a painting by W. Langdon Kihn,
1924.**
Photo courtesy of National Museums of Canada.

8000 B.C.: The little ice-age in Gitksan and Wet'suwet'en territories; many of the people retreat to refugeos in non-glaciated valleys.

1000 B.C.: Norse community in L'Anseaux Meadows, Newfoundland.

1200: The English aristocracy begins to divide and fence the common lands in England, Scotland and Ireland. The practice of colonialism begins upon the Irish and Scottish Clans.

1492: Christopher Columbus is discovered by America.

1498: England's John Cabot travels the coast of Labrador and Nova Scotia. Names New Found Isle, later known as Newfoundland.

1534: Jacques Cartier enters the Gulf of the St. Lawrence river. Their ship is frozen in the ice and the Iroquois, taking pity on the scurvy-ridden crew, feed them spruce, high in vitamin C, saving their lives. They will return.

1613: The Beothuck people in Nova Scotia cover themselves in red ochre, thereby becoming known as "red Indians." From 1613, French and English fishers hunt them into extinction and keep track of the murders with notches carved into their guns.

Dutch and English settlers unite to slaughter the Pequots in 1637.

1670: Charles II of England grants a charter to the "Hudson's Bay Company" with complete jurisdiction over Rupert's Land, a vast land area surrounding Hudson Bay.

1680: The Haudenosaunee (Iroquois) Confederacy creates an historic compact with the English, recorded in the Two-Row Wampum. The two rows symbolize two peoples, two paths; and peace, friendship and respect. The oldest democracy in America includes power for both sexes and a voice for all.

1700: Bini—a Wet'suwet'en prophet and spiritual leader—sees the coming of the white man, missionaries, trains, Jesus, air travel and the telephone.

1752: The Seven Years' War between the English in New Canada ("Canada" is the Ottawa word for villages) and the French in New France. Both the English and French seek Indian allies from the various Nations. England gains permission from several of the Indian Nations to build forts on their land throughout the area surrounding Detroit up towards Ottawa.

1755: The English expel Acadians from the mouth of the St. Lawrence; many exiles end up in Louisiana.

1759: James Wolfe arrives from England and burns the countryside around the St. Lawrence near the Québec Fortress; his men take scalps. After a siege by bombardment on the starving civilian population of Québec city for six weeks, he defeats Louis-Joseph Montcalm on the plains of Abraham. England wins the Seven Years' War.

—The articles of Capitulation of Québec signed between France and England pledge that "The savages, or Indian Allies of His Most Christian Majesty, shall be maintained in the lands they inhabit, if they choose to remain there; they shall not be molested on any pretense whatsoever."

1763-64: Chief Pontiac organizes a confederacy of Ottawa, Wyandot, Potawatomi, Miami, Kickapoo, Wea, Peoria, Ojibway, and Seneca warriors and lays siege to British forts in the Great Lakes region. Seven of ten forts are burning and two are under siege when the British agree to negotiate—resulting in the Royal Proclamation of 1763.

1763: The Treaty of Paris ends all French claim to Rupert's Land.

—On October 7, King George III issues the Royal Proclamation, the Imperial affirmation and recognition of the fundamental principles upon which the legal relationship between Indians and the Crown are to be resolved. The Proclamation does not have in its terms a condition that one Indian Nation speaks for all. Instead, a process is outlined in which England must obtain the consent of the Indian Nation in whose territory the English want to settle.

1775: The American War of Independence from British rule is fought. It ends in 1783.

1776: Captain James Cook is instructed: "You are also with the consent of the natives to take possession in the name of the King of Great Britain of convenient situations in such countries as you may discover, that have not already been discovered or visited by any other European power."

1778

CAPTAIN JAMES COOK ON HIS THIRD MISSION IS DISCOVERED BY THE NOOTKA PEOPLE.

(Much of present day British Columbia remains taken without consent or treaty.)

1778: British Columbia Natives discover Captain James Cook at Nootka Sound.

1792: Captain Robert Gray, a trader from Boston, kidnaps a Clayoquot Nation Chief. After the Clayoquots attack Gray's fort, Gray leads a massacre and total destruction of their village.

1793: A bill for abolition of Negro and Pani (Indian) slavery in Lower Canada is defeated.

1803: Maquinna, a Nootka chief, successfully attacks the American trading ship "Boston" after Captain John Salter's men rape two Nootka girls. It is two years before another ship returns to Nootka Sound.

1805: The North West Company's Simon Fraser founds "New Caledonia" at McLeod Lake, the first permanent trading outpost in the southern interior of British Columbia.

1815: Between 1815 and 1839, 431,089 immigrants are landed through the port of Québec. Lord Durham notes: "Reduced to pauperism by the results of centuries of plundering, extortion and exploitation of the ruling class at home, these emigrants were herded in foulships and packed off to Canada under the most inhuman and horrible conditions."

1820: A huge rock slide in Hagwilget Canyon (Gitksan territory) prompts the move of the Wet'suwet'en village from Kya Wiget (Moricetown) to the present Tse Kya. The Gitksan permitted the move of their southern neighbors and called the new village Hagwilget—"place of the gentle people."

—The Hudson Bay Company of England sets up an outpost at Babine Lake, penetrating that previously Gitksan-, Wet'suwet'en- and Nisga'a-controlled economy of the Northwest Interior. The company introduces flour, rice, beans, bacon, tea and sugar to the interior Nations; and sets up a credit system which advances supplies against a season's trapping, effectively binding trappers to the post.

1823: February 24: William Brown, a trader, becomes the first white man in Gitksan Territory.

1832: The cholera epidemic which kills 3,800 in Québec City and at least 4,000 in Montréal, is born in the jammed hold of *The Voyager* which limps leaking into Québec Harbour on June 7, 1832.

1837: Two unsuccessful farmers' revolutions take place in Québec and Ontario.

1839: Lord Durham describes the rules of colonialism in the colony of Canada: "It seems... to have been considered the policy of the British

Government to govern its colonies by means of division, and to break them down as much as possible into petty isolated communities, incapable of combination, and possessing no sufficient strength for individual resistence to the Empire. Indication of such designs are to be found in many of the acts of the British Government with respect to its North American Colonies...."

1849: Vancouver Island is established as a British Colony. The Crown grants the land to the Hudson's Bay Company, which becomes effectively wedded to the Crown.

1850: Fourteen treaties are entered into on Vancouver Island by James Douglas, who is both Governor of the colony and Chief Factor of the Hudson's Bay Company. A dispute as to who would bear the cost of treaties (the colony, the Hudson's Bay Company or the imperial government) blocks treaty-making after 1854. Douglas relates his understanding of the Native population's feelings about land in a petition to the Duke of Newcastle: "As the native Indian population of Vancouver Island have distinct ideas of property and land, and mutually recognize their several exclusive possessory rights in certain districts, they would not fail to regard the occupation of such portions of the colony by White settlers, unless with the full consent of the proprietary tribes, as national wrongs."

1861: New settlers in Victoria begin to press for agricultural land. A man named Amor DeCosmos

Gitsegukla Village on the Skeena River, at the turn of the 19th century.
Photo courtesy of Glenbow Archives, Calgary, Alberta.

A BRITISH SQUADRON, COMMANDED BY REAR ADMIRAL J. DENMAN ATTACK AN INDIAN VILLAGE IN CLAYOQUOT SOUND.
(After an illustration by Lieut. E.C. Hall, 1864)

(lover of the universe), who is soon to become a British Columbia Premier, writes in his Victoria newspaper *The British Colonist*, "Shall we allow a few red vagrants to prevent forever industrious settlers from settling on unoccupied land? Not at all…. Locate reservations for them on which to earn their own living and if they trespass on white settlers punish them severely to form a correct estimate of their own inferiority and settle the Indian title, too."

1862: Smallpox, introduced to British Columbia a year earlier in Victoria, rampages up the coast, and into the interior. The Haida people, who receive first contact, in Victoria, lose 80 percent of their kin. Gitksan and Wet'suwet'en Nations lose 30 percent of their people. Houses amalgamate in order to survive. Protestant and Roman Catholic missionaries seek to usurp the power of the Medicine people. They hold out the whites' immunity as "proof" of the superiority of Christ's magic. A vaccine stockpile remains untouched in Victoria.

1864: Until the admission of British Columbia into Confederation in 1871, Indian policy comes under the influence of Joseph Trutch who represents the ideology of the frontier: "The Indians have really no right to the lands they claim, nor are they of any actual value or utility to them, and I cannot see why they should… retain these lands to the prejudice of the general interest of the colony."

—Captain Denman destroys a village in Clayoquot Sound on the coast of British Columbia.

1866: The Collins overland telegraph line pushes its way through the British Columbia interior. The idea is to link America with Europe by way of a route through British Columbia, Alaska and Russia. When the competing Atlantic Cable finally holds, the work on the overland route stops. They go as far as Gitksan territory—some of the first whites to be seen in the area. The present Bulkley River receives its name from American engineer of the project, Colonel Charles Bulkley who never sees the river. The Wet'suwet'en and Gitksan use the tons of wire left behind to fortify the bridge at Hagwilget canyon.

1867: On July 1, the British North America Act is passed for the legal creation of Canada as a nation. The Colonies in Canada which originally form the Confederacy are Nova Scotia, New Brunswick, Upper and Lower Canada.

1868: The new Canadian Parliament passes an "Act for the gradual civilization of Indian Peoples." Under this policy, the Indian Act becomes a key legislative tool for assimilation. There are three major functions under the Indian Act intended to assimilate Indian Peoples:

1. Creation of vastly reduced "Reserve" lands which do not reflect the traditional tribal territories of the Indian Nations.

2. Creation of puppet "Band Councils" which replace and undermine the authority of traditional tribal governments.

3. Defining who is an "Indian" under the Indian Act.

1871: British Columbia joins the Dominion of Canada. For a while the Native Nations of British Columbia are hopeful that this may mean a different policy toward them and the land. Canada makes treaties, although forced, in the prairies. But through "Article 13," and political chicanery,

Genocide or Assimilation?

Genocide is the practice of wholesale physical slaughter of a people by means which would remove them as obstacles to taking the lands and its resources. Assimilation is the practice of using certain processes and tools for the killing of a people's spirit. In assimilation, governments can tell their citizens, "See, we are being good to the Indian people because we have not killed them. They are whole and living among us." While at the same time, they have our souls in their welfare pockets or have caused our death by other means not directly tied to them.

In the choices facing Canada for gaining control of Indian lands and resources, *assimilation* was the policy by which Canadian governments proceeded to weaken the Indian Nations. Their goal was to get the Indian to cease to be Indian and become white.

—**Rosalie Tizya**, United Native Nations historian.

British Columbia's Chief Commissioner of Lands and Works, Joseph Trutch, manages to retain the status quo, as Native people suffer racism, neglect and political disenfranchisement.

1872: In response to the burning of twelve Gitksan houses and six poles, caused by a group of miners, Gitsegukla Chiefs blockade the Skeena River to all trading and supply boats. After gunboats arrive at the mouth of the Skeena from Victoria, British Columbia, the "Skeena Rebellion" ends peacefully when Gitsegukla Chiefs meet with Lieutenant Governor Joseph Trutch and receive compensation for the burning.

1876: The Governor General, the Earl of Dufferin, gives a speech in Victoria condemning the "error of the provincial government in not recognizing Indian title:" "In Canada... no government, whether provincial or central, has failed to acknowledge that the original title to the land existed in the Indian tribes...."

1877: The first gill net fishing boats arive at the mouth of the Skeena River. By the end of the century the canneries have developed, and Native fishing rights and trade are abolished.

1883: U.S. Supreme Court rules that Native Americans are "aliens."

A shot of the Grease Trail bridge at Tse Kya in 1872, taken by Charles Horetzky.

One of the dozens of Gitksan stone clubs, over two thousand years old, found near Tsekya, Hagwilget, on Nikateen's territory.

Photo: courtesy *Stone Age B.C.*, by Wilson Duff.

1884: Gitksan Chiefs of Gitwangak tell the Provincial Government that the influx of miners to Lorne Creek within their territory, without their consent, is wrong and has to be stopped.

—A.C. Youmans, a freighter for miners, fails to notify and compensate a Gitsegukla family of the drowning of their son, Billy Owen, while in his employ. Three years earlier, Billy's brother had also been drowned while in Youmans' employ. Youmans had also refused compensation then as is required by Gitksan law. He is killed by Billy's father, Haatq, who is charged and sentenced to ten years imprisonment. He dies later in jail.

—Canada's federal government passes a law prohibiting feasts, making the traditional Gitksan and Wet'suwet'en system, and other feasting nations in British Columbia, illegal. Feasting continues secretly. Gitksan Chief Gyetim Galdo'o openly holds a feast in Hazelton and is arrested by Royal Canadian Mounted Police.

1885: November 16: Louis Riel, after the second Métis "rebellion" and in spite of a recommendation for mercy from a jury, is hanged in Regina, Saskatchewan.

1889: Original surveys for the establishment of reserves is completed on Gitksan and Wet'suwet'en territories.

—The Babine Agency is established at Hazelton by the Department of Indian Affairs. The first Indian Agent, Richard Loring, is appointed for the Gitksan and Wet'suwet'en territory.

—The Federal Fisheries Act is passed, prohibiting Indians from selling fish or owning fishing licences. Indians who work for fish companies are paid five cents a fish, while white fishermen are paid ten cents a fish.

1893: The notorious Residential Schools are established; the Superintendent of Indian Affairs makes it clear that it is the intention of the federal government to destroy Indian language and lifeways. "...in boarding or industrial schools the pupils are removed for a long period from the leading of this uncivilized life and receive constant care and attention. It is therefore in the interests of the Indians that these institutions should be kept in an efficient state as it is in their success that the solution of the Indian problem lies."

—The government blasts rocks out of the Skeena River to improve steamer traffic. At Gitsegukla, the fishing sites and smokehouses of five families are destroyed.

1898: Johnny Muldoe, a Gitksan, while digging a house post below the Hagwilget Canyon, discovers 35 2000-year old stone clubs cached together. A.W. Vowell, Superintendant of Indian Affairs, in British Columbia, takes them and sells them to collector G.T. Lemmons. They eventually end up at the Museum of American Indians in New York.

1900: Genocide has reduced the indigenous population north of the Rio Grande—estimated at between 12-15 million in 1492—to 300,000.

1900: Father Morice and Bishop Dentenwill burn Wet'suwet'en feast regalia in Hagwilget (Tse Kya) in a Catholic effort to suppress traditional beliefs.

1901: As a result of the South African War scrip scheme, whereby volunteers from British Colum-

Totem poles were seen as objects of pagan worship by established missionaries. Many were cut down. Ceremonial regalia was gathered to be burnt during special masses held by the Catholic Church. At one of these burnings on Wet'suwet'en territory, Father Morice admitted he "felt a pang at the sight of the miniature museum going up in smoke."

bia who had served in the Boer War are given 160 acres of "unoccupied, unclaimed and unreserved land," many Wet'suwet'en families are forced from their homes. Clusters of Wet'suwet'en hunters, trappers, and fishermen, having completed the season's fishing at Moricetown or Hagwilget, return home to find their homes and ancestral lands seized. The bitterness of this invasion of their homes is followed by severe hardship and a record-breaking, cold winter.

1906: A Southern British Columbia Indian delegation goes to England to raise the land question with the Crown.

—Simon Gunanoot and his cousin, Peter Himadam, are charged with the murder of a white and a mixed-blood on the Babine trail. They evade posses, police and Pinkerton agents for 13 years. In 1919, they finally walk out of the bush on promise of a fair trial and are acquitted on both counts.

1908: Three Wet'suwet'en men are convicted and fined for threatening at gunpoint white settlers who have taken over Moricetown reserve land.

—In Hazelton, the army is called in, as Indian Agent Richard Loring digs trenches at Hazelton, expecting an attack from Kispiox. No such attack is ever made.

—A Gitksan delegation meets with Prime Minister Wilfred Laurier, in Ottawa. They speak eloquently about white incursions into their territories.

1909: Kispiox Chiefs stop road building in their valley; the Royal Canadian Mounted Police arrest seven.

—Kitwanga people stop a group of surveyors at gunpoint and demand meetings over land grievances. At the meetings, they quote from the Royal

Proclamation of 1763 as one of the bases of their claim.

1910: Kitwancool and Kitwanga Chiefs pin notices of their land claims along trails in Hazelton district and invoke the Royal Proclamation of 1763 to challenge the white presence.

1912: The McKenna-McBride Commission is established to address the question of Indian reserves. During the Commission hearings, the Gitksan and Wet'suwet'en Chiefs insist on talking about their territories and reject the idea of reserves.

1915: The first pan-tribal organization in British Columbia—The Allied Tribes of B.C.—is created to address "the land question."

1921: The Dene people sign Treaty 11 in the Northwest Territories.

—After white owners of South African scrip get a court order to remove Wet'suwet'en, Jean Baptiste, from his land, he sends his family away and threatens to kill anyone who tries to remove him. Dr. Horace Wrinch of Hazelton declares, "He is a desperate man." The Department of Indian Affairs acquiesces and creates Jean Baptiste reserve No. 28.

A Gitksan family gathering the winter's wood at Gitanmaax, around 1910.
Photo courtesy of British Columbia Archives & Records Service.

1922: The Royal Canadian Mounted Police seizes over 600 objects in a "potlatch" raid at Alert Bay on Vancouver Island, and divide the spoils between the Royal Ontario Museum in Toronto and the National Museum in Ottawa.

1923: Holland and Persia support Iroquois sovreignty claim at the League of Nations. Canadian Mounties storm and occupy the Six Nations Council house at Osheweken (near Brantford) and read aloud a proclamation dissolving the ancient assembly; they seize all legal documents and wampum belts. The government installs Band Councils under police protection.

1927: The Canadian federal government amends the Indian Act, making it an offense, punishable by imprisonment, to raise money to press for land claims in Canada.

—During the 1920s and 30s, the paddle-wheelers ply the Skeena River to Hazelton less and less as the railroad has taken over. Illegal feasts continue with the aid of look-outs. Caribou disap-

pear because of rail lines and fencing; moose take their place. Work on poles and rail-ties is available for the Gitksan and Wet'suwet'en. However, the skills of fishing, berry-picking and hunting continue, making depression days easier for the people. In Hazelton a horn is sounded at 9.00 p.m. to signal Gitksan to leave town and go back to the "reserve."

1947: First Nations peoples are given a vote in provincial elections for the first time. They still have no federal vote.

1951: Sixty-seven years after it is outlawed, the Potlatch Law is repealed. It is now legal to raise funds on behalf of indigenous land claims.

1959: The federal Fisheries Department blows up the huge rock, used by the Wet'suwet'en of Tse kya and the Gitksan of Gitanmaax for fishing. It had fallen into Hagwilget Canyon in 1820, 140 years earlier. Wet'suwet'en women throw rocks off the bridge to discourage the work; they are restrained by local collaborators. After the rock is

People wait for the boat at Gitanmaax, now Hazelton, around the year 1910. Shingles, flour and boards can be seen on the beach, with Gitksan houses and poles in the background.
Photo courtsey of British Columbia Archives & Records Service.

The canyon at Tse Kya, in 1915. On the near side are the fishing platforms and traps used by the Wet'suwet'en; on the far side, the structures belong to the people of Gitanmaax. In between lies the rock that was blasted out by the Federal Fisheries department.

Photo by Harlan I. Smith, from *The Gathering Place*, by Maureen Cassidy.

In the 1940s and 1950s, South Africa sent Commissions to study Canada's (and the United States') reservation systems. They studied Canada's treatment of original people in order to create their own "reservations" under APARTHEID...

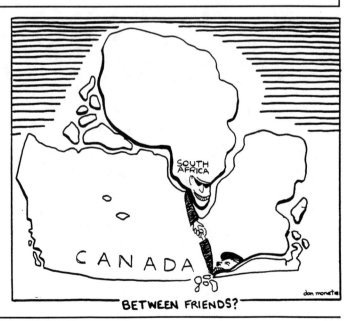

blown, the people become fish-poor, and experience the split-up of many families.

1960: First Nations peoples are given a vote in Canadian federal elections for the first time.

1967: The W.A.C. Bennett dam floods the homeland of Ingenika and Mesilinka people in British Columbia's interior. Hydro-power is sold to Vancouver and Seattle. Wolliston Lake (reservoir) is 200 miles long. A huge tract of forest still lies rotting below, making the "lake" useless for travel or drinking; tons of debris line the shore.

1969: Jean Chrétien and Prime Minsiter Trudeau put together the White Paper policy which repeals the Indian Act and amends the Constitution to eliminate all references to Indian people. Because of organized Indian resistance, Trudeau is forced to shelve the White Paper and consult with Indian peoples about their rights.

1973: The Canadian Supreme Court rules against the Nisga'a people, northern neighbors to the Gitksan, in the landmark "Calder Case." Three judges ruled that their aboriginal title is still in existence, three ruled that their rights were "extinguished by legislation," and the seventh ruled on a procedural point of error against the plaintiffs. Mr. Justice Hall, Canadian Supreme Court justice in the case, refers to the 1763 Proclamation as the Native Magna Carta: "The Royal Proclamation is not the source of aboriginal rights but an affirmation of their existence."

—A letter from Jean Chrétien to Pierre Trudeau spells out Canada's new land claim policy: to promote negotiations and avoid the courts as a way of resolving title, since courts could rule in favor of the Indian people; to avoid confirmation of title; to shift jurisdiction of Indians to the provinces; to negotiate only with those groups willing to accept extinguishment of their title; to give priority to those areas of high development potential; to set rigid time limits on negotiations and threaten legislated settlements; and to avoid Indian political organizations.

1974: A Québec Supreme Court injunction stops the massive James Bay hydro-electric project in northern Québec from drowning 8000 square kilometres of Inuit and Cree homeland. Québec negotiates with the Inuit and Cree: the first settlement in Canada since 1921. The people are given $225 million and reserve lands; their title is extinguished, as per Trudeau's policy.

Gitksan-Carrier Declaration

Since time immemorial, we, the Gitksan and Carrier People of Kitwanga, Kitseguecla, Gitanmaax, Sikadoak, Kispiox, Hagwilget and Moricetown, have exercised Sovereignty over our land. We have used and conserved the resources of our land with care and respect. We have governed ourselves. We have governed the land, the waters, the fish and the animals. This is written on our totem poles. It is recounted in our songs and dances. It is present in our language and in our spiritual beliefs. Our Sovereignty is our Culture.

Our Aboriginal Rights and Title to this land have never been extinguished by treaty or by any agreement with the Crown. Gitksan and Carrier Sovereignty continue within these tribal areas.

We have suffered many injustices. In the past, the development schemes of public and private enterprise have seriously altered Indian life and culture. These developments have not included, in any meaningful way, our hopes, aspirations and needs.

The future must be different. The way of life of our people must be recognized, protected and fostered by the Governments of Canada and the Laws of Canada. Only then will we be able to participate fully in Canadian society.

We, the Gitksan and Carrier people, will continue to exercise our Sovereignty in the areas of Education, Social and Economic Development, Land Use and Conservation, Local and Regional Government.

We have waited one hundred years. We have been patient. Through serious negotiation, the basis for a meaningful and dignified relationship between the Gitksan and Carrier People and the Governments of Canada and of British Columbia will be determined. These negotiations require mutual and positive participation by the Federal Government and the Provincial Government.

Today, the Governments of Canada and British Columbia undertake a bold new journey to negotiate with the Gitksan and Carrier People. During this journey, we will fulfill the hopes and aspirations of our ancestors and the needs of future generations.

Let us begin negotiations.

Recognize our Sovereignty, recognize our rights, so that we may fully recognize yours.

—KISPIOX, B.C.
November 7, 1977

Note: "Carrier" has since been discontinued; "Wet'suwet'en" is back in use.

1977: The Federal Government accepts the Gitksan and Wet'suwet'en declaration for land claims negotiation.

1980: The assembly of First Nations in Ottawa

issues a Declaration of The First Nations.

1981: The federal government issues a restatement of its 1973 "White Paper" policy in a booklet entitled, "In all Fairness."

1982: Creation of a United Nations committee on Indian rights represented from all parts of America, Scandinavia, Australia, New Zealand, and Asia.

1984: October 24: Gitksan and Wet'suwet'en Chiefs file a statement of Claim against the Provincial government seeking a declaration that they have a right to ownership of, and jurisdiction over, their House Territories.

—The Supreme Court of Canada decides *Guerin vs. The Queen.* A trust action against the Department of Indian Affairs, Chief Justice Dickson states that in the Calder case the court had "recognized aboriginal title as a legal right derived from the Indians' historic occupation and possession of their tribal lands." He also quotes a decision of the U.S. Supreme Court that Indian tribes were "the rightful occupants of the soil, with a legal as well as a just claim to retain possession of it."

—The government of Canada and the Inuit people of the Mackenzie Delta sign a final agreement settling title claims. Extinguishment, Canada's desire, is attained.

1985: Gwiis Gyen, Stanley Williams, stands in front of a train on the main line from Prince Rupert to force Canadian National Railways to compensate Gitwangak for 100 acres taken from the reserve in 1910. The Grand Trunk Railway was built right through the village cemetery; the village had been given $100 to bury the 14 bodies the railway had disturbed, but nothing for the land itself.

In opposition to pesticide spraying, Gitwangak Chiefs stage a successful blockade of the Canadian National Railways tracks.

—The British Columbia Court of Appeal in *Macmillan Bloedel vs. Mullin* (the litigation over Meares Island on Vancouver Island's west coast), upholds an interim injunction on the basis of a claim to aboriginal title.

1986: Hugh Brody's *On Indian Land,* a film about the Gitksan Wet'suwet'en, is shown on British Broadcasting Corporation television, in the United Kingdom. It is banned by the Canadian Broadcasting Corporation due to its being "too one-sided."

—At Anki-iss fish camp, Gitwangak, marshmallows are thrown at the heavily-armed Fisheries officers, causing them to retreat. The news creates international attention.

1987: The case of *Delgam Uukw vs. Her Majesty The Queen* begins in a crowded Smithers court room. The Gitksan and Wet'suwet'en people, as plaintiffs, put the colonial government on trial.

—After massive cuts by the government of Canada, the staff of the Gitksan Wetsuwet'en Tribal Council go on Unemployment Insurance Compensation.

—The Tribal Council changes its name and begins a process of diverting power back to the Chiefs. It is now called "The Office Of The Hereditary Chiefs."

1988: Kispiox Chiefs blockade their huge valley from logging. Thirty Royal Canadian Mounted Police officers are rounded up from the entire north. They bring an empty school bus for arrests. The blockade is lifted before they arrive.

—Gitwangak Chiefs assert their jurisdiction and seize logging equipment on Eagle territory; they begin to selectively log with horses and without "permits."

—Dozens of Innu people are arrested in Labrador, Québec, for blocking a NATO runway, used by Germans and Americans for low-level jet-bomber test-flights—more than three thousand per year over Innu land.

—Gitksan Chiefs blockade a logging bridge under construction at Sam Greene Creek. The bridge was to have spanned the Babine River into untouched territory. The Chiefs win a counter-injunction in British Columbia Supreme Court, stop-

GENERAL K. FOSTER APPEARS ON TELEVISION TO SAY; GENERAL ROI HAS ALL THE ORDERS HE NEEDS... WE ARE NOW IN A MILITARY OPERATION." AUGUST 27, **1990.**

Mohawks defending a traditional burial ground from being developed as a golf course spark Canada's "Oka crisis" in the summer of 1990. The response of civilians, the Québec police, and the military confirms that racism against Indian people is alive and well in Canada.

ping the bridge until the main action is decided.

—Lubicon people and supporters, seeking recognition as a people and a halt to oil and timber extraction from their homelands, are arrested in Alberta. A boycott of the Winter Olympics "Spirit Songs" (stolen) Native art exhibition receives international attention.

1989: The Kispiox Chiefs blockade the valley again; this time, a task force is arranged among loggers, contractors and the Chiefs.

—Gitksan and Wet'suwet'en people blockade the Suskwa valley; the contractors co-operate and remove equipment.

—McLeod Lake people of British Columbia's southern interior blockade a huge convoy of Canadian Army soldiers seeking to play war games on their homelands.

1990: The Mohawk people of Kahnesatake near Oka, Québec, defend their sacred burial grounds from a golf course expansion. The Québec police charge into their own tear gas and a gun battle erupts. A police participant is killed in the fire. Police refuse to say whether it was by their own gunfire or not. A long seige behind barracades begins. In solidarity, the Mohawks of Kanawake block the Mercier bridge into Montreal. In a series of racist incidents against Mohawks, the police stand by, while rocks thrown at children and Elders kill a man and wound a baby. Canadian federal forces move in.

—Nations across Canada blockade roads to support the Mohawks. In Alberta a huge wooden train bridge is burnt to the ground. The Wet'suwet'en at Moricetown and the Gitksan at Gitwangak block the main highways.

—The Canadian Army moves in on Oka and arrest the Mohawks.

—Sixty people from the Mount Currie band close to Vancouver are arrested for blockading a road into their land. Not recognizing the authority of the court, they refuse to give their names; they are held for three weeks as Jane and John Does, then released.

—The trial of *Delgam Uukw vs. Her Majesty The Queen* ends.

—At the front door of the Federal Fisheries Office, Wet'suwet'en Adam Gagnon illegally sells fish to non-native, Richard Overstall.

March 8, 1991: *Delgam Uukw vs. The Queen* is decided in favor of the government by Chief Justice Allan McEachern, who describes indigenous life as "nasty, brutish and short" and announces that indigenous title was extinguished in 1858. Academic and media commentary expresses shock at the reasons for judgment.

April 1991: Gitksan and Wet'suwet'en Chiefs launch an appeal of the decision. The estimated cost to pursue the case is $5 million, to be raised by government, church and individual grants and donations.

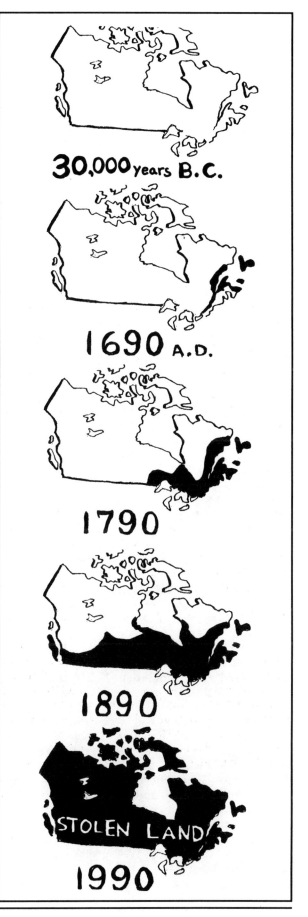

30,000 years B.C.

1690 A.D.

1790

1890

STOLEN LAND

1990

Chapter 2

Culture, Law, Language:
The Trial Begins

May 11, 1987. A warm sun beams down on the small northern town of Smithers, British Columbia. Early morning traffic streams steadily by as a crowd gathers on a grey expanse of concrete leading into the equally colorless backdrop of a government building. A fresh breeze, flowing down from the nearby mountains, tosses well-combed hair and the vibrant red, black and mother-of-pearl button blankets. The sound of a gentle drum and low chant is heard. It grows in force and energy as new voices join in. On a final beat, there is silence... the sudden caw of the ever-present raven is quickly followed by the clicking shutters of countless cameras.

In the ageless language of their ancestors, a Wet'suwet'en Chief welcomes the visitors to his territory, a Gitksan Chief reminds all who are gathered the reason for their assembly, and a prayer is offered to the Creator. The robes and headgear of the Chiefs are quietly removed and carefully bundled away.

The crowd has grown. As he drives by, a man in a pick-up truck yells "White Rights!" The curious stares and questioning glances of the townspeople go unanswered as the crowd slowly files into the building. Inside, the clerks and court officials are busily preparing the old county courtroom for the opening of the Supreme Court of British Columbia presided over by the Chief Justice, Allan McEachern. The trial of *Delgamuukw vs. the Queen* has begun.

Along the crowded corridors and packed wooden benches of the spectators' gallery ripples a mood of relief mixed with trepidation. Relief, that after a century of battling the governments and their partners in business, finally, finally, the issue of ownership and jurisdiction will be dealt with. Trepidation, because for the first time in their history, the Gitksan and Wet'suwet'en will unlock a treasured wealth of knowledge and history passed down through countless generations, to be poked and prodded and dissected and questioned by a society that has neither shown itself to be receptive nor respectful of those treasures.

"It is necessary" are the guiding words that have brought the Gitksan and Wet'suwet'en to this foreign arena where the weight of evidence falls squarely upon their collective shoulders. Unan-

swered questions are the cause of the trepidation. Will the necessity of educating the courts and the Canadian public balance the intense public scrutiny to which they will be subjected? Will this foreign system with its seemingly contradictory rules be able to adjust itself to understand the fundamental basics of Gitksan and Wet'suwet'en laws? Will the world views and philosophies of the Gitksan and Wet'suwet'en be seen through corporate eyes and discounted merely as being archaic, mythical and irrelevant? Will Canada understand and respect the painstaking journey the Gitksan and Wet'suwet'en have charted for themselves?

The two principal plaintiffs—Delgamuukw for the Gitksan, Gisdaywa for the Wet'suwet'en—step into the arena and utter the first of millions of words that will become the public record of this most unprecedented land title action. There is no hesitancy. What must be, will be.

The activity evident today is both a culmination of years of preparation as well as a springboard of effort yet to be expended. What is not evident in the formal setting of the courtroom is the vast coordination of hundreds of details that the Gitksan and Wet'suwet'en community undertook and continue to undertake.

Every important occurrence becomes part of a House's history that will pass down to the generations yet to be born. *Delgamuukw vs. the Queen*, in all its aspects, is a momentous event that will figure prominently in the history of all Gitksan and Wet'suwet'en Houses. It is only in the telling of personal involvements that the truest depiction of the history of our land title court action will be recounted. The versions are many and varied; all are true.

This chapter of our history reflects the first two months of the trial in Smithers—the courtroom setting and players; the departure from the norm where, instead of legal counsel, the principal plaintiffs for the Gitksan and Wet'suwet'en provide the opening statement; the daily debriefing sessions of the Gitksan and Wet'suwet'en in their newly-rented offices directly across the street from the courthouse; the barriers erected against the first four witnesses as they attempt to educate the courts on the Gitksan and Wet'suwet'en system; the reluctance of the Chief Justice to hear evidence of a "spiritual nature," and how the courtroom atmosphere would noticeably change during the telling of that evidence; the key role played by the Gitksan and Wet'suwet'en translators who diligently translate the knowledge of the Elders and Chiefs into sterile English words that lack the necessary backdrop of cultural understanding; the tactics of government lawyers to delay the proceedings knowing that time and money are precious to the Gitksan and Wet'suwet'en; the relationships that develop between the plaintiff and defendant counsels; the resistance by the Gitksan and Wet'suwet'en to the change of venue for the convenience of the courts.

All children, for generations to come, will hear stories of the courage of their ancestors in travelling a new path into an alien world; they will hear how the young people of our time, guided by the vision and wisdom of the Elders, educated and trained themselves in the white man's system to do what was necessary; how once we feared the white man's courts, came to understand it, then used it to show the abuses of their history; how, true to the prophecies of our Elders, those same courts showed great disrespect to the people and their culture; how, in the face of astounding adversity, the strength of the Gitksan and Wet'suwet'en people carried them through the first turbulent months of *Delgamuukw vs. the Queen.*

Our histories now have an added element to enrich the telling of the stories—the cartoons and drawings of Don Monet. There is an understanding with the Gitksan and Wet'suwet'en that there is no such thing as coincidence. What is meant to be, will be. So it is with Don Monet. It was no accident that a young man journeyed into Gitksan and Wet'suwet'en territory shortly before the trial began. It was no accident that this same young man had the ability to see beyond the superficial and understand what was unfolding before him. It definitely was no accident that he had the ability to depict his understanding on to paper to become a part of the history of the Gitksan and Wet'suwet'en.

—Skanu'u (Ardythe Wilson)

In the Supreme Court of British Columbia
(BEFORE THE HONOURABLE THE CHIEF JUSTICE)

No. 0843
Smithers Registry

BETWEEN:

DELGAMUUKW, also known as ALBERT TAIT, suing on his own behalf and on behalf of all other members of the HOUSE OF DELGAMUUKW, and others,

Plaintiffs;

AND:

HER MAJESTY THE QUEEN IN RIGHT OF THE PROVINCE OF BRITISH COLUMBIA and THE ATTORNEY GENERAL OF CANADA,

Defendants.

Plaintiff: A person who brings an action; the party who complains or sues in a civil action and is so named on the record. A person who seeks remedial relief for an injury to rights; it designates a complainant.

Defendant: The person defending or denying; the party against whom relief or recovery is sought in an action or suit, or the accused in a criminal case.

—**Black's Law Dictionary** (Definitions of the Terms and Phrases of American and English Jurisprudence, Ancient and Modern)

The Claim Against The Crown

The Respondents, as plaintiffs in Action No. 0843 in the Supreme Court of British Columbia against Her Majesty the Queen in Right of the Province of British Coulumbia (the "Delgamuukw case") and Canada, claim the following relief:

1. A declaration that the Plaintiffs have a right to ownership of and jurisdiction over the Territory.

2. A declaration that the Plaintiffs' ownership of and jurisdiction over the Territory existed and continues to exist and has never been lawfully extinguished or abandoned.

3. A declaration that the Plaintiffs' rights of ownership and jurisdiction within the Territory include the right to use, harvest, manage, conserve and transfer the lands and natural resources, and make decisions in relation thereto.

4. A declaration that the Plaintiffs' rights to jurisdiction includes the right to govern the territory, themselves, and the members of the Houses represented by the Plaintiffs in accordance with Gitksan and Wet'suwet'en laws, administered through Gitksan and Wet'suwet'en political, legal and social institutions as they exist and develop.

5. A declaration that the Plaintiffs' rights to ownership of and jurisdiction over the territory include the right to ratify conditionally, or otherwise refuse to ratify, land titles or grants issued by the Defendant Province after October 22, 1984, and licences, leases and permits issued by the Defendant Province at any time without the Plaintiffs' consent.

6. A declaration that the aboriginal rights of the Plaintiffs, including ownership of and jurisdiction over the Territory, are recognized and affirmed by Section 35 of the Constitution Act, 1982.

7. A declaration that the Defendant Province's ownership of lands, mines, minerals and royalties within the Plaintiffs' Territory is subject to the Plaintiffs' rights to ownership and jurisdiction pursuant to Section 109 of the Constitution Act, 1867.

8. A declaration that the Defendant Province's jurisdiction over the Territory, the Plaintiffs and members of the Houses represented by the Plaintiffs is subject to the Plaintiffs' right to ownership and jurisdiction.

9. A declaration that the Defendant Province is not entitled to interfere with the aboriginal rights and title, ownership and jurisdiction of the Plaintiffs.

10. A declaration that the Defendant Province cannot appropriate any part of the Territory through grants, licences, leases, permits or in any other manner whatsoever.

11. A declaration that the Defendant Province cannot issue or renew grants, licences, leases or permits authorizing the use of any resources within the territory of the Plaintiffs by the Defendant Province, its agents or by third parties without the consent of the Plaintiffs.

12. A declaration that the Plaintiffs are entitled to damages from the Defendant Province for the wrongful appropriation and use of the Territory by the Defendant Province or by its servants, agents or contractors without the Plaintiffs' consent.

13. A *lis pendens* against the Defendant Province over the Territory described in Schedule "A" and delineated in the map which is set out in Schedule "B."

14. A declaration that this Honorable Court shall retain jurisdiction to resolve all outstanding disputes between the parties as to the implementation of the Declaration and Orders of this Honorable Court.

15. The costs of this action.

16. Such further and other relief as to this Court may seem just.

This document explains to the judge just what it is that the Chiefs are coming to the court for.... It asks him for a declaration that all of these items are true.

Opening prayer outside the courtroom, Smithers, British Columbia, May 11, 1987.

The Address Of The Chiefs, May 11, 1987

THE ADDRESS OF THE GITKSAN AND WET'SUWET'EN HEREDITARY CHIEFS TO CHIEF JUSTICE ALLAN McEACHERN OF THE SUPREME COURT OF BRITISH COLUMBIA

My name is Gisday Wa. I am a Wet'suwet'en Chief and a Plaintiff in this case. My House owns territory in the Morice River and Owen Lake area. Each Wet'suwet'en plaintiff's House owns similar territories. Together they own and govern the Wet'suwet'en territory. As an example, the land on which this courthouse stands is owned by the Wet'suwet'en Chief, Gyolugyet, in Kyas Yax, also known as Chief Woos' House.

My name is Delgam Uukw. I am a Gitksan Chief and a Plaintiff in this case. My House owns territories in the Upper Kispiox Valley and the Upper Naas Valley. Each Gitksan Plaintiff's House owns similar territories. Together, the Gitksan and Wet'suwet'en Chiefs own and govern the 22,000 square miles of Gitksan Wet'suwet'en territory.

For us, the ownership of territory is a marriage of the Chief and the land. Each Chief has an ancestor who encountered and acknowledged the life of the land. From such encounters come power. The land, and plants, the animals and the people all have spirit they all must be shown respect. That is the basis of our law.

The Chief is responsible for ensuring that all the people in his House respect the spirit in the land and in all living things. When a Chief directs the House properly and the laws are followed, then that original power can be recreated. That is the source of the Chiefs' authority. That authority is what gives the 54 Plaintiff Chiefs the right to bring this action on behalf of their House members—all Gitksan and Wet'suwet'en people. That authority is what makes the Chiefs the real experts in this case.

My power is carried in my House's histories, songs, dances and crests. It is recreated at the Feast when the histories are told, the songs and dances performed and the crests diplayed. With the wealth that comes from respectful use of the territory, the House feeds the name of the Chief in the feast hall. In this way, the law, the Chief, the territory and the Feast become one. The unity of the Chief's authority and the House's ownership of its territory are witnessed and thus affirmed by the other Chiefs at the feast.

By following the law, the power flows from the land to the people through the Chief; by using the wealth of the territory, the House feasts its Chief in order that the law can be properly fulfilled. This cycle has been repeated on my land for thousands of years. The histories of my House are always being added to. My presence in this courtroom today will add to my House's power as it adds to the power of the other Gitksan and Wet'suwet'en Chiefs who will appear here or who will witness the proceedings. All of our roles, including yours, will be remembered in the histories that will be told by my grandchildren. Through the witnessing of all the histories, century after century, we have exercised our jurisdiction.

The Europeans did not want to know our histories; they did not respect our laws or our ownership of our territories. This ignorance and this disrespect continues. The former Delgam Uukw, Albert Tait, advised the Chiefs not to come into this court with their regalia and their crestblankets. Here, he said, the Chiefs will not receive the proper respect from the government. If they are wearing their regalia, then the shame of the disrespect will be costly to erase.

Officials who are not accountable to this land, its laws or its owners have attempted to displace our laws with legislation and regulations. The politicians have consciously blocked each path within their system that we take to assert our title. The courts, until perhaps now, have similarly denied our existence. In your legal system, how will you deal with the idea that the Chiefs own the land? The attempts to squash our laws and extinguish our system have been unsuccessful. *Gisday Wa* has not been extinguished.

If the Canadian legal system has not recognized our ownership and jurisdiction, but at the same time not extinguished it, what has been done with it? Judges and legislators have taken the reality of aboriginal title as we know it and tried to wrap it in something called aboriginal rights. An aboriginal rights package can be put on the shelf to be forgotten or to be endlessly debated at Constitutional Conferences. We are not interested in asserting aboriginal rights; we are here to discuss territory and authority. When this case ends and the package has been unwrapped, it will have to be our ownership and our jurisdiction under our law that is on the table.

Our histories show that whenever new people came to this land they had to follow its laws if they wished to stay. The Chiefs who were already here had the responsibility to teach the law to the newcomers. They then waited to see if the land was respected. If it was not, the newcomers had to pay compensation and leave. The Gitksan and Wet'suwet'en have waited and observed the Europeans for a hundred years. The Chiefs have suggested that the newcomers may want to stay on their farms and in their towns and villages but, beyond the farm fences, the land belongs to the Chiefs. Once this has been recognized, the court can get on with its main task which is to establish a process for the Chiefs' and the newcomers' interests to be settled.

The purpose of this case then, is to find a process to place Gitksan and Wet'suwet'en ownership and jurisdiction within the the context of Canada. We do not seek a decision as to whether our system might continue or not. It will continue.

May 11, 1987
Delgam Uukw (Ken Muldoe) delivers his opening
address to the court. The trial begins.

Supreme Court of British Columbia, Smithers, B.C.
May 11, 1987

ALLAN McEACHERN
Chief Justice of the
Supreme Court of B.C.

MICHAEL
GOLDIE
Q.C.,
Province of
B.C.
—Defendants

JAMES MACAULAY
Q.C., Government of
Canada—Defendants

Never before has a Canadian court been given the opportunity to hear Indian witnesses describe *within their own structure* the history and nature of their societies. The evidence will show that the Gitksan and Wet'suwet'en are and have always been properly counted amongst the civilized nations of the world; that their ownership of their territory and their authority over it has always existed; and that they have shaped a distinctive form of confederation between House and Clans. The challenge for this court is to hear this evidence, in all its complexity, in all its elaboration, as the articulation of a way of looking at the world which pre-dates the Canadian Constitution by many thousands of years.
—Opening Statement.

GEOFF PLANT
Province of B.C.
—Defendants

MURRAY ADAMS
The Plaintiffs

STUART RUSH
The Plaintiffs

LOUISE MANDELL
The Plaintiffs

MARVYN KOENIGSBERG
Govt. of Canada
—Defendants

PETER GRANT
The Plaintiffs

MICHAEL FREY Govt.
of Canada
—Defendants

MICHAEL JACKSON
The Plaintiffs

Excerpts From The Opening Statement By Lawyers For The Gitksan and Wet'suwet'en Peoples

The opening statement prepares the judge for the evidence he will hear. It sets the tone for the case.

The Western world view sees the essential and primary interactions as being those between human beings as part of an interacting continuum which includes animals and spirits. Animals and fish are viewed as members of societies who have intelligence and power, and can influence the course of events in terms of their interrelationship with human beings. In Western society, causality is viewed as direct and linear. That is to say, that an event has the ability to cause or produce another event as time moves forward. To the Gitksan and Wet'suwet'en, time is not linear, but cyclical. The events of the "past" are not simply history but are something that directly effects the present and the future.

* * *

You will hear how each Gitksan House is identified by its crests and images which encapsulate and provide a visual record of the major historical events experienced by the ancestors of this group. The Gitksan crests—*ayuks*—commemorate the groups' origins, odysseys from ancient villages, moments when the people drew upon the assistance of spirit power, the defeat of neighboring peoples who threatened their security, or the discovery of new ways to survive the natural disasters they periodically experienced. With the crest goes the *adaawk*—the verbal record of the event. Key images within the *adaawk* are evoked by songs—*limx'ooy*—that come out of the ancient past, literally from breaths of the ancestors, to take the listener back in time by the very quality of their music and the emotions they convey.

* * *

There is yet more to the role of the Chief. Along with the Chief's name and the House territory, the Chief inherits the crests infused with spirit power. Gitksan and Wet'suwet'en Chiefs exercise their authority and carry out their responsibilities with the aid of this spiritual power. In the course of the trial, you will also hear evidence from the Gitksan witnesses as to *naxnox* performances which take place in the Feast Hall. Some of these dramatize the implications for a people whose members lack respect for the rights and territory of others and who lie, boast or disdain their social responsibilities. If ignored, these dark qualities grow to become a destructive force that threatens the social order and welfare of the society. The performance is the ritual taming and controlling of this negative force, thereby creating order, peace and harmony. The Chief, as the embodiment of the House and the individual whose spiritual strength is most evolved, must use that strength to contain or mitigate these destructive qualities. The Chief controlling one of these forces takes on its name. Each Chief holding such a *naxnox* name tames that anti-social force for the House and for the society as a whole. *Naxnox* performances of this kind can be considered an enactment of the process of civilization.

You will also hear about other forms of *naxnox* and the power of the *halayt*. You will also hear evidence that the authority of the Wet'suwet'en Chiefs derives not only from the assumption of the High Chiefs' names, but also from individual contact with the spirit realm which comes from dreams, visionary experiences and what the Wet'suwet'en will refer to as *habo'stat*.

* * *

Both Gitksan and Wet'suwet'en witnesses, in identifying their place in their respective societies, will refer to their Houses and Clans. Houses and Clans are the two most important units of Gitksan and Wet'suwet'en society. A person is born into a particular House and Clan by virtue of laws of matrilineal decent. The four Gitksan Clans are *Lax Gibuu* (Wolf), *Lax Xskiik* (Eagle), *Giskaast* (Fireweed) and *Lax Seel / Lax Ganeda* (Frog). There are five Wet'suwet'en Clans: *Gitdumden* (Wolf), the *Gilserhu* (Frog), the *Laksilyu* (small Frog Clan), the *Laksumshu* (Fireweed) and the *Tsayu* (Beaver). Within each Clan there are a number of related Houses, which are identified in the Statement of Claim. These groups are called Houses because, in the past, their members would live under one roof. Over the course of history, some Houses, as a result of population increase and decline, have split off from, or amalgamated with, other Houses. In terms of difference between House and Clan, a House is a matrilineage of people so closely related that the members usually know their relationship. In the case of Clan affiliation, there is the assumption that all the Clan members are related, although the precise nature of that relationship may or may not be known. As you will hear in the evidence, the relationship between House and Clan is complex and is differently expressed in the Gitksan and Wet'suwet'en systems.

The chief counsel for the plaintiffs, Stuart Rush, reads from an extensive opening statement. Depicted is his telling of the powerful Gitksan *Naxnox* performance.

Gyolugyet (Mary McKenzie), Lax Gibuu Clan, Guldo Village by Peter Grant, May 13, 1987

Q: Could you tell the court your Chief's name, please?

A: My Chief's name is Gyolugyet.

Q: What does that name mean?

A: It means to stand in one accord.

The Court: I am sorry, Mr. Grant, I am confused already. She says "my Chief's name." Does that mean her name or his chiefly name, or is somebody else being her Chief's name? I am not sure what this means.

Mr. Grant: It may have been my questioning, my lord, and I will try to be careful.

Q: Do you hold the name Gyolugyet?

A: Yes, I do.

* * *

Q: Does the piercing of the ears when you were three years old, does that signify anything with respect to the fact that you are a Chief today?

A: Yes, it does. When I had my ears pierced, and I wear these earrings, it gives in Gitksan law it means that I won't take or hear anything that's wrongful.

Q: Um-hum.

A: And by wearing my ear rings and my bracelets—to the Gitksan it's not jewelry, it's our identification. In the olden days it's only very few women and men would be able to have their ears pierced.

Q: And those men and women that were able to have their ears pierced, were they all—I will use your translation—of the children of royalty, I think as you tried to make an analogy?

A: Yes. That's what it is.

* * *

The Gitksan and Wet'suwet'en translators worked day and night preparing a huge word list for the court transcript. One sat next to the witness, and another next to the recorder.

The Translator: G-W-I-N-E-E-K-X-W-' -M-D-A-K

The Court: Thank you.

Mr. Grant: What does that name mean?

A: It means the coal bark of a tree.

Q: Is this a name in the House of Gyolugyet?

A: Yes.

Q: Now, you've described a number of the names that you've received. Can you tell the court the significance of receiving these—of you taking on different names at different times in your life?

What is the significance to the Gitksan of holding names?

A: The way I describe myself from birth up to what I just said in Gitksan shows the preparation to become a Chief. In Gitksan law you have to work yourself up to become a Chief. You don't get a Chiefly name just if you want it today, you'll have it—it will be given to you. It doesn't work that way. In the Gitksan law, right from infancy we have to prepare our children to reach the stage of becoming a head Chief of a House or to become a Chief, the wing of a Chief of the House. Now, when names are changed, there's Feasting given every time, and this is the strength of the names, and it's the strength of the Feasting, because in a Feasting this is where we make our laws. Our names are given in a Feasting, marriage is taken to a Feasting, and the territory we hold, we say what part of the territory each Chief holds; so each Feasting has a meaning, and each Chief has to work himself up to become a head Chief.

* * *

A: *Ada'awk* in Gitksan language is a powerful word describing what the House stands for, what the chief stands for, what the territory stands for is the *adaawk*. It's not a story, it's just how people travelled is the *adaawk*. And it's the most important thing in Gitksan is to have an *adaawk*. Without *adaawk* you can't very well say you are chief or you own a territory. It has to come first, the *adaawk*. Names come after, songs come after, crests come after it and the territory that's held, fishing places, all those come into one: that's the *adaawk*. It's not a story, it's *adaawk* to the Gitksan people.

...I think I have tried to illustrate what all goes into *adaawk* and what it means to the Gitksan people. The *adaawk* is the most important. Today these *adaawk* are told. The Gitksan people didn't write anything, it was all oral, from one generation to another. But today these *adaawk* will go because our young people have educated themselves to write these and we have our language, our own alphabets that they can put on paper, black and white, it will never diminish at all. It will still be there, like it has been before. It goes around like a windmill, it goes around and that's how our *adaawk* are. It goes from one generation to another and no one changes.

* * *

Here the judge displays his cultural bias and impatience with the evidence.

The Court: Mrs. McKenzie, we are getting beyond the realm of evidence.

GYOLUGYET
(Mary McKenzie)
Days 2-11, May 1987

"My Chief's name...means to stand in one accord."—Gyolugyet (Mary McKenzie)

A: I am trying to put this...
Mr. Grant: I think...
The Court: This is not evidence, Mr. Grant.
Mr. Grant: She is trying to—let her explain

what *adaawk* is.
The Court: I understand all that but I think you really have to get on with some evidence. We had all this yesterday.

Gitksan Marie Wilson, from Gitanmaax sits in the press box and reports back to the villages in this weekly newsletter.

Gitksan Wet'suwet'en Newsletter, May, 1987

The court began in earnest when Gyolugyet (Mrs. Mary McKenzie) of the Wolf Clan, began her testimony. It was a strange afternoon as Peter Grant laid the ground work for the following days of evidence. He carefully introduced the judge with the Indian names of clans, crests, relationships, leadership and territories.

May 14, 1987: Mrs. McKenzie continued her evidence for the rest of the day. She is a strong, knowledgeable witness exhibiting great self-control, balanced by a sense of humor. She gave evidence on the Feasting system, the types of feasts, the procedures and the seating arrangements for all feasts and the purpose of each event that occurs in the Feast Hall. The avalanche of Gitksan and Wet'suwet'en words (calling for instant spelling and interpretation) has a numbing effect on those new to the language and the culture. It was clearly evident which lawyers were familiar or had done their homework. Others simply submitted to making jokes and not paying attention during the long afternoon. Mr. Grant assured Judge McEachern that a glossary of terms was being prepared.

May 15, 1987: Witness Mary McKenzie continued her explanation of the Feasting System and her own preparation to become a hereditary Chief worthy of that system. Her evidence was detailed and personal, reviving strong memories of the past. In the presence of a respectfully quiet court audience she presented a history of her own personal training and the happy, painful events that kept her memory lively.

The Gitksan Wet'suwet'en Tribal Council has established an administration office in a building directly across from the Smithers Court House. It contains office space for the lawyers, the administration staff, library and Tribal Council Leaders. There is also a large assembly room where

Gitksan and Wet'suwet'en gather after the afternoon court session to discuss the day's events and to receive a legal interpretation to those events.

Lunch is served in the assembly room of the Tribal Council building every court day. The Gitksan and Wet'suwet'en are a caring and sharing people. We demonstrate this quality daily as we share food, encouragement and power together.

—Marie Wilson

Gitksan Wet'suwet'en Bulletin, May 29, 1987

The Courtroom is full, with a good mixture of Indian and non-Indian observers.

Chief Justice McEachern called on Mr. Rush to explain why he believed that oral history, particularly the *adaawk*, should be considered admissable evidence in this trial. He would also like to know exactly what evidence can be included in the *adaawk*.

Mr. Rush gave a spirited argument favoring acceptance of the *adaawk*. He believes that the history of the Gitksan and Wet'suwet'en has been tested repeatedly through time in the feasting system. The history is sifted through Gitksan minds continuously and each generation must agree to its purity. History is not static. The truth, as witnessed by the community, comes forward in time and includes all events that affect the people. In open forums of discussion, the people, through all ages, have verified the truths of their origins, their territories and their laws. Mr. Rush made many legal references, and in particular he referred to court cases involving oral history.

Chief counsel for the Government of Canada taking a nap during testimony.

Debriefing, May 19, 1987: "The Gitksan have to show the judge not just the time, but how to make a watch."

Gyolugyet (Mary McKenzie) by Peter Grant

Q: You described the beginning, before you started to tell your *adaawk*, that this *adaawk* has been told in the Feast, could you tell the court now when, in the Gitksan Feast process, are *adaawks* told? In other words, at what kinds of Feasts and why are they told and to whom are they told?

A: In a Feasting of a burial of a Chief, these *adaawks* are not told deeply, it's just a changing of a successor, in a burial Feast. But when a totem pole is erected, that's when these *adaawks* come out of, of the erection of a totem pole, our crests are carved on these totem poles and they, these questions tell the *adaawk* of the family and erecting of a totem pole, the Chiefs all gather at an erection, the Chief tells, illustrates or tells the story of the *adaawk* of these crests. Now, there is a pause there somewhere, if one person thinks that one crest is not supposed to be on that totem pole, they say it right then. So, if everything, all the crests are on there, everybody says, it's alright, that's when these Chiefs come with their speeches, putting the power and the blessing on what this totem pole represents. This is the kinds of Feasting. And this is done in a Feasting House where the Chiefs give their blessing and their power to the Chief who erects the totem pole.

* * *

Q: Okay. If a Chief is injured, is hit for example, is there a Feast for that process?

A: There is.

Q: What is it called?

A: In English we call that the Shame Feast, but there are different types of Feasts when a Chief is hurt or shamed, embarrassed. If, like in just recent times I have three, just to tell the court that this is still continuing today. While fishing last year down at the coast one of the Chiefs fell in the ocean. He was taken out. Now, when he returned to Kispiox he put a Feast on, and we called it *Gil k'al gimpks*, to wipe off the ocean from him.

The Translator: *Gil k'al gimpks*, G-I-L-K-'-A-L-G-I-M-P-S.

* * *

Q: What about if there's a settlement of peace between the Gitksan and another group, is there a Feast ceremony for that?

A: Yes.

Q: And what is that called in Gitksan, or in English, if you want to explain it that way?

A: I can't find a name for peace in my language right away. But when this Feast is I'll find the court an explanation of this Feast. When this Feast of peace is put on, this is when Eagle down is used

HALAYT SONG
"The *Halayt* find their own medicine song by fasting and praying beside a waterfall. They exercise to keep bodies strong. Slowly, as they listen and listen, the words of their *Halayt* song become louder and clearer. Then they have second sight."—Gyolugyet.

Mix Kaax is used.

Mr. Grant: Would you spell that, please.

The Translator: *Mix Kaax*, M-I-X K-A-A-X.

Mr. Grant:

Q: Um-hum.

A: After things are settled there would be quite a bit of argument, of course, but when both sides agree, and then the both parties have a young nephew to make a dance for the parties. They put on their regalia. They have their headdress on, and in that top of that head dress are the Eagle down, and these dancers, these nephews of young Chiefs, they have each one was their song of one side. This person does the dance with the flowing of the Eagle down to the people. That means peace, and the same way with the other, so Eagle down is very important to us. When if you don't enter into a Feasting House, a Chief doesn't enter right away, words keep going to that Chief and he's still not there. That's when Eagle down is used again. They take the Eagle down and take it to this Chief. They put it on him. He can't say no, and he can't say he can't come, because that Eagle down is put on his head. He has to come, as the importance to the Eagle down is peace.

Assault tied to claims

MORICETOWN — Young people in Moricetown are being beaten and verbally harassed, the band says.

In the first incident, Aug. 8, the son of a band employee was knocked unconscious while walking home, pulled onto a pickup truck and then dumped by the side of a road, according to a Moricetown band councillor.

Victor Jim said the youth was struck with an object carried by a person in a blue, shortbox GMC pickup near the Moricetown Canyon information pull out on Hwy16.

"The last words he heard were: 'this is for the land claims'," Jim said.

"They then drove him about four miles away to Blunt Creek Road where they dumped him," he said.

In another incident two weeks ago, Jim said one of his sister-in-law's daughters was stopped by several people in two cars and verbally harrassed with "derogatory things about land claims."

A spokesman for the Smithers RCMP detachment said that, although patrols in the Moricetown area have been stepped up, there was little police could do until the victims made a formal complaint.

"There haven't been any actual reports — these are only rumours until we get the facts," said Sgt. Herb Schmidt last week.

Jim said that he spoke to RCMP following the incidents, but he said he understood the RCMP could do nothing until it had the licence plate numbers of the vehicles involved.

"We'll certainly be talking to them now," he said last week.

Jim said there had been "rumbles" in the past, and he attributed the latest incidents to people's emotions running high over the Gitksan and Wet'suwet'en land claims case before the courts.

The Moricetown band is a member of the Gitksan-Wet'suwet'en tribal council.

"A lot of people don't understand what the land claims are all about, and things can get heated up," said Jim.

Although he says he does not know if the people involved in the two incidents are from Smithers, Jim said he is trying to meet with Smithers mayor Brian Northup to discuss the issue.

He said the RCMP have been very co-operative whenever their assistance has been required at Moricetown.

Earlier this year, a native special constable was assigned to the detachment to provide a liaison with bands in the area.

—*Interior News*, Smithers, September 2, 1987.

Gaxsgabaxs (Gertie Watson) and Gwaans (Olive Ryan) witness daily.

OBSERVERS

Victor Jim

Debbie Brauer
Canadian Press

Art Wilson

Lelt

Katie Ludwig

Albert Wilson
translator

School children
from Morice town

Antgulilbix
Mary Johnson

Bev Anderson

LE PETIT ROI

LAWYERS

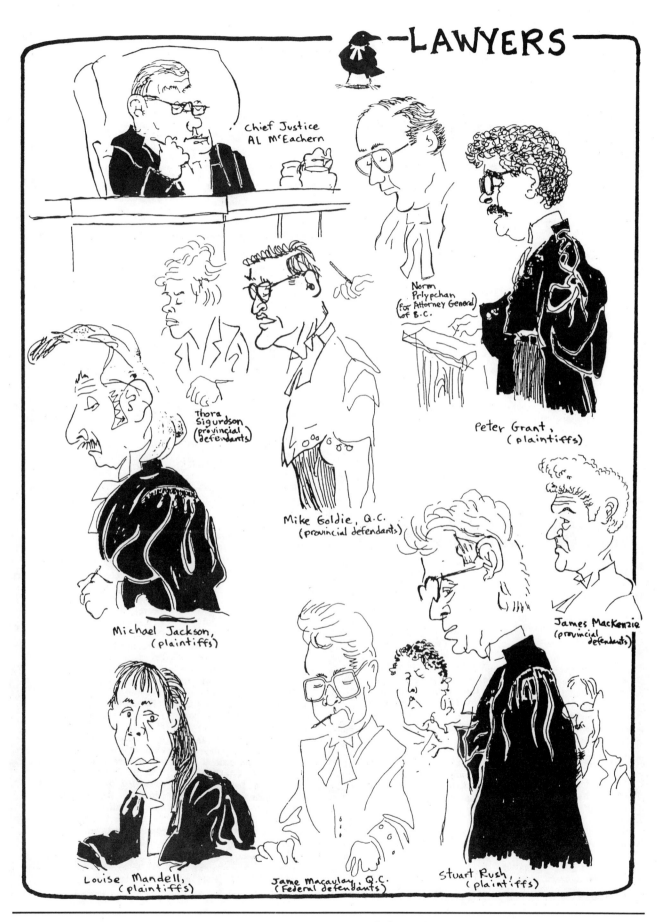

Chief Justice Al McEachern

Norm Prlypchan (for Attorney General of B.C.)

Thora Sigurdson (provincial defendants)

Peter Grant, (plaintiffs)

Mike Goldie, Q.C. (provincial defendants)

Michael Jackson, (plaintiffs)

James MacKenzie (provincial defendants)

Louise Mandell, (plaintiffs)

Jame Macaulay, Q.C. (Federal defendants)

Stuart Rush, (plaintiffs)

Chief testifies on Gitksan culture

Ken Muldoe, using his Indian name Delgam Uuk, wore a ceremonial red-and-black button vest decorated with his family's crest during Tuesday's hearing.

He said the judicial system has tried to turn aboriginal title into a package called aboriginal rights.

By DEBORAH BRAUER

"My chief's name is Gyologyet."

With these words Mary McKenzie, 68, of Gitanmaax, began testimony May 13 as the first witness in the B.C. Supreme Court trial expected to be one of the stiffest tests aboriginal title claims have yet faced.

At issue is the ownership of more than 57,000 square kilometers (22,000 square miles) of northwestern B.C., an area about the size of Nova Scotia. McKenzie was one of 54 Gitksan and Wet'suwet'en hereditary chiefs who said the land was theirs. They are suing the provincial and federal governments for recognition.

The chiefs said they had continued to own, occupy and exercise jurisdiction over the territory. To prove it, they decided to put their culture and its traditions on trial through testimony such as McKenzie's.

During more than five days of direct testimony, McKenzie drew a detailed and vibrant portrait of Gitksan society and its culture. Speaking about her own family, she introduced the court to the house and clan system and explained how chiefs were chosen and trained.

The feast's social, spiritual, economic and political importance to the Gitksan came into sharp focus as McKenzie described how feasts were given to mark the passages of life: Birth, marriage, death. It was in the feast house, she said, that laws were made, disputes were settled and rights and territories were affirmed.

The Vancouver Sun, Thursday, May 14, 1987   ★★★   A1

Oral history of Indians held as truth

Gitksan was spoken during feasts, she said, to underline their solemnity and importance. "You have to speak right from the heart," she said. "If we speak in English a lot is left out, the feeling isn't there."

An integral part of feasts is the reciting of the ada'ox, the oral history of a house, McKenzie said. The ada'ox tells of important events in a house's history and names a chief's rights and territories. It is considered the very personal and private property of the house.

Afraid scholars and researchers would use transcripts of the trial to publish articles retelling their ada'ox, the Gitksan and Wet'suwet'en asked that access to court transcripts be restricted. Chief Justice Allan McEachern, who is hearing the case, reserved judgement on the request.

The ada'ox itself has become something of an issue in this trial. The chief justice has not yet ruled what parts of it might be admissible evidence as an exemption to the hearsay rule. A decision on the matter is expected this week.

During her testimony, Mary McKenzie said under Gitksan law, all ada'ox are true. This was challenged by counsel for the province, who asked, "Isn't that a conclusion for his lordship [the chief justice] to draw?"

McKenzie responded with an impassioned defense of the ada'ox. "How can the ada'ox be repeated to the Gitksan people if they're not true?" she said. "They have to be accurate."

continued on page 16

continued from page 13

Later, she answered what she perceived to be yet another challenging of the ada'ox by saying, "It's not a story. It is ada'ox to the Gitksan people."

The province began its cross-examination of the witness last Thursday and was expected to finish Monday, May 25. Its opening questions were grounded in the framework of its defense: Aboriginal title, if it ever existed, has long since been extinguished or surrendered.

McKenzie was asked whether she voted in provincial and band council elections and whether she received a federal retirement pension, questions she answered in the affirmative.

Earlier in her testimony, McKenzie described the particular territory her house held in the claim area, explaining its importance in spiritual and economic terms.

The province sought to counter this evidence by questioning her about house members' other sources of income. It noted none of McKenzie's house actually lived on the territory and more than half lived outside the claim area altogether.

"They're still Gitksan, no matter where they live," she answered.

Despite her long and grueling days of testimony, McKenzie proved a formidible witness, giving her evidence with confidence and, at some points, humor.

Mary Johnson of Kispiox is scheduled to be the next witness in the case, which daily has attracted between 30 and 40 spectators to the 40-seat courtroom since its opening May 11.

THE HAZELTON SENTINEL, Thursday May 28, 1987

Antgulilibix (Mary Johnson) Giskaast Clan, Kispiox Village by Stuart Rush November 28, 1987

Stuart Rush argues with Judge McEachern about seeing the truth of this witness' adaawk

Mr. Rush: And perhaps I should leave your Lordship with this, that the evidence of the oral history, the evidence of the *adaawk*, is led not for the purpose of the beliefs that are held. They are led here for the purpose of the truth of the contents of those histories and that in my submission they cannot be reduced or demeaned on the basis of relegating them to the fact that this is what people today believe in, but rather because of the very process contemplated in the Catherine Millings case we find authenticity contemplated by that case.

The Court: Well, do you advance Mrs. Johnson's evidence about the destruction of the village by a supernatural bear as proof of that fact? That's what you just said I think.

Mr. Rush: Well, what I say is that that *adaawk* will be—may be repeated and may be explained in the context of a scientific event at that time. What we will endeavor to do, My Lord, is to put that event in the context of a very specific moment in time that we can demonstrate scientifically

The Court: But—yes, but she said that the belief is that the village was destroyed by a supernatural bear. And I think you said a moment ago, and I want to make sure I have your submission right, that you were putting forward the history of the *adaawk* as proof of the truth of the facts stated in it. I think that's what you said.

Mr. Rush: Yes.

The Court: Yes.

Mr. Rush: Well, again, as I what I say is the sifting process has to bring you to the acceptance, in my submission, of the truthfulness—

The Court: Yes.

Mr. Rush: — or whether it was a bear with unusual powers, a large bear, what has been—what has been brought forward to the present time is the cast of a supernatural bear.

The Court: Yes.

Mr. Rush: It doesn't mean that the event, wherein the supernatural bear or the bear with extraordinary powers is located, didn't happen. And it's my submission, My Lord, that to say that there was a supernatural or an intertwined, inter-related aspect of the supernaturality, if you will, of the bear with the natural element, the bear itself, to say that that occurred, and that in my submission—

The Court: You mean the destruction of the village?

Mr. Rush: That's right.

* * *

Antgulilibix by Peter Grant May 29, 1987

The Registrar: Order in court.

The Court: Mr. Grant.

Q: Mrs. Johnson, is there a plant that you know of that's referred to as Devil's Club?

A: Yes.

Q: And is it used by the Gitksan?

A: Yeah. They call it *hwa'uumst*.

Q: Okay. What is it used for by the Gitksan?

A: It is used for medicine, they drink it.

Q: Can you explain how it's used?

A: They gather it and they scrape off the outside and scrape the inside and the white spot, and they dry it for future use.

Q: Did you know a man named John Brown at Kisgagas?

A: Yes. He comes from Kispiox, but he got sick while in Kisgagas when he was young.

Q: And what kind of sickness did he have?

A: He got T.B..

Q: Can you tell the court what was done for him?

A: They made some Devil's Club for him and they dried like I said, ready for him, and then about—and they roll it in little balls like the size of the large pea and he chews those things and swallow them. He was dying they said, he is got nothing but skin and bone. And they call this disease *X'yansxw*.

The Translator: *X'yansxw*, X-underlined Y-A-N-S- X-W.

A: And another word they call it is *X'yaahlxw*, both *X'yansxw* and *X'yaahlxw*.

Mr. Grant:

Q: And do you know what it's called by the non-Gitksan?

A: They call it T.B.

The Court: Just a moment, I think we need a spelling.

The Translator: X underlined y-a-a-h-l-x-w.

Mr. Grant:

Q: And did—did—what happened to John Brown after he took this Devil's Club?

A: He got better and he got his strength back again. And in later years after he is an elder man, he works for the coast. He is a contractor of some boats, and a government boat happens to come around to X-ray the Indians. And people are still in the suits or clothes when they stand to have an X-ray and there was one of his lungs is half gone they said, and they were really amazed to see what happened. This was long before the white people

ANTGULILIBIX
(Mary Johnson)
Days 12-15, May-June 1987

Antgulilibix (Mary Johnson)—"Whirlpool in the Ocean."

"...they put a fence around us like they did to the pigs or animals. I am hoping and praying that the Queen will know what they did to us... in the olden days when they took away our inheritance."—Antgulilibix.

find out cure for T.B. If they got T.B. they would die right there, but not among the Indians.

Q: Do you know another plant that's referred to in Gitksan as *mulgwasxw?*

A: Yeah, *mulgwasxw.*

The Court: Mr. Grant, how is this going to help this resolution of this case? There must be a great many of these herbal remedies that are common all over the world. How is it going to help us resolve this case?

Mr. Grant: Well, the part of the defence, of course, is the people's use of the territory and use of the resources of the territory, My Lord. And I understand that there is a thesis that that's not what is done and that that's a major defence being used, mounted, and—

The Court: Well I can understand—

A: —and the position is the use of these.

* * *

Q: Did your grandmother talk to you—I mean your great-great-grandmother talk to you about the first white man that she saw?

A: Yeah.

Q: What did she tell you?

A: She said she happened to be staying with her grandmother, and—and a dog barked so she went out and she came back running in, telling her grandmother that some monsters came and they were holding a kind of roots that they made out of—roots that they made to—as a rope, and they call these roots *dakkhla wist.*

The Province claims that the culture is not valid because it is "watered down."

The Translator: *Dakhla wist* is d-a-k under-lined-h-l- a, space, w-i-s-t.

A: And after that, they understand it was the telegraph wire that she called *dakhla wist...*

* * *

Q: ...Did she talk to you about any other white people that she saw when she was younger, I'm talking about your great-great-grandmother?

A: Yeah. Perhaps about middle-aged, when she was middle- aged,and they live at the same cabin because that's Hawaaw' territory. And a young man came along, he said—and he got—this young man got nothing to eat. And he—on his pants were worn out under—on the knee and below the leg, and they took—took him in and feed him and this is—they got another custom among the Indians, they called Chief's names—their dogs the Chief name, and that's what they called him *Hluuhlxwm os.*

* * *

Q: But why do they why did they do that? Why did they give names to their dogs?

A: Because they love the dogs.

Q: This man who was given this name, was he given any rights to any territory?

A: No. They just call him *Hluuhlxwm,* that's why—they just like what they did to the ordinary dogs, that's what they did to him when they took care of him, and gave him the name.

* * *

Antgulilibix (Mary Johnson) Cross Examination by James Macaulay, Government of Canada, June 9, 1987

Mr. Macaulay: When you say that Mr. Heavener, the old soldier, got land on your grandfather's territory, you mean that the government granted Mr. Heavener some land on the traditional House Territory.

A: Yes. That's how they are. They stole away the ancestors' territory, but grandfather know it and he didn't know what to do until some folks, when I was small, started the land claim and they go to Ottawa.

Q: That was in 1927 wasn't it?

A: No. Long before that. As far as I could remember, I used to hear the—the Elders talk about it. They called the House of Parliament *Wilp alalgyax.* That's where people get together to talk, and they call the land claims *liseewa yip.* They talk among themselves about the land. They even go to Ottawa to talk about it.

The Law vs. Ayook
Written vs. Oral History

idea:
Gertie Watson
Gitsegukla

don monet /87

Some of the arguments surrounding the Judge's problem of hearing Antgulilibix' song.

The Court: How long is it?

Mr. Grant: It's not very long; it's very short.

The Court: Could it not be written out and asked if this is the wording? Really, we are on the verge of getting way off track here, Mr. Grant. Again, I don't want to be skeptical, but to have witnesses singing songs in court is, in my respectful view, not the proper way to approach this problem.

Mr. Grant: Well, My Lord, with respect, the song is what one may refer to as a death song. It's a song which itself invokes the history and the depth of the history of what she is telling. And, as counsel, it is my submission that it is necessary for you to appreciate...

The Court: I have a tin ear, Mr. Grant, so it's not going to do any good to sing it to me...

The Witness: The reason for the sad song is when they raise the pole, and when the pole is half-way up, they tell the chiefs who pull the rope to stop for a few minutes, and they sing the song and they cry. They remember those who used to raise the pole before them, and all those that were dead before the new pole is raised. So after they sing what they call *Limx oo'y*, then they put up the pole.

Q: These are the poles that are raised, like a pole that is raised even in your life-time, they would sing this song?

A: Yeah, yeah.

Q: Okay.

A: Well, if the court wants me to sing it, I'll sing it.

The Court: No, I don't Mrs. Johnson, but apparently counsel does. And I think I'm in a position where if counsel in the responsible discharge of their duties say this has to be done, then I have to listen to it. But I don't think, with respect, that this is the way this part of the trial should be conducted. I just don't think it's necessary. I think it is not the right way to present the case.

Mr. Grant: You can go ahead and sing the song now.

(WITNESS SINGS SONG.)

Q: Can you tell us what the words of the song mean in English?

A: They sing about the grouse flying, flying, how the grouse flies, those are the first words. And another word says, "I will ask for you to tell him to give it to me." That means when the first sister grabs just the tail end of the grouse. And another words says, "It will make noise underneath your wings." That means when you hear the drum, when the grouse drums and it makes a loud noise. And then another word says how the grouse gave him-

self up to die for them to help them save their lives. So that's the end of the song. And today the young lady that caught the grouse stood at the foot of our totem pole that we restored in 1973, and she is holding the grouse with tears in her eyes.

Q: And that pole is in Kispiox?

A: Yes.

The Court: All right now, Mr. Grant, would you explain to me, because this may happen again, why you think it was necessary to sing the song? This is a trial, not a performance.

more letters

Interior News
July 15, 1987

cartoons

Dear Sir:

In his criticism of Don Monet's cartoon of Chief Justice Alan McEachen, lawyer Tom Buri accuses the Hazelton cartoonist of not understanding the Gitksan and Wet'suwet'en Chiefs' aboriginal title case.

But it is Buri's understanding that has failed. Rather than attempting to constuct bad puns or inconsistent metaphors, Monet was merely recording events as he saw them.

All the elements in the cartoon took place in the courtroom. For example, while protesting that he should not hear witness Mary Johnson sing a dirge song that is part of her House history, the chief justice admitted to having a tin ear.

On another occasion, Mrs. Johnson did refer to the judge as "Your Highness" — doubtless her own parody of the quaint tradition in the legal business of calling the chief justice "Your Lordship."

By bringing these incidents together, Don Monet is doing what artists are supposed to do, directing our attention to some larger truth.

In this case, that truth seems to be the difficulty we all have in hearing and acknowledging information from cultures other than our own.

Yours sincerely,
Richard Overstall
Telkwa. B.C.

A cultural hearing aid

Very few people who live within the 57,000 square kilometres of Gitksan and Wet'suwet'en territory managed to sit in on the supreme court hearings of the title action case in Smithers during May and June.

Cartoonist Don Monet spent many hours listening to the powerful explanation of Gitksan and Wet'suwet'en culture by four hereditary chiefs.

One of his most effective interpretations of Chief Justice Alan McEachern's cultural hearing problems (*The Interior News*, June 24, 1987, page A2) cannot be fully appreciated unless people know what actually happened in court.

When lawyer Peter Grant asked Chief Mary Johnson to sing a Gitksan song as an essential part of her evidence on the "Ayook," the ancient but still effective Gitksan law, Judge McEachern objected. He said he did not want any "performance" in his court of law. "I can't hear your Indian song, Mrs. Johnson. I've got a tin ear."

In the cartoon, Mrs. Johnson says, "That's okay, your highness, I've got a can opener." As a matter of fact, Chief Mary Johnson did once address the judge as "Your Highness." It may have been a slip of the tongue, but it certainly expressed the customary respect shown to

"I could sing that song for you folks, but this court doesn't like me to sing."

I can't hear your INDIAN song Mrs. Johnson, I'VE GOT A TIN EAR!

S'OUP

That's OK your highness, I've got a can opener!

KLICK! KLACK! KLICK!

don monet

any Canadian judge, albeit in a most unusual form. The whole courtroom, including Chief Justice McEachern, broke out in friendly laughter.

The cartoon shows Chief Johnson using her "can opener" to overcome the cross-cultural deafness caused by the judicial "tin ear."

Most of us non-aboriginal Canadians also wear a tin ear. It seems natural because we have worn it all our lives. We are not even aware of the significant sounds we cannot hear.

What we are missing may be a valuable key which could help to open the way toward peace with justice on earth and in the Bulkley and Skeena valleys.

—Walt Taylor, Smithers

— **The Three Rivers Report** — Wednesday, July 15, 1987

Culture, Law, Language: The Trial Begins 43

Gwaans (Olive Ryan), Giskaast Clan, Gitsegukla Village by Peter Grant

Mr. Grant: Yes. Can you explain for the court what *Gwaans* means?

A: When the eagle flies around and landed on top of the tree, *Niigwaant*, that's what the meaning of my name. That's Tsimxsan language, *Gwaans*.

* * *

Q: Did your—did your grandmother use maps to teach you?

A: No.

Q: Do you use maps to teach your children?

A: No.

Q: I'd like to ask you a bit about caring for the older people and what your grandmother taught you about that.

A: Well, that every time she talks about it and she says one of the older people, when they needed help, you go and help. You give part of your life to them and I asked, you know, how and she explained it to me. You should help when they needed help. That's what they said.

Q: Do you do that today?

A: I'm still doing it today.

* * *

The Court: I didn't get the name of the village.

Mr. Grant: Gitwanga<u>x</u>, G-i-t-w-a-n-g-a-<u>x</u>.

Q: And that's the village the same place that some persons may refer to as Kitwanga; is that right?

A: Kitwanga, I guess, pronounced in Gitksan, Gitwanga<u>x</u>.

Q: The white people pronounce it as Kitwanga and the Indians as Gitwanga<u>x</u>.

A: Uh-huh.

* * *

A: There was no mill that time.

Q: There's no what?

A: No sawmill that time.

Q: There's no sawmill?

A: Yes. The old people don't use chain saw.

Q: But did they cut the trees—

A: Yes.

Q: —when they used them?

A: They used *da wiis* when they cut the trees.

Q: That's a—

A: They have to be tough when you use the *da wiis*.

Q: Okay. And can you describe what the *da wiis* was?

A: Well, Norman's going to explain.

Mr. Grant: Can you translate *da wiis*?

The Translator: That is—that is what the Na-

tives used as axes.

The Witness: *Da wiis* (adze).

* * *

Q: Now, you were talking about the bark or the inside of the hemlock tree that was used for food?

A: Yes.

Q: And was it dried the same way as the berries?

A: Yes.

Q: Do your people still collect this bark of the hemlock?

A: No, because of the forester get after the Gitksan when they go out and get the *tsoo'*. They don't allow us to do the things to the tree.

Q: And that has happened to you?

A: Yes.

* * *

Gwaans sits in the witness box for two days. Her eyes half closed, she recites all of the House and clan fishing sites down river from Gitsegukla. Meanwhile the lawyers and judge frantically turn pages and try to locate them on maps and documents.

Q: I'd like to ask you some questions about the type of plants or what you were taught about the type of plants that were used for medicines. Now, did your grandmother, did she use—make medicine?

A: Yes.

Q: And did she used to help other people like—

A: Yes.

Q: Some of the other witnesses have referred to Devil's Club, the use of Devil's Club. Did your Grandmother use Devil's Club?

A: Yes.

Q: Did she use it for when you were young on you?

A: Mm-hmm, yeah.

Q: Do you still use it?

A: Yes.

* * *

Q: Were waterlily roots used?

A: Well, that's medicine too.

Q: And have you seen them being used?

A: Yes.

Q: Yourself? What are they used for?

A: They make medicine out of it. They boil them and they they drink it, for the ones that are sick, yeah.

Q: For what kind of sickness is it used?

A: Well, any type. Well, I notice Mrs. Marsden was in the court today. That's what she was taking when she had disease.

* * *

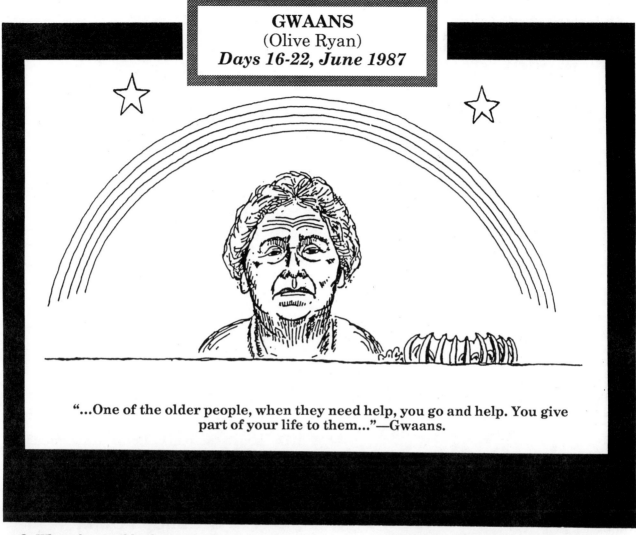

GWAANS
(Olive Ryan)
Days 16-22, June 1987

"...One of the older people, when they need help, you go and help. You give part of your life to them..."—Gwaans.

Q: What about wild celery roots?
A: Well, they used for when you be aching, arthritis, and they cook the roots and they pound it like a paste, and you put it on and put the rocks, keep the heat in.
Q: And this is a plant that you've used and that your grandmother used?
A: Yes.
Q: Do you know of the inner bark of the balsam tree, is it used for medicine?
A: That's what they used when someone was hurt and the flesh was open, and that's where they used, you know, the—taking all the infection out.
Q: How was it used that way?
A: Well, they take the ouside bark and then they roll it and put it in where—and they drain everything out.
Q: They put it in the wound?
A: Yeah.

* * *

Gwaans (Olive Ryan) Cross Examination by Geoff Plant for the Province, June 16, 1987

Q: Do you know how many members there are on the band list?
A: No.
Q: Do you know how many people live on the Reserve?
A: No.
Q: Do you have an approximate idea of how many people live on the Reserve?
A: No.
Mr. Plant: Is it in the order of hundreds of thousands, tens of thousands of people?

* * *

About five to six hundred people live on the Reserve.

Q: Is there electric lights on the Reserve? Is there electric lights there, an electric light on the Reserve?

A: Are you going to pay the bill?

Q: Do you pay the bill Mrs. Ryan?

A: Yes, I did.

Q: For the electric light?

A: Yes.

Q: And the members of the band that live on the Reserve own automobiles and trucks, don't they?

A: Repeat again?

Q: Yes. So far as you know, do the members of the Band who live on the Reserve, do some of them own automobiles and trucks?

A: Well, I seen some cars there, but I didn't ask.

* * *

The province theorizes that if Native people use automobiles, electric lights, eat pizza...that they are really just like Europeans, they have somehow given up their birthright.

Q: You have seen some cars on the Reserve?

A: Well, they will call me nosey if I ask them, the people there.

Q: You have seen people who live on the Reserve drive cars?

A: Oh, yes.

Q: And there is a school on the Reserve?

A: Yes.

Q: Is there a church on the Reserve?

A: Yes, two churches, Salvation Army and United Church.

Q: Which Church do you go to?

A: Salvation Army.

Norman Moore — interpreter.

Now suppose I was to be silly, and stand in the middle of the stream, who's land am I on?

The above cartoon of Peter Grant got a big laugh during one of the breaks in the hall.

Gisdaywa (Alfred Joseph), Gitumden Clan, Tse Kya Village (Hagwilget) by Stuart Rush

Q: Mr. Joseph, when you participated as a councillor or chief councillor at the Hagwilget band, did you consider that your participation was in any way giving up of your rights as a hereditary Chief to your land and to your name?

A: No. The advice that I was given all my life was that we have lost a lot of things in the past and that we were told the same thing, we all heard the same thing in the Feast hall, that this loss of our land had to be dealt with sometime in the future and that's the first thing in your mind when you are on a reservation, you are fenced in, you are looking out and then if the people want to go through your reserve, or make a bridge, build a highway, blow it up, they don't need your permission to do that. We have opposed everything that's been put on us, but it's always been carried out by the government. Or whoever was in charge. So everyone, every Gitksan and Wet'suwet'en person, has in the back of your mind that you have a duty to perform. Your Elders, what your Elders have told you, how they suffer,

"When House Chiefs take a name, they take on the responsibilities that go with the name. One of them is to make sure that, on the territory you have taken to protect, the people using it make sure there is no pollution, and that the area the animals are using and game trails and beaver dams and fishing sites are free from any obstructions, and you have to make sure that the people using it don't clear out the animals that are there for reproduction."—Gisdaywa (Alfred Joseph).

the humility they have gone through, is something that we have witnessed and that is why we have to listen to what the Elders said in the Feast hall. It wasn't visible, it wasn't heard by the outside, because the Feast was going on in the reserve or wherever they gather, but the message was always there, we have to deal with this land that's been taken from us.

Q: As the chief councillor and, to your knowledge, while you were a councillor, did the people at Hagwilget or the Wet'suwet'en people accept the reserve system?
A: No.

Gisdaywa worked for many years before the trial began to prepare for the case. Between 1977-1984 he and Leonard George interviewed Wet'wuet'en elders.

Whenever Judge McEachern hears something spiritual, he gets a strange look on his face.

Gitksan Wet'suwet'en Bulletin
Marie Wilson
June 10, 1987

Mrs. Ryan was called to the witness stand to speak for the House of Hanamuuxw. Mr. Norman Moore was sworn in as interpreter. Mr. Goldie challenged the use of Gitksan persons as interpreters, suggesting fear of biased interpretation, or improper interpretation of Gitksan words. He asked that all evidence be taped so that he could have an evaluation of the work being done by a local Gitksan interpreter. A provincial language expert (Gitksan) will then examine these tapes to monitor and correct any poor or irregular interpretation. Chief Justice McEachern agreed to the taping on the condition that the expert language critic would present himself to defend his interpretations in the court at some future date. Chief Justice McEachern granted permission for mixed language evidence and it was agreed that Mrs. Ryan would be questioned in English and could reply in English or Gitksan.

* * *

Gitksan Wet'suwet'en Bulletin
About Mary McKenzie's
Evidence

Mr. Macauley asked Mrs. Mckenzie to examine a document that he held in his hand. She recognized her signature and handwriting on the paper. Mr Macauley then identified the document as copy of a probated will. This copy was taken from the estate files of the Department of Indian Affairs in Hazelton where the agents of the D.I.A. acts as executor for all estates entrusted to their care. It is a private relationship between client and counsel. No other persons are allowed entry into the estates files. The content of the wills remain in the confidential custody of the legal authorities involved. That the Federal Government would sanction an invasion of these files to provide defense evidence is shocking and distasteful. Mr. Macauley waved the papers in front of the witness and proceeded to reveal the name of the deceased client, her residence and the content of her will. The Gitksan and Wet'suwet'en observers in the court room stared in angry amazement at this blatant betrayal of trust. Mr. Grant appealed to Chief Justice McEachern to stop this public diclosure. It was decided that, for the moment at least, the will in question would not be open to public disclosure.

Chief Counsel for the Attorney-General of Canada, James Macaulay.

Maxlaxlet (Johnny David), Lax Silyu Clan, Gitsegukla Village, Videotaped Commissioned Evidence (1st Witness), October 19, 1985

The Witness: What am I telling you now, I have not made it up. What I am telling you now I've learned from my Elders from the early days. I told you about how we were treated by the white man. The game wardens had sticks which they threatened us with, similar to the stick I have behind the door. The trees that they have taken off our territory, the government has been receiving the money and they're putting it in their pockets—now we want the stumpage fees. We want the stumpage fees from all the traplines they have logged. Where do they get the money to be driving nice cars, to have a railroad system or to be flying in the air? This is our money that they're using and I am walking on my feet. In the old days these people that trapped each territory, they protected the trees in blocks so that the animals would flourish. Now the government has trapped all our territories and they have all the money and the way they treat us, they throw us little bits and pieces of things to eat. That's it.

* * *

Gaxsgabaxs (Gertie Watson), Ganeda Clan, Gitsegukla Village June 15, 1987

Gitksan and Wet'suwet'en Strength

Tribal land and River
Traditional foods and Harvesting
being one with the land and Rivers
Potlatch and Spiritual Law
Tribal Family Membership and Unity
is following the ways of our ancestors
a sense of Place Identity
a sense of belonging
Strength
We have to be strong to
follow the ways of our
Forefathers.

Submission by the Chiefs' Lawyers Against The Direction that the Trial Resume in September in Vancouver

The Prejudice to the Integrity of the Process

It is a fundamental precept of the common law that the court process be subject to public scrutiny. This is the touchstone of the legitimacy of the process.

It is a fundamental precept of Gitksan and Wet'suwet'en law that statements regarding the rights and titles of the Hereditary Chiefs, their assertions of ownership of territory, of crests and of histories be publicly witnessed in order that those rights and titles be legitimated, authenticated and validated.

We submit that while significant Indian evidence remains to be given moving the trial to Vancouver will render the court process illegitimate under both the Common Law and Gitksan and Wet'suwet'en law.

The Province has alluded to inclement weather and the difficulty of perceiving Smithers through snowflakes. We can advise both Mr. Goldie and the Court that September and October are not months in which the weather in Smithers takes it outside the pale of civilized transportation and communication.

To the extent there is a question here of balance of convenience this court should take into account the fact that it is within the financial means of both Defendants to participate in this trial to the full extent necessary in the Town of Smithers. It is not possible for the Plaintiffs to participate in a like manner in Vancouver. That fact must overshadow all others.

Ken Muldoe (Delgam Uukw), Herb George and Victor Jim in the courtroom.

DAN SCOTT

PROTEST RALLY: Gitksan-Wet'suwet'en Indians at Robson Square Wednesday

Several protests are made in Smithers outside the courtroom, and again in Vancouver, demanding that the trial stay in the territory.

The Vancouver Sun, Thursday, July 9, 1987   ★★★

Natives say moving trial hurts case

By KIM BOLAN

Haida elder Minnie Wilson Croft thinks the white man and his courts don't make enough of an effort to hear what native elders like her have to say about land claims.

And she says the decision of B.C. Supreme Court Chief Justice Allan McEachern to move the unprecedented land-claims trial of the Gitksan and Wet'suwet'en Indians from Smithers to Vancouver will make it even tougher for the elders to get their day in court.

McEACHERN

A letter from McEachern says he does "not have the endurance to continue a case as difficult as this one for any appreciable time out of Vancouver."

But Wilson Croft and other native leaders told a rally of 150 supporters Wednesday that elders who have hundreds of years of relevant history to tell may be too fragile to make the long trip to Vancouver.

"The old man says he can't stand that area (Smithers) because he's too old," Wilson Croft said. "Well think of our native elders who can't stand all the noise and goings on down here."

The tiny woman, who has been in court many times on native issues, said: "A hundred years ago, no Indians could speak their mind, no Indians could be heard and Indians weren't supposed to be seen. But now we have to be heard, we have to be seen and we have to speak out for ourselves."

Native leaders from around the province offered support for the Gitksan and Wet'suwet'en and their court fight, while others carried signs critical of the justice system and the 61-year-old McEachern.

Herb George, spokesman for the Gitksan-Wet'suwet'en Tribal Council, said despite pleas from the coun-

cil's lawyers, McEachern refused to budge on his position to move the trial to Vancouver when it reconvenes in September.

"The move jeopardizes us from getting our best case on the record," George said. "The move will cost us $1 million more to bring people to testify."

McEachern did not respond to phone messages left for him Wednesday.

But the memorandum he sent to the Gitksans' lawyer July 3 says: "The anticipated length of this trial, which is uncertain and indefinite, makes it necessary that the trial be moved to Vancouver now or at some early date ... I frankly admit that I do not have the endurance to continue a case as difficult as this one for any appreciable time out of Vancouver."

He wrote that court reporters also "cannot be expected to continue such a regime."

But George and other leaders said McEachern should not put his personal comfort above their presentation of the case.

"By forcing us to move out of Smithers to Vancouver, the chief justice is using it to get us to spend less time in court," George said.

GITKSAN-WET'SUWET'EN PROTEST CHANGE OF VENUE

THE GITKSAN-WET'SUWET'EN PEOPLE ARE PROTESTING CHIEF JUSTICE McEACHERN'S ORDER TO MOVE THEIR LAND CLAIMS CASE TO VANCOUVER. HIS UNFOUNDED DECISION SERIOUSLY UNDERMINES THIS MILESTONE CASE FOR INDIAN PEOPLE'S LAND RIGHTS.

IMPORTANT EVIDENCE WILL NOW BE UNAVAILABLE DUE TO THE HIGH COSTS OF HOLDING THE TRIAL IN VANCOUVER. DESPITE PLEADINGS BY THE GITKSAN-WET'SUWET'EN TO RECONSIDER HIS ORDER, CHIEF JUSTICE McEACHERN DENIED THEIR REQUEST.

BY ARRIVING AT THIS DECISION, THE CHIEF JUSTICE DID SO KNOWING FULL WELL THAT FUNDING FOR THE GITKSAN - WET'SUWET'EN HAD BEEN CUT BACK BY THE FEDERAL GOVERNMENT. NEVERTHELESS, HE MAINTAINED HIS STAND AND CITED ONE OF HIS REASONS TO BE THAT HE DID NOT HAVE THE "ENDURANCE TO CONTINUE" THE CASE OUT OF VANCOUVER. PERSONAL PREFERENCE HAS NO PLACE IN JUDICIAL PROCEEDINGS, ESPECIALLY OF THOSE WHO ARE TO UPHOLD THE LAW TO ITS FULLEST AND TO ENSURE THAT JUSTICE IS DONE!

—from a poster for a protest rally in Smithers.

KWEESE (Florence Hall)

"Theres a lot of sentimental value and reasons in that territory, because of that territory most of our elders have through hardship passed on.

Every time there is a death in the clan and feast to be conducted, they all went out on the territory to prepare for the feast."

Florence Hall
(Kweese)
Oct. 15/87
commissioned
evidence

SINCE 1987 THERE HAS BEEN NUMEROUS WITNESSES APPEARING AS COMMISSIONED EVIDENCE IN THE JURY ROOM AT SMITHERS LAW COURTS, THE SALVATION ARMY CHURCH IN GITANMAAX, AND IN THE HOMES OF SOME ELDERS.

COMMISSIONED EVIDENCE OF KWEESE.
Smithers Law Courts. OCT. 1987

Chapter 3

Our Box Was Full:
The Chiefs Witness In Vancouver

January 3, 1988. The same sun whose rays warmed my face outside the courthouse eight long months ago still beams above me as I make my way into the Smithers airport. Today, however, the solid gray mass of winter clouds and the sharp bite of the north wind denies me the sun's warmth. A chill of apprehension shivers through me as the glass doors to the airport slide open, signalling the time to bid farewell to my daughter and reminding me that a new phase of my life is about to begin. My apprehension is balanced by a warm thrill of excitement at the unknown challenges that lay before me. Many of us have been swaying between these two emotions as this day drew nearer. We are the last of a group of Gitksan and Wet'suwet'en people journeying 1200 kilometres south to the City of Vancouver to resume the trial of *Delgamuukw vs. the Queen.*

Judging by the faces around us, it is equally wrenching for our children, our parents and grandparents to release us from their strength as it is for us to distance ourselves from them. Our comfort lies in the knowledge that our kinship system will guarantee their well-being. Since 1984, when our Chiefs filed suit against the Province of British Columbia, we have been challenged, individually and collectively, to do many things over and above the normal course of our lives. Our journey to the city is but the latest. Overriding our protests of moving the trial to Vancouver, Chief Justice Allan McEachern deemed the inconvenience to the courts to be greater than that of the Gitksan and Wet'suwet'en. We would ask ourselves, over and over in the months to come, if he, at any time, considered the added burden this move would make to us.

This chapter of our history centres around the six months we were literally transplanted to a totally different environment and the necessary adjustments we made in our lives to accommodate this change of venue.

Foremost was the issue of finances. Having filed suit against the Province of B.C. which, in turn, enjoined the federal government as co-defendants, we were experiencing the financial squeeze of cutbacks and cut-offs with the already limited program budgets under which we operated. In an area of high unemployment and stressed economy, we were forced to raise the bulk of funding from our communities to carry us through this phase of our litigation. The logistics of our transplantation were being carried out even as we scrambled around trying to raise the funds to pay for it. Not only did we need to maintain our home office with a skeleton crew, we must now find premises in Vancouver to accommodate the support staff and resources necessary to our legal team. Since the weight of evidence was being shouldered by our Chiefs and Elders, it was necessary to find appropriate living quarters to soften the impact of the "Big City." Through the assistance of numerous volunteers, we acquired office space kitty corner from the monolithic glass structure of the B.C. Law Courts and accommodations with a local inn. These two premises became the anchor points for our people over the next six months.

If we, the "young legs" of our Elders, had any thought of complaining about our situation, we were silenced by the quiet resolve of our Chiefs and Elders who took the stand to give evidence on our behalf. For most of them, two words will describe this year in their lives, "First time." The first time out of their territories... the first time on a plane... the first time in a city... the first time in a courtroom. Coupled with the strangeness of their new surroundings were the peculiarities of city life—the fast pace, the pollution, the noise, the anonymity, the isolation.

In every possible way, we tried to be buffers for our Elders when they reached the city, but we were helpless once they reached the witness box. On the hard, narrow, wooden bench of the witness seat, they suffered the increased arrogance of government lawyers emboldened by the absence of our people from the public gallery of the spacious courtroom. I marveled at the discipline and perserverance of our Elders and often wondered what tested their resolve the most: the continuous battery of ignorant assumptions and questions, the subtle slurs and side comments, the long hours and days spent on that wooden bench, the intrusive snoring of chief counsel for Canada who would slumber as evidence was being led? Or was it the assaults of city life: the violent attempt to rob an Elder in an elevator, the physical attack of another, the propositions made on the street? We would never know, for the more they were subjected to these alien forces, the more persistent our Elders were in offering us encouragement and boosting our sometimes lagging morale. We were witnessing, first hand, that which had been taught to us throughout our lives—seek your truth, strength, and guidance from your Elders and you will learn humility.

Out of the ashes of our sacrifices emerged a determination to meet and conquer each new challenge that was thrown at us. Turn the inconveniences into opportunities. Use the distance imposed by the courts to increase and extend the education of the public, for it is only in ignorance that a blind eye can be turned. And so it happened. The judge,

lawyers, and clerks were uttering Gitksan and Wet'suwet'en words, the court recorders spelling them. From a faceless number on the court dockets, we became living, breathing, identifiable individuals who make up a greater whole. Much to the chagrin of the government lawyers and their employers, we refused to don the cloak of invisibility they so desperately tried to wrap around us in their efforts to convince the courts and the general public of our non-existence as Gitksan and Wet'suwet'en people.

Our histories teach us that we have existed and maintained our generations by understanding our relationship with the world around us. "The land and all its resources is like our bank," the Elders tell us. "It is the Treasure Box from which all Gitksan and Wet'suwet'en life flow." To ensure the continuity of life, it has been our responsibility to care for the treasure box. "What the governments are doing to us is robbing our bank," says one Chief. "If we went into one of their banks and robbed them of their money, they would throw us into their jails. Our box was full... overflowing, and now it is nearly empty."

The wealth of our resources may be dwindling, but the wealth of spirit and determination continues to flow steadily from that treasure box.

—**Skanu'u (Ardythe Wilson)**

SCALES OF JUSTICE?
THE GOVT. OF CANADA CUTS GITKSAN – WET'SUWET'EN FUNDS WHILE THE PROVINCIAL JUDGE MOVES THE VENUE 1300 km's FROM THE PLAINTIFFS HOME. EXACERBATING THIS HISTORIC CASE WITH EXTRA COSTS AND FAMILY HARDSHIPS.

Law Week

Welcome!

Here's Your Guide to the
Vancouver Law Courts Open House

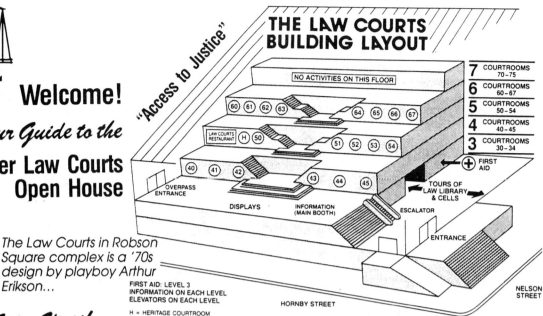

THE LAW COURTS BUILDING LAYOUT

"Access to Justice"

7	COURTROOMS 70–75
6	COURTROOMS 60–67
5	COURTROOMS 50–54
4	COURTROOMS 40–45
3	COURTROOMS 30–34

NO ACTIVITIES ON THIS FLOOR

60 61 62 63   64 65 66 67

LAW COURTS RESTAURANT H 50   51 52 53 54

40 41 42   43 44 45

⊕ FIRST AID

TOURS OF LAW LIBRARY & CELLS

OVERPASS ENTRANCE

DISPLAYS

INFORMATION (MAIN BOOTH)

ESCALATOR

ENTRANCE

NELSON STREET

FIRST AID: LEVEL 3
INFORMATION ON EACH LEVEL
ELEVATORS ON EACH LEVEL

H = HERITAGE COURTROOM

HORNBY STREET

The Law Courts in Robson Square complex is a '70s design by playboy Arthur Erikson...

Enjoy Your Visit!

On every day, a rotation shift of court reporters uses a type of shorthand to record every word said in court ...for the public record.

They are really good at it, but do make mistakes. Some examples on one day are: "They rot the salmon" instead of **got** the salmon; "deranged pieces," instead of **arranged** pieces!

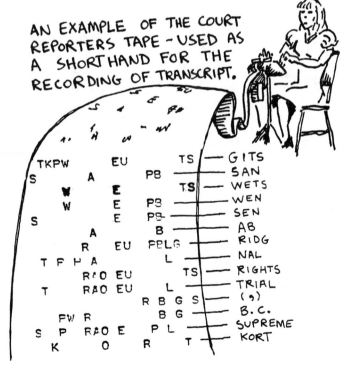

AN EXAMPLE OF THE COURT REPORTERS TAPE – USED AS A SHORTHAND FOR THE RECORDING OF TRANSCRIPT.

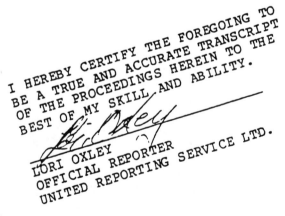

I HEREBY CERTIFY THE FOREGOING TO BE A TRUE AND ACCURATE TRANSCRIPT OF THE PROCEEDINGS HEREIN TO THE BEST OF MY SKILL AND ABILITY.

LORI OXLEY
OFFICIAL REPORTER
UNITED REPORTING SERVICE LTD.

B.C.S.R.A. 232 Number

SATURDAY AFTERNOON GRANVILLE ST.
ALFRED JOSEPH ANSWERS A
FAMILIAR QUESTION.

WHAT THEY TEACH IN
LAW SCHOOL

Since the trial began, the press has been conspicuous in absence.

OPINION

Local Case, Local Court

Shall we go, cap in hand, to beg at the court of our masters?

That is the question, as the historic court case presented on behalf of hereditary chiefs by the Gitksan Wet'suwet'en Tribal Council nears its court date.

As matters stand, the chiefs and their witnesses will now have to travel to Vancouver, where they will plead their case in front of a judge on the home turf of the two groups who have wrested control of this land from the native peoples - the provincial government and the major forest companies.

This land case, in which the native leaders claim stewardship of a vast territory, will undoubtedly have an effect in the Vancouver boardrooms. But it will have a much more profound effect here, where the people and the land are situated. It is therefore only logical that the court proceedings be conducted here.

Further, with the several claimants and their many witnesses now facing the costly expense of travelling to Vancouver - an expense not all may be able to bear - staging the court case in the metropolis could actually jeopardize the fairness of the hearing.

It would seem much more sensible to bring the court to the case, in this instance, than the reverse. The stylish new Gitanmaax hall would be a suitable venue for this monumental event, or, should that building not meet the court's requirements, perhaps the provincial court building in Smithers could be put into use.

Either way, the people who stand to gain or lose most from the case have the right to expect justice to be served in their own community - not to have to travel hundreds of kilometres to a strange and forbidding city.

To the justices who determine where the case will be heard we offer a reminder: Justice must not only be done, it must be seen to be done - in the affected community.

THE REASONS GOLDIE AND McEACHERN WANT TO LEAVE SMITHERS

TOO COLD

TOO BAD!

NOW YOU SEE THEM, NOW YOU DON'T

RAILROADED IN SMITHERS

"THE COURTS RULING TO CHANGE THE VENUE OF THE TRIAL FROM OUR AREA TO VANCOUVER WILL HAVE THE EFFECT OF TORPEDOING THE PLAINTIFFS ABILITY TO ADVANCE THEIR CASE." from submissions to Justice McEachern.

MOVING THE TRIAL MEANS THAT THE 'LAW' IS NOT SEEN TO BE DONE. A tenet of both 'Laws'.

IT MEANS THAT MANY HARD-SHIPS WILL BE IMPOSED ON THE WITNESSES AND FAMILIES.

IT DIVERTS VALUABLE TIME TO SUBSISTANCE FUNDRAISING, AND STOPS LOCAL SPENDING.

Vicky Russell, Alice Sampson and Sadie Howard having
lunch at the Vancouver office. The wall behind them
displays on-going illustrations from the trial.

Photo: Dan Muldoe.

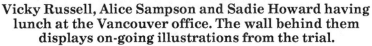

MY BROTHER CALLED ME
FROM SCOTLAND... HE
MANAGES A BAR IN
GLASGOW. THE '60 STITCHES'.
HE ASKED ME WHAT I
WAS DOING TO SUPPORT
THE GITKSAN + WET'SUWET'EN.
'WHO'? I SAID. RIGHT.
HE HAD SEEN "ON INDIAN
LAND" ON THE B.B.C.,
AND EVERYBODY IN
SCOTLAND WAS TALKING
ABOUT IT... NOT VANCOUVER!
I CAME RIGHT DOWN
AND VOLUNTEERED.
THE REST IS, AS
THEY SAY... HISTORY!
LINDA O'HARA
2 YEARS LATER.

Gene Joseph managed the huge library, and the tiny
budget, in the Gitksan and Wet'suwet'ens' Vancouver
office on Hornby Street.

Photo: Dan Muldoe.

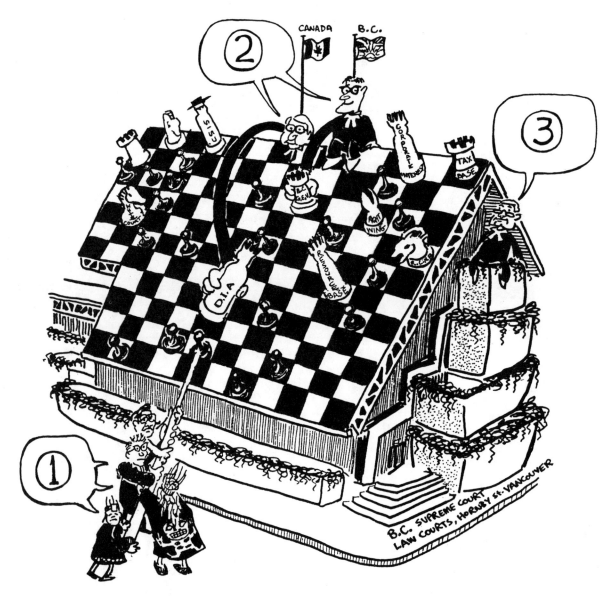

**Anonymous suggestions for these balloons
made at the Tribal Council Office:**

(1)
- This is not all for nothing.
- A pawn for a rook—typical move by the Feds…
- Does the public understand the gravity of the situation??

(2)
- If you want to play fair, play by our rules—*CHEAT!*
- Two for one move—stalemate!
- You go. No, you go, first.

(3)
- How is it possible to lose a downhill battle?

- When it was *my* move, I moved the whole board to Vancouver!
- Where the heck did all these pawns come from?
- Gardening is my specialty!
- I miss my garden.
- I feel left out.
- I'll wait in the weeds, then I'll make my move—eh Boris?
- My partner, Goldie, sits on glass, but I'm safe, I've covered my ass! (Goldie, the Province's lawyer, was once in the same law firm as Chief Justice McEachern.)
- The pieces must keep still or I'll lose my judgment…

AUGUSTANA UNIVERSITY COLLEGE
LIBRARY

Gisdaywa (Alfred Joseph), Cross-Examination by Michael Goldie for the Province

Q: Now, do you know how big that territory is of Gisdaywa in terms of square miles? Just approximately.

A: Yes. 40 square miles.

* * *

Q: There's been that mining there all your life, has there not?

A: Mining activity is without Gisdaywa's permission.

Q: Without permission?

A: Yes.

* * *

Q: But logging has been going on there since the 1950s, has it not, to your knowledge?

A: Yes.

Q: And that would be without your permission?

A: Without my permission. And if I try to prevent that it's—it's always happened that our people went to jail if they opposed anything that was happening on their territory.

...But since that time it has been really cut out. At the time my uncle was doing the trapping in the fifties there was no clearcut. It was selected logging.

* * *

Q: So as far as hunting is concerned, anybody that gets a hunting licence can hunt on Crown land in the territory at the present time, is that right?

A: They are hunting there without my permission.

...we were camped at Owen Creek back in 1983 and as we were camped there an Elder was with us and it was a cold morning and he related to me how we used the territory, how we used the resource of the land. And while we were talking there was a logging truck going by every two or three minutes and that interrupted him, so he had to stop. So he finally said to me, "Those logging trucks going by there and the trees you see on the back of that truck," he asked me, "Who—who protected that when they were small trees?" He asked me, "Who protected that?" And I didn't know. So he said, "Gyologyet protected those young trees when they first started to grow up because he was using the territory. He didn't want to see any burns." He said that Gyologyet protected those trees. That's why those trees are going by here now. There was no B.C. Forest Service. There was no Department of Indian Affairs at the time. So that is why I say that we owned the territory. We owned the resources that are on it, because our ancestors protected those resources before the coming of the government or any Federal or Provincial Government.

* * *

...And then there was areas of culture where we had our regalia and old articles that were used in ceremony were all burnt.

Q: That was done by your people as a result of encouragement by your Church, was it not?

A: The Church, yes, is the one that asked the people to do it.

* * *

...My grandfather's house at Owen—at the mouth of Owen Creek—is no longer there. There is a sign there. It's a big hole in the ground and it is used as a dump site by the Parks Branch, I think. So it's right on the house site where this hole is. I was looking for a place to camp, to show where my children where my grandfather had a house, but then when I seen this I couldn't bring them up. I seen the dump, the hole in the ground filled with garbage.

Q: This is your grandfather Joseph Nahloochs, is it?

A: Yes.

* * *

In his cross-examination of Gisdaywa, Mr. Goldie tries again and again to get him to admit to being a "normal" British Columbian. Gisdaywa slowly and thoughtfully reduces Goldie's questions to a shadow of repetition.

Q: ...Any resident in British Columbia can go up there and have a picnic; isn't that right?

A: Yes.

Q: Including you and the members of your house?

A: It is for that purpose it's put there, but then my uncle also had cabin sites and fish sites and fish weirs or traps right there, but he cannot do that with the recreational facility there.

"Looks like they're playing oragami with Wet'suwet'en territory."
—Ardythe Wilson

"When a House Chief takes on a name, they take on the responsibilities that go with the name."—Gisdaywa (Alfred Joseph)

Dzee (Madeline Alfred), Lax̱ Silyu Clan, Kyah Wiget Village by Stuart Rush

Q: Okay. Now, once the hide has been smoked and tanned, do you—do you use the hide yourself?
A: We make moccasins out of it and coats.
Q: How do you use the Devil's Club, Mrs. Alfred?
A: We use a sap from the Devil's Club. We put it around our neck and also for children so they won't catch cold, or as a remedy for colds.

* * *

Dzee explains how she discovered a white man destroying their cabin.

A: There was a heavy argument but he didn't touch him. They argued and I didn't understand what they were saying, enough. And after the argument the white man just picked up his axe and he went back across.
Q: And did you understand what the argument was about?
A: He was arguing with him because this man was dismantling that house.
Q: Is this the house you had lived in—Jim's house?
A: Yes.

* * *

GEOFF PLANT CROSS EXAMINES DSEE.

A: ...And when you're handling fish, you always put down a bed of leaves and you always take care of the handling. You make sure you don't mishandle them at all at any time?
Q: What—is there anything that could happen if you do mishandle them?
A: Long time ago it was said that if the fish when they come back, they would say, "This person here mishandled me, so I won't go to him," and that is why they take care to handle them properly.

* * *

A: Our ancestors who have passed on before us, when we are out on the territory they try to communicate with us. When you hear a whistling noises from the fire and then we immediately take a piece of smoked salmon or something, and we throw it in the fire. This whistling noise is our ancestors way of trying to get our attention. And they are asking for something. And that is why we do that.

* * *

A: Yes, there has been a long-standing belief in reincarnation, because when children recognize things that they have never seen before or recognize places where they haven't been before, and that's where the understanding is that their ancestors have been there before. And that they are the reincarnation of their ancestors.

Cross-examination by Geoff Plant, for the Province

Q: Did your late husband ever work as a saxophone player?
A: Yes, he played saxophone.
Q: Did your late husband, Peter Alfred, speak English?
A: Yes, he spoke English.

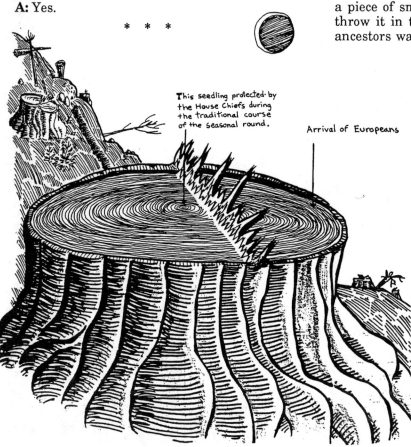

This seedling protected by the House Chiefs during the traditional course of the seasonal round.

Arrival of Europeans

DZEE
(Madeline Alfred)
Days 40-48, January 1988

"We take care of the land and respect it as well as the animals. You don't use one area over and over again and deplete one area, you always take care of the land and go to another area."—Dzee (Madeline Alfred)

Gitksan Wet'suwet'en
Information Pamphlet, 1988

A radical idea with a long history is being asserted in northwestern British Columbia. It is simply this. That people should be personally responsible for the well-being of their neighbors and of the land they all live on. The idea has been the basis of law and politics on the upper Skeena for the period of at least 10,000 years the Gitksan and Wet'suwet'en peoples and their ancestors have lived here.

The Gitksan (GITkSAN), people of the misty river, (Skeena), and the Wet'suwet'en (WET SO WETAIN), people of the Wedzen Kwe (Bulkley River), are presently in the Supreme Court of British Columbia. Their Hereditary Chiefs, (not the Department of Indian Affairs or the tribal council), have decided to take B.C. to task in the Province's own court system.

Claiming ownership to their House territories, (some 22,000 square miles) and jurisdiction over the land and their people, they have begun to call their own people to the stand as witnesses. One after the other, from both Nations, they have shared with the judge and other witnesses key elements of their unique societies, previously kept well guarded. In a spirit of hope and generosity they have detailed the Feast system which is the expression of their law, their *adaawk* and *kungax*, (oral histories), crests, poles, ancient songs, their spiritual lives and beliefs, medicines, Clans and Houses, revealing the matrix of the distinct nature of their societies.

Over the past one hundred years, Wet'suwet'en and Gitksan people have watched with interest the emerging Canadian society and have found it wanting. It does not respect political decisions based on face-to-face relationships and made among a network of relatives. It does not see economic transactions based on sharing, on affection, rather than competition. It forcibly prevents the Chiefs from obeying their own laws which say that the land they inherited from their grandparents must be looked after so that it can be passed on in good health to their own grandchildren.

This other way of relating to the world is usually hidden behind the stereotypes of Indian life which many Canadians rely on to dismiss assertions of indigenous title. In the courts, the Chiefs had hoped to find a Canadian institution where their words and lives, rather than stereotypes, prevailed. This has not happened and much of the expensive trial time has to be spent overcoming the biases of the colonial judge and lawyers.

The first three months of this historic trial, which has implications the world over, were held on the peoples' own territory. However, by the judge's design, it was moved away from the region and people in question, closer to the home of the government's power, Vancouver. Not only does this prevent justice from being seen to be done, but creates an added financial and physical burden for the Chiefs' Houses.

This trial, which will continue until the end of June, is presently being held in Chief Justice Allan McEachern's cavernous courtroom #53 at the Law Courts on Hornby Street, Vancouver, 10:00 a.m. to 12:30 p.m. and 2:00 to 4:00 p.m., daily.

Your supportive presence would be appreciated by the Chiefs and their Houses, but not by the judge or the crown who are anxious to see justice done — in private.

Come out and be a part of history.

IF you have come to help me
You are wasting your time
But if you have come because your liberation
is bound up with mine
Then let us work together.

Lilla Watson

(Lilla Watson is an Australian Aboriginal woman)

Wah tah keg'ht (Henry Alfred), La<u>x</u> Silyu Clan, Kyah Wiget Village by Louise Mandell

...If clearcut logging should go any further than it is now, and if it should be destroyed further into the area, we wouldn't have any place else to go.

Q: Um-hmm. Have you been taught how many beaver to take from a house?

A: Yes.

Q: Who taught you?

A: From quite a few people. Specially my Uncle Peter Bazil, but I learned it from Alfred Mitchell, he knows the most, he knows a lot about beavers.

Q: And what's the general law that you follow in terms of how many beaver you'll take from a dam?

A: When we trap for beaver we generally try to take big ones and we try leave the little ones so when they grow up they will produce other smaller ones for future use.

Q: If there is a beaver house which may have ten beaver in it, how many beaver would you think would be proper to trap from that house?

A: If there is a beaver in one house with ten, the most you catch four and then the rest is small.

Q: Okay. Has there been a Laksilyu Feast

recently which you can recall where beaver meat from Wah Tah K'eght's territory was announced at that Feast?

A: The last one that has been announced was at my Dad's funeral Feast.

Excerpts from Opening-Statement:

The Feast is a legal forum for the witnessing of the transmission of Chiefs' names, the public delineation of territorial and fishing sites, and the confirmation of those territories and sites with the names of the Hereditary Chiefs. The public recognition of title and authority before an assembly of other Chiefs affirms in the minds of all, both the legitimacy of succession to the name, and transmission of property rights. The Feast can also operate as a dispute resolution process and orders peaceful relationships both nationally, that is within and between Houses, and internationally with other neighboring peoples.

...You will hear evidence how, through its many facets, the Feast weaves each generation into the fabric of Gitksan and Wet'suwet'en history and sustains them as they move forward into the complexities of their future. Despite the efforts of missionaries and Indian agents, aided by the legal prohibition of the Feast from 1884 to 1951, the Feast has remained a bastion of Gitksan and Wet'suwet'en societies. It has remained so because the system of ceremonial, reciprocal relations expressed in the Feast remains a model for everyday interpersonal transactions between kin, Houses, Clans and villages as well as between human beings and the non-human world with whom they share their territories. The transactions in the Feast hall give meaning to what it is to be Gitksan and Wet'suwet'en.

"When we trap for beavers, we generally try to take big ones and we try to leave the little ones so when they grow up they will produce other smaller ones."— Wah tah keg'ht (Henry Alfred)

WAHTAHKEG'HT
(Henry Alfred)
Days 49-51, February 1988

Txemsim (Alfred Mitchell), La<u>x</u> Samashu Clan, Ans Payaxw Village by Louise Mandell

Q: What is your first language? What's the first language that you were taught to speak?

A: Gitksan.

Q: And what is your second language?

A: Wet'suwet'en and English.

Q: What language do you speak at home with your wife?

A: Wet'suwet'en.

Q: Do you have problems in completely understanding or speaking English?

A: In English in our words I couldn't understand. Like lawyers, like you guys, I can't understand you.

The Court: I can't either, Mr. Mitchell.

* * *

A: ...Even we staying in a camp where we used to camp, me and my father, seems like he's with me all the time. All the things he teached me through that territory, how to trap, how to hunt, all that comes back to me. Even our grandfather, if I go the Namox lower part, I remember what he says. He always telling us stories by the campfire at night. Not only that one night they teach me this—all this territory, lakes, peaks, boundaries, they keep telling us year after year. If— if I don't remember that mountain, I'd ask them again to make sure. Their spirit—yes, what our ancestors have spoken about in the past and what I believe is that our ancestors are reincarnated or reborn and they come back to the territory, and that is what I believe.

* * *

A: I get a very eerie feeling when you ask me this question because when you're out in the territory, if there should be—if we have a campfire, if there should be a whistling sound or—or like a whistling sound, that is when the ancestors that have died and gone before you are trying to communicate with you...

HEADS I WIN. TAILS YOU LOSE!

IF YOU USE PERMITS YOU ACCEPT OUR LAW. YOU LOSE.

IF YOU DON'T USE PERMITS YOU ARE LAWLESS. YOU LOSE.

Jim Macauly, head of the federal legal team, is saved by the quick thinking of his assistant Marvyn. Luckily, his afternoon nap during important testimony, was undisturbed.

Jan 6, 88

* * *

A: Yes. Well, the animal relationship to human life is sort of a communication. Like they can feel what is going to happen to you. For example, when my father was going to die or before his death, I went hunting, and I was unsuccessful. A deer was standing almost right in front of me, and I was unable to shoot it because I missed it, and that to me is a message to me from the animal telling me something is going to happen. And after my father's death, I didn't have any problems shooting the moose after that.

* * *

Txemsim is a skilled, respected hunter who outlines most of the Wet'suwet'en territories, names, boundaries, game and floral life.

A: That's my lucky charm. You guys like to buy a lucky charm in store. May I take it out? That's what you call *C'un yee.* I always carry it, trapping, bingo game.

Ms. Mandell: My lord, would you like to see it?

The Court: Thank you.

The Witness: Always use that for cleaning rifles too.

The Court: This is a root, is it?

The Witness: That's a root of that *C'un yee.*

The Court: Thank you.

The Witness: It's got a name for it in white. I don't know. I forgot the name for it in white man.

Ms. Mandell: George, do you know the name?

The Interpreter: Indian Hellabore.

A: ...our responsibility within the territory is as caretakers. Our—my father had told me that any

"Our ancestors, they didn't go by square miles, they go by their boundaries and that's what they have it in, their head, and that's what I am using. I don't know about square miles."—Txemsim (Alfred Mitchell)

time when you're hunting or trapping you do not take everything, you only take what you need, like beaver and marten. You only take what you can—what you can use. And the same goes with the big game. Some time back there used to be lots of moose, moose was plentiful, but now there's hardly any around.

A: Yes. The information that our great, great, great grandparents had handed down from generation to generation. They all resided in the same area and then we today still live in the same territory. We never came from anywhere but where we are today.

Txemsim
Cross-Examination by James Mackenzie for the Province

Q: Maybe I could put that again. Do you understand that the Gitksan Chiefs and the Wet'suwet'en Chiefs are now seeking compensation for the loss of territory?

A: When you speak of compensation, we are not trying to sell out, but we're seeking to have the territories the way they were before, the way our ancestors had governing the land and that is what this litigation is all about.

Q: Thank you very much. You want the court to recognize your ownership of the territory; correct?

A: What we want is to be recognized as our ancestors. They own that territory and we want to follow their footsteps. Now, government has taken it away from us, all the timbers, even water taking it away from us.

Q: So you want the territory back again, don't you?

A: The way it was governed our—like our ancestors.

* * *

…And that is when Dan was shovelling snow at the cabin and you yourself sneaked up on him and took pictures, and that's when Dan caught you.

Q: Thank you very much. You already mentioned that.

A: You're welcome.

* * *

Mr. Rush: What's the relevance of this cross-examination? I would like to object to this. I would like to know why it is relevant that a doctor looked after a witness who was injured in a motor vehicle accident in the Smithers Hospital?

Mr. Mackenzie: Well, my lord, there is quite a lot of evidence called about medicinal plants, and healing on the territories, and the use of the sweat lodges, as Mr. Mitchell in fact said they are hospitals for the ancestors and the Wet'suwet'en. And this it seems to me, this evidence is relevant to

show that the times have changed and the Wet'suwet'en people are moving with the times, as we all are, in some cases.

* * *

Ms. Mandell: Excuse me, my lord. Before we adjourn I seek the court's leave to be excused. I think I'll go have a baby.

The Court: I hope you are. We extend all best wishes. What would you have said if I had said no? Two o'clock.

The Registrar: Order in court. Court will adjourn until two o'clock.

Txemsim
Re-examination by Stuart Rush

The Witness: All these questions they been asking me, the government, I just wondered why don't they ask me where we from and where we're originated from?

*Later in the debriefing, Txemsim answers, "The lawyers ask us over and over about our family tree. I would like to know what is **their** family tree? We know ours—the spruce tree out on the hunting grounds where our mothers gave us birth and life.*

idea George Holland

Watching Peter Grant argue points of law with Justice McEachern is much like a game of badminton. Back and forth, back and forth...

Every hour and a half the court takes a fifteen minute break in the cavernous hallway.

Wigetimstochol (Dan Michell), Tsayu Clan, Tse Kya Village by Stuart Rush

A: Well, it's an ongoing thing with all our clan, and especially the ones that hold the names, the Chief names. We get together and we all have meetings and discuss what we're gonna do. Like for the use of it, and how it's going to be arranged, who's gonna look after each area of the territory, and how it's to be used.

* * *

Q: And can you tell me how are decisions reached among the House members and the Chiefs of the House? How do you arrive at a decision?
A: Well, we usually decide that at the Feast hall.
Q: Okay.
A: Where we can speak about it openly at the Feast hall with other Chiefs listening in as witnesses. And there that final decisions are made to whatever is gonna happen.

* * *

Q: ...What do you consider your authority to regulate these resources to be?
A: Well, it's always been that way in the past. It was handed down to us by our ancestors. And we are brought up in those territory which we know that we belong to the land and the land belong to us. That's one way of putting it. And all the resource in it that we are entitled to it. And that is the reason why we are always taught to respect the land and everything that's in it.

...You see like even from experience I learn from our ancestors that we are created by our Creator, and the land that we live on was created by the Creator. And he provided for us the resources that's on the land, and we look after it. And we look after the resources, as I would explain it, like it would be like money in the bank with the white man. He don't clean it out and get it empty. He always took care of it and just use so much of it and leave the rest for like safe keeping. You look after it, eh. You don't kill off all the moose or all the other animals. You always took just what you need off the land. And the same thing with the berry patches. They really protect that. I believe they were told that the girls in the clan before they come of age, I don't know exactly what year, 11 or 13, when that happens they're not allowed to go into the berry patches otherwise, you know, berry patches wouldn't produce any more berries for the future. This is what I meant by that's what I was told by our grandparents. That's how they really look after it, and they really believe it. And same thing for the animals too, you know, when at that age they don't—they're not allowed to eat fresh meat that is killed on the territory.

Excerpt From The Opening Statement of The Chiefs

The Gitksan and Wet'suwet'en, in asserting their rights of ownership and jurisdiction over their territory, are affirming the foundations upon which their civilizations are based and have been based for over 5,000 years. In denying that these rights exist, the Province of British Columbia and the Federal Government of Canada are denying the very existence of those civilizations. The foundations of Gitksan and Wet'suwet'en societies are firmly entrenched in their own laws. But in the face of Provincial and Federal disrespect for these laws and the injustice this has brought, the Gitksan and Wet'suwet'en have come to this court to secure those foundations in Canadian law, law which the Province and Federal Governments can be compelled to respect. Only then will the Gitksan and Wet'suwet'en be able to negotiate a just resolution of their relationship with Canada. This case is therefore a search for the legal pathways to justice.

Colonialist justice: step by step.

① Claim the land. Ignore owners.

② Steal resources and make laws.

③ Create courts and be just!

"We belong to the land and the land belongs to us. And that is the reason why we are always taught to respect the land and everything that's in it."—Dan Michell

Knedebeas (Sarah Layton), Gilseyu Clan, Tse Kya Village by Murray Adams

A: When Johnny David spoke he also expressed himself with kind words, words of encouragement, and he also spoke about the name Knedebeas, how it had been passed on from generation to generation from way back. He remembers the name Knedebeas when he was just a child himself. The name had been always been passed on when he can remember as a child.

* * *

Q: Mrs. Layton, why did you decide to come to court and to be a plaintiff in this court case?

A: As in the past, Knedebeas, the name Knedebeas goes on like my grandmother's brothers and uncles before her, and my uncles and brothers before me. We are not here to lose the territory, but to let you know that we are— we are still here, we are not going to lose it, and that is why I am here.

* * *

A: This territory has always belonged to us, and when we travelled in our territories, we were happy when we travelled through our territories. And nobody block our ways, stop us and block us and try and give us permits, and things like that when we travelled within our territories. And that is one of the reasons why I am here—they might find a way to let us use the territory without anybody blocking our way.

Q: And do you want the court to stop people from blocking your way?

A: I am here to let my feelings be known that our feelings are with the territory, and we want to see justice being done, and the way our ancestors had used the territory. And we don't seem like we mean anything to anybody now, the way the logging takes place, clearcut the place, make money on it, and then they move out leaving us with nothing. Just like our ancestors who had been living there in the past and lived off the land, now there is nothing to live off in there.

Q: Mrs. Layton, do you want money from the government to pay for your territory?

A: I don't want no money from anybody and I still maintain that. I want it back the way the territory was in the past for our future children's use, our grandchildren, and our great-great grandchildren, so they will be able to use it the way our ancestors have in the past.

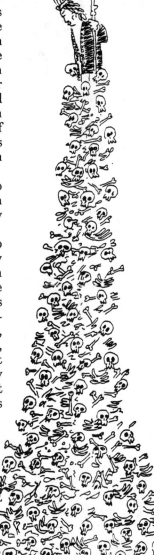

SOME TYPICAL EXCUSES BY CANADIAN MEDIA FOR **NOT** COVERING THIS HISTORIC TRIAL...

NOT SEXY, TOO BORING!

NO VISUALS, NO MONEY.

UNINTERESTED, STUPID AUDIENCE.

WE WILL "OBJECTIVELY" REPORT THE END.

TOO EMBARASSING! We don't want the people to know too much ... it may make our judge look silly at the end of the day.

SOUTHAM - THOMPSON

"This is our territory; nobody's going to take it away."
—Knedebeas (Sarah Layton)

KNEDEBEAS
(Sarah Layton)
Day 65, March 1988

Yaga'lahl (Dora Wilson), Lax Gibuu Clan, Gitanmaax/Tse Kya Village
by Peter Grant

Q: Yaga'lahl....Can you tell the court what that name means?

A: It means taking a rest on the mountain side. It's the way a person is taking a rest on the mountain side, and it's hard to describe. It's like the mountain goats, they lay side by side taking a rest on the mountain side.

* * *

Q: Now, your mother is Margaret Austin?
A: Yes.
Q: And does she hold a name?
A: Yes. Her name is Saaniilen. Saaniilen.
The Translator: 261.
Mr. Grant: 261.
Q: And what does that name mean?
A: Saaniilen means looking at the moon.
Q: Is it a Wet'suwet'en or a Gitksan word?
A: Wet'suwet'en word.

* * *

Yaga'lahl describes the action that the women of the village of Tsekya took when Fisheries Canada decided to blow up the rock in the canyon, the rock that was the place from which the people used to fish for salmon.

Q: And you were present there. Did she do anything else? Did she participate in any other efforts to prevent this rock from being destroyed in the canyon?

A: Well, there was a group of the women who went down to the bridge that pelted those workers down below with rocks, tried to get them to stop.

Q: And was your grandmother involved in that?

A: Yes. So was my aunt and quite a number of the women.

...We don't get any fish any more from that canyon. You know, during our Feasts sometimes

AND DID YOUR LITTLE BAND CONSULT A PROFESSIONAL FORESTER BEFORE COMPLAINING ABOUT CLEAR CUTS.

NO.

"We keep them wild animals sacred; we don't use them for fun."—Dora's mother, Saanii Len (Margaret Austin) at de-briefing

some of our personal debts that we pay up concern fish that's given to us, because when we're given something, you know, we pay it back in the Feast with a gift.

* * *

Yaga'lahl describes what effect the provincial highway had on their village.

Q: And how does it affect your village?

A: Well, that highway, that went over some of the grave sites I remember. I'm sure there is still some that are covered. There were a few that were moved.

* * *

A: Well, that's what I mean. There was discrimination from the non-Indians and some of the Indian people. It's just like anywhere else. Just because we are Indian people doesn't mean that we don't have feelings, we don't have emotions, we don't experience sorrows and joys. We have the same feeling as anybody else. And if somebody says something to us that hurts, we hurt just as well as anybody else would hurt if it was said to them.

* * *

Q: ...What is the Wet'suwet'en word for student? Can you give me the word? What do the Chiefs call a student?

A: The way I've heard the Chiefs use it, the word for student is *Distl'us Nuu Bee Bodilegh*.

A: I've heard it used in the Feast house when the chiefs speak, and this is usually when they see someone who has been in school and is doing really well. They recognize them and they say "*Distl'us Nuu Bee Bodilegh*." It is learning about these papers for us. It's not said just once. I've heard it many times. It's so that they learn to understand what is written, what the written word is and how to write it.

"I'd like to see the government's geneology charts!"
YAGA'LAHL

"I'm right here in front of you. Look at me, listen to me talk. How can you deny that I exist if I am right here?"—Yaga'lahl (Dora Wilson)

Tenimgyet (Art Mathews), Lax Gibuu Clan, Gitwangak Village by Peter Grant

Q: And you hold the Chief's name Tenimgyet today?

A: Yes.

Q: And you're a member of the Wolf Clan?

A: Yes.

Q: Can you tell the court what the name Tenimgyet means?

A: Tenimgyet in our language, the first part, *"Tenim,"* means a half bear/half human. It also means that *Tenimgyet*, to break it down more, it's a bear without a den that walks around all winter; it doesn't hibernate. We also use the name *Tenimgyet* as a *nax nox* performed before a Feast is held.

* * *

A: I would say I would be trained from a young age; these *adaawks* being told to me in short form, in medium form. Like when I say that, I mean when you're just a young kid, they just give you the

FOOD
FROM THE
TERRITORIES.
THE PLACE IS
CALLED OUT
AT THE FEAST.
WHEN YOU
DIGEST IT,
YOU ARE
AFFIRMING
THE PLACE.
IT IN TURN
AFFIRMS
YOU.

general outline of an *adaawk*, and as you get older more detailed as you get—progressed until the full form of the *adaawk* is fulfilled and its full length and the *yuuhlxamtxw*, *gan didils*, everything that's in it, you have to understand.

* * *

A: Short versions would be similar to Barbeau's stuff.

Q: You're referring to the type of notes that Barbeau would have taken?

A: Yes.

* * *

A: These types of thing, they expand and expand, but with the territorial names, the trails, the cabins, the exterior boundaries. It encloses everything after, it just expands, expands. It's similar like going to university where you hear these lectures daily, hammered into you.

* * *

The Translator: S-i-s-a-t-x-w.

The Court: And what is that, please; spirituality?

A: Yeah. It's a purification, the purifying of your very soul, your spirit, not physically, external.

* * *

The Interpreter: *Yuuhlxamtxw* is when they give you advice on when—how to live your life and show respect to people. And *gan didils* is—

A: Okay, I'll say. *Yuuhlxamtxw* is wisdom, to give me wisdom, the understanding, the various spirituality of our land. *Gan didils* is the way of life, how to react, how not to react. In other words, it's a doctrine of one's *adaawk*, it's a realism, it's philosophy, and it's epics, both life and death.

* * *

A: I don't want to be too negative, but this is caused by the white man. When they came they brought disease amongst my people. You might say that was the first germ warfare they have had with us, but this is what happened, that over half of our House was wiped out by disease....

* * *

A: Yes. As a matter of fact, they have a name for the train in their language. If they are mad at that train, the name of the train it was given is mobile disease carrier. That's how they are known, the trains.

* * *

Tenimgyet desribes his initiation as a boy.

...And he killed him, shot him once. And as the bear was still half dead, you might say, it's still

TENIMGYET
(Art Mathews)
Days 73-79, March 1988

"Tenim means a half bear/half human. *Tenimgyet* is a bear without a den that walks around all winter; it doesn't hibernate."—Tenimgyet (Art Mathews)

going like that, he grabbed me and rubbed my face on its mouth, indicating that we will be fearless and fear nobody; we would have power, same power as this grizzly had. And that's one of the trainings I had.

Q: How old were you when that happened about?

A: I was early teenager, probably about 13 years old.

* * *

Tenimgyet describes the food taken from the territory

A: ...They were announced as an *adaawk* and they were announced when you bring your soup, your tea, your bread, whatever, they are announced and said this so and so, this meat comes from, and they specify each mountain or its territory where it comes from. Each creek is mentioned. So in our rule and laws we say that if you eat and digest the words, it's within your very soul.

That's why they do these things.

* * *

Q: When you stop, when your House stops for the sockeye or when the pink come, what do they do next?

A: That's generally the signal to go out picking berries and the first site or the first place we go is on the *Tsihl Gwellii* side where we pick salmon berries.

* * *

Q: And what do your House members do, then, after the closure of the smoke house in October?

A: Besides the trapping, the hunting—one of the hunting things we do is we go up the mountain directly above Wilson Creek to go hunt for goats. These are mountain goats we are after now.

A: *Daiks* is when we take snow, oolichan grease and berries and mix it together. It's like an ice-cream. It's a real tasty dish if you will try.

* * *

Art Mathews (Tenimgyet) opens his family's box (ada'ox) before House members from Gitwangak.

Stephane Morrison sewing an owl vest at de-briefing.

Q: Do you know if the Westar mill is involved in clearcut logging operations?

A: That's their whole name, clearcut. We always call them clearcut. It is their general practices that they have.

Westar is the major logging corporation operating on the land. Westar is owned by B.C., Toronto and New York investors.

*   *   *

…Gitksan, Wet'suwet'en all work there, and what we then receive through wages and obtain through these hourly works that we perform, if you would compare that with the vast amount of wealth that's been extracted out of the territory, it's just a drop in a bucket…

*   *   *

A: When you clearcut, the very word clearcut means they cut everything down right from underbrush to the very food, you might say, of these moose, like poplar. It's not been utilized in any way,

shape or form, it's just been cut down and burnt.

*   *   *

…Kinship is essential for the very survival of our ancestors to live as they've lived and continue this into today's world and we do these things as they have done through *amnigwootxw* and do the helping and sharing of your territory.

*   *   *

…Geoffrey, Wallace and Jack and my grandfather Charley Smith said that the phrase about our Gitksan and Wet'suwet'en relations, interconnections of marriage, we are like a *sgano*, a woven fabric, solid. That is the way we look at ourselves as a woven fabric together.

*   *   *

Tenimgyet (Art Mathews) Cross-Examination by Geoff Plant for the Province

Q: And that reserve has running water?
A: It wouldn't flow if it didn't run. Yes, it runs.
Q: There is water servicing the houses?
A: Yes.
Q: And there is electric power?
A: Yes.
Q: The roads are paved?
A: Yes.
Q: There is a primary school on the reserve now?
A: We had to fight like hell to get the school. We couldn't get any funding from Department of Indian Affairs so we converted our band council meeting room into a school, yes.

*   *   *

A: No, we don't have a baseball team. We have a soccer team, we have a softball team, and we have a fastball team.
Q: But no hardball?
A: No.
The Court: Only in this lawsuit.

A crew was digging up 4 foot holes for hydro lines. In Dora's village Tse Kya.

One crew member found a human skull on his shovel … They stopped working.

When they called the boss-he said, "Keep working, just toss the bones into the canyon.

Dora's Grandmother Martha Wilson made them stop. The bones were properly taken care of and re-buried in the cemetary. By people from Hagwilget. (Tse Kya)

HOW OFTEN DOES THIS HAPPEN?

IS it all going in,
or is there a leak
somewhere?

Gil Ts'ek'
March 10, 1988
Vancouver.

Land-claims testimony proves private ordeal for native clan chief

TENIMGYET

By TERRY GLAVIN

GITWANGAK Wolf Clan Chief Tenimgyet hosted a traditional Gitksan feast in a downtown Vancouver office building Tuesday evening, symbolically closing the bent-cedar box that contains his family's most precious possessions.

Under fluorescent lights in a third-floor office suite across Hornby Street from the Robson Square law courts, about 40 guests ate chicken and oolichan grease, dried seaweed, cake and blueberries. There were gifts, speeches, prayers and songs.

It was a feast of thanks, a prayer for blessings, and Tenimgyet's chance to say goodbye.

Tenimgyet, whose English name is Art Matthews, was returning to his job at Westar Timber's Kitwanga sawmill near Terrace today after spending three weeks in Vancouver as a key witness in the boldest land-claims case ever heard in a B.C. courtroom.

For the past eight trial days, three of which consisted of cross-examination by lawyers for Attorney General Brian Smith, the 47-year-old sawfiler endured the painful task of recounting his ada'ox, the contents of his symbolic treasure box.

Ada'ox is a Gitksan word for which there is no easy English translation — it consists of histories, sagas, myths, laws, geneologies, social rank and duties. And ada'ox is guarded fiercely.

McEACHERN

Since last May, ada'ox has comprised the bulk of the evidence submitted by 13 native witnesses to date in a landmark B.C. Supreme Court case in which 54 hereditary chiefs representing 76 houses of the Gitksan and Wet'suwet'en are claiming ownership of 57,000 square kilometres of land in northwest B.C.

Unsuccessful move

The use of ada'ox (pronounced, roughly, adowk) has posed a legal conundrum at times for B.C. Supreme Court Justice Allan McEachern — an exception to the hearsay rule that the judge allowed but describes as "almost unknown in our law."

And it was the subject of an unsuccessful move by the chiefs to have the court transcipts copyrighted to prevent misuse of ada'ox.

But the plaintiffs are forced to open their bent-cedar boxes, as they say, because the provincial government's lawyers' position

is as unequivocal as the native stance.

The attorney general's office has told the court there is no such thing as aboriginal title, no such thing as a distinct Gitksan or Wet'suwet'en people and no such thing as distinct Gitksan or Wet'suwet'en law. Ada'ox is dismissed as a mere collection of folktales.

As a result, lawyers for the chiefs have been obliged to demonstrate a continued practice of ownership in the tribal territories that began several thousand years ago and continues to this day. So the hereditary chiefs have relied on their adao'x to prove the point.

Evidence that Tenimgyet drew from his ada'ox for the court proceedings includes an account of a fierce lion that made its way up the Skeena River countless generations ago. It devoured a weeping woman and threatened the countryside until it was chased into the river and drowned.

The account is vital in determining place-names within Tenimgyet's house territory, and the story itself belongs to his house.

Another chapter from his ada'ox that provides instruction in hunting and conservation methods, along with providing precise locations of Tenimgyet's house boundaries, is the account of a young woman kidnapped by grizzly bears in what is now called the Sand Lake area, northeast of Gitwangak.

The knowledge of bear-

hunting methods among Tenimgyet's house members derive from lessons learned during the young woman's captivity. Tenimgyet's name means half man, half bear.

But the hereditary chiefs' claim of unsurrendered ownership is also grounded in contemporary constitutional law.

Colonial agreements

It is based partly on the fact that aside from a handful of colonial agreements on southern Vancouver Island, no treaties were concluded with native Indians west of the Rockies. The Royal Proclamation of 1763 required treaties in advance of colonial settlement, but the B.C. government has denied, since its emergence in 1871, any responsibilty to conclude treaties.

As a result, the entire land mass west of the Rockies is subject to 21 separate native land claims.

The Nisga'a, the Gitksans' neighbors, are engaged in the only current talks in B.C. All 20 other groups are awaiting their turn to negotiate with the federal government (the B.C. government has declined to participate in negotiations).

The Nisga'a came close to winning recognition of their continued title to their traditional territories in a split Supreme Court of Canada decision in 1973, and nothing approached that case in galvanizing native hopes until the Gitksan and Wet'suwet'en chiefs brought their case to trial last May. *Vancouver Sun, May 23/88*

Hanamuxw (Joan Ryan), Giskaast Clan, Gitsegukla Village by Michael Jackson

Hanamuxw describes the responsibilities of being a House Chief.

The Witness: ...You have to accept the fact that you will be responsible in protecting the smaller creatures in your environment. You have to be sensitive. You have to be an independent thinker. You have to be a good listener. You have to learn to be a servant, yet at the same time you hold the highest title that the Gitksan nation can bestow upon you. You have to learn to handle many different situations with dignity, including under duress...

...You have to learn how to co-operate. You learn how to, or at least—how to be part of a group. You have to learn how to make split-second decisions when necessary. You have to be courageous. You have to be committed to the idea that it's your job to make life better for everyone within your Nation, not just for your house, but for everyone within your Nation, and including those outside of your Nation as well.

* * *

A: *Hlaa niin xsi gyalatxwit dim ant guuhl hli dax gyets dip niye'en. Dim guudinhl wa midim'y ama gya'adihl Lax yip.*

Q: Do you have a translation of those words that were given to you?

A: Roughly the translation would be that you are the one that has been selected to take the land that was your inheritance, to hold it, and to take care of it...

...It also means that you as the Chief have the responsibility of training the younger members of your family so that all the traditions, all the cus-

toms, all the rituals within your House are maintained. So in a sense the Chief is also the teacher for the younger people as well as a counsellor, as well as a spiritual leader.

* * *

Q: What is the significance of the raising of a pole of the former Hanamuxw, Jeffrey Johnson, and the raising of your pole, the present Hanamuxw?

A: First and foremost, it means that what I am doing now is preserving the past for the nieces and nephews that we have now and the future members of my family. Also following the tradition that is required for the Chief that you put up your own pole, which indicates that there is continuity in the history of the house, and that putting up of the pole indicates that you intend to maintain that link with the past, it means that you are careful about preserving the history of the house. One way of ensuring that the history is there. It also indicates too that you do have a House. I mean, without the pole it certainly would be difficult to identify the House of Hanamuxw because your pole records experiences of your House. It's like a history book of your House. It's evidence that Hanamuxw's House did exist, does exist and will continue to exist. So maintaining your poles is really important. It's a very important evidence in the Gitksan Nation, that you are what you are.

* * *

Q: Is there any special training or any special way in which you prepare yourself to gain that spiritual strength?

A: Certainly by listening to our Elders is one way of gaining understanding of what we mean by our spiritual values. One of the ways in which you incorporate into your life is to exercise every day, one of the ways in which you try and enhance the presence or increase the presence of the Creator in your life is to prepare your body, your mind and your spirit, and one form of doing that is by fasting, and this is where guidance from your Creator is very important, the length of time that you do your fasting depends on the instructions that you get from your Creator, so it may be for a short period of time, it might be a fairly lengthy time, but at all times you are protected by him.

Q: Do you yourself engage in that, in fasting?

A: At times, yes.

HANAMUXW
(Joan Ryan)
Day 80, March 1988

Pole from the House of Hanamuxw.

"Your pole records experiences of your House. It's like a history book of your House. It's evidence that Hanamuxw's House did exist, does exist, and will continue to exist."—Hanamuxw (Joan Ryan)

I tried out the witness box: a totally uncomfortable bench. The Province's lawyer—Geoff Plant—said, "It's not meant to be comfortable!" But I pointed out that an eighty year-old woman sat here last week. "Then, the moral is, don't make them sit here," he replied.

Hanamuxw (Joan Ryan) Cross-examination by Geoff Plant for the Province

Q: Chief Hanamuxw, by becoming a Chief of the Gitksan, do you acquire spiritual power?

A: We don't believe that you acquire spiritual power, we feel that the spirit is always a part of you, right from the start. And it is up to you to develop and strengthen that spiritual power.

Q: But does the same spirit, is the same spirit part of every Gitksan person or is it limited only to those who are Chiefs or are destined to become Chiefs?

A: We believe that every human being has a spirit so it would be in every Gitksan person as well as anybody else.

One day a couple of Canadian Astronauts were lost in space.

Finally they found a strange uninhabited planet to land on.

They planted a big plastic flag and claimed this NEW planet in the name of Canada! JUST THEN A STRANGE FIGURE APPROACHED...

"What's Canada?" said the stranger. "Oh no," said the Canuk, "do we have to call all the witnesses again?!"

Taxwok (James Morrison), Lax Gibuu Clan, Kitwancool Village by Stuart Rush

Q: And this feast was held in Kispiox at the community hall there?

A: Yes.

Q: And why was Elsie Morrison and Pete Muldoe at your Wilksiwitxw; what were they invited to do?

A: They were invited to put the blanket on the crest.

Q: Put the blankets on you?

A: Yes.

Q: And, is this done in accordance with Gitksan law?

A: Yes.

Q: And why were Elsie Morrison and Pete Muldoe, why were those Chiefs chosen to put it on you, were they high chiefs of your Wilksiwitw?

A: No, the same, Wilksiwitw on the father's side, that's why you never miss that.

Q: Okay. Now, at the feast, were there speeches made about your taking the name?

A: Yes. First thing is, you have to go back where this memorial song is sung at that time before they put the blanket on.

Q: Was the memorial song sung then?

A: Yes, by Gordon Robinson, the late Gordon Robinson.

Q: That's the same Gordon Robinson from your House?

A: Yes. That were sung at that time. And they put the blanket on and then goes on to the speech.

Q: Just before you go on to talk about the speech, I just wanted to ask you about when the memorial song is sung, what is the purpose or the effect of the singing of this song?

A: Well, when, while they ever singing that song, that's memorial, that's today, when they are singing it and rattle, when they are singing it in a quiet way, while they are singing that song, I can feel it today that you can feel something in your life, it memories back to the past what's happened in the territory. This is why this song, this memorial song. While the chief is sitting there I can still feel it today while I am sitting here, I can hear the brook, I can hear the river run. This is what the song is all about. You can feel the air of the mountain. This is what the memorial song is. To bring your memory back into that territory. This is why the song is sung, the song. And it goes on for many thousands of years ago. And that's why we are still doing it today. I can feel it. That's how they know the law of Indian people, as this goes on for many years and I know this is how they have been handled in the feast, the first one has to be the one that sung the song.

Sakxum Higookx (Vernon Smith), Lax Xskiik Clan, Gitwangak Village by Murray Adams

Q: Mr. Smith, you hold the Gitksan chief's name Sakum Higookw, is that right?

A: Yes.

Q: And that is number 56 on the plaintiff's list. And could you tell the court what that name means in English?

A: It means the person that starts something energetically, but never finishes it off.

Q: Now, did you have to make a choice between restoring the pole that had fallen and starting a new one?

A: Yes.

Q: And what series of events is involved if you had made the decision to start a new one?

A: It is going to run into a few grand if I start a new one because if my Wilksiwitw go out into the forest and look for a pole that would fit the size of the totem pole that I would like him to carve, it would take him a few days to look for one particular pole, a cedar pole. And once he found the cedar pole and reports back—reports back to me, then we have to set up another Feast celebrating the tree that went down. And then every time the pole moves there is a gathering. And we feed the people every time we move the pole until it gets to its location. And it takes a series of Feasts in order to do that and it runs into a few grand by the time it's over.

* * *

THE COURT COSTS ARE HUGE, WHILE THE TRIAL (LIKE A CHESS GAME) IS MOVING ALONG AT LESS THAN A SNAILS PACE.

TAXWOK
(James Morrison)
Days 82-88, April 1988

"I can still feel it today while I'm sitting here, I can hear the brook, I can hear the river run.... You can feel the air of the mountain. This is what the memorial song is. To bring your memory back into that territory."—Taxwok (James Morrison)

"If you know the territory well, it is like your own skin. Sometimes you can even feel the animals moving on your body as they are on the land, the fish swimming in your bloodstream..."

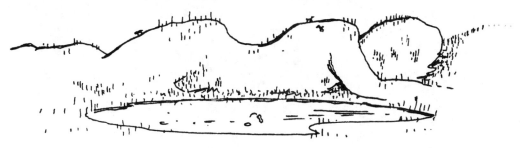

"If you know the territory well enough, you can feel the animals."—Johnny David, Wet'suwet'en, 108 years old.

THE CLEAR CUT!

BRITISH COLUMBIA'S NEW FASHION CRAZE!

Partners in Crime, Hon. Dave Parker Min. of Forests.

A: In the old days you live off your own resources, inside your own territory's resources. And there is hardly any money involved before the clearcut logging came in. And with the clearcut logging, there is nothing out there for us to live on so we have to rely on other sources to do what we traditionally do. That's why I go out and be a commercial fisherman or bus driver or grab whatever job I can get.

Q: And do you say that you don't have the use of your territories now?

A: No, we are restricted because of the laws of the province. We can't go out and do what we usually do. And if we do go out, we get charged. So we are very limited to whatever we do even if there is space left to do our traditional lifestyle.

* * *

Q: And can you give an example of that process of the Hereditary Chiefs giving direction to the Tribal Council in relation to territory and land claims?

A: A few years back I was in one of the meetings where they were concerned about the logging operations on their territories and seen that the whole resource is being wiped out. The province keeps saying that the trees will—they are going to replant the trees. But the Hereditary Chiefs think that the next generation will grow old and have nothing to do by the time the planted trees are mature and their children will grow old before the trees mature. So the concern is to try and slow down the logging and save something for our children to live on. And they have instructed the Tribal Council to follow up on the concerns. And, in turn, the Tribal Council went and did some research after those few meetings that they have and it all boils down right up to today in this court case.

Sakxum Higookx
Cross-Examination by James Mackenzie for the Province

Q: And can you tell me why in 1977, November 1977, the Kitwancool Hereditary Chiefs decided to submit their own claim independently of the other seven villages?

A: They claimed that they've never endorsed to have a reserve within their territory. They want to keep the whole territory as it stands and they don't agree with the government to put them in the reserve. They confronted the surveyors and they were arrested, they were shipped to Oakalla. So in turn when they come back the reserve is set up already while they were gone, so they call that Kitwancool-Oakalla Prison Reserve.

Mr. 'Map' Kenzie

I'll use both your lordship.

"Why do you use Indian names, can't you just use their english name? Why does everybody use both? I have to struggle to catch up every time you use one... I just can't see why?" JUSTICE McEACHERIN

SAXUM HIGOOKX
(Vernon Smith)
Days 89-91, May 1988

"The Hereditary Chiefs think that the next generation will grow old and
have nothing to do by the time the planted trees are mature. So the concern
is to try and slow down the logging and save something for our children to
live on."—Sakxum Higookx (Vernon Smith)

Xamlaxyeltxw (Solomon Marsden), Ganeda Clan, Kitwancool Village
by Peter Grant

Q: Mr. Marsden, your Chief's name is Xamlaxyeltxw?
A: Yes.
Q: And you are the head Chief of a House?
A: Yes.
Q: And you are a member of the Ganeda or Frog Clan of Kitwancool?
A: Yes.
Q: And the name Xamlaxyeltxw is a *nax nox* name which means "going back and forth?"

* * *

A: In the ancient times they have their own tools to use on whatever they are doing, carving poles, cooking.
Q: When you were taught the *adaawk*, were you taught what these tools were made of?
A: What they would do is they would sharpen a rock until it was sharp like a knife and it does work like a knife. And these tools are also used when they are preserving their fish and their meat. The tool that they used to carve the totem pole is known as the *dax winsxw*.

* * *

A: In the ancient times when the people acquired

Solomon Marsden holds his grand-daughter during a break in his Cross-examination.
May 10/88

their crests they go through a hardship, and some of the people suffer while acquiring the crest. And this is how they acquire these crests.

* * *

A: When the *Limxoo'y* is sang, it is very important and it's very powerful. It is used only when important events are happening, and this is why we sing these songs. There is power in these songs. We put the power, the *Daxgyet* on to the person that is raising the pole.

* * *

Xamlaxyeltxw has described the severity of Gitksan law on trespassers.

Q: Now, can you explain why that is so, that this law is so severe?
A: This is why the Indian people, Aluugigyet, call their territories a storage place, *An luu to'os't*.
Whenever they would need anything for survival or whenever they want the resources, it's just like opening a storage bin and taking what you need out of that, the storage place. And this is why they have respect for the land for survival.

Xamlaxyeltxw Cross-examination by James Macaulay

Q: And in the same long house lived sub-Chiefs of the House to the left and to the right?
A: I want to tell you an *adaawk* while concerning the long houses what happened. It will only take about five minutes. In the beginning of time when people become chiefs, what the law they have to follow is that they sleep in the back centre of the long house and what they do is they take a name and they're responsible for the House members and we don't write anything down becasue there was no writing done in those days. So what happens is as soon as the Chiefs wake up early in the morning, they get up and start telling the history to the people from the beginning of time and then they start telling the *adaawk*, what *adaawk* they had in that House and then they tell their other House members what to do and how they should do it. And this was the law of the Gitksan people. It gets passed on from generation to generation. And the hard work of the Chiefs in the ancient times was to pass the *adaawk* and the history from generation to generation and their hard work reached us. This is why we know our *adaawk* and our history. Because this is what the Chiefs did back then, passing from generation to generation...

Michael Goldie (for the Province of B.C.,
"And before the highways, before horses,
you people never went that far into the
territory, did you?"
Xamlaxyeltxw (Solomon Marsden),
"Before then we carried 100 pound packs
and we walked in."

Gitludahl (Pete Muldoe), Giskaast Clan, Kispiox Village
by Stuart Rush

Q: Mr. Muldoe, you are 79?
A: 78, something like that.
Q: Okay.
The Court: Sure doesn't look it.

* * *

Gitludahl explains what is expected by the House Chiefs attending a Feast.

Q: And can you tell us generally what the Chiefs said when they spoke?
A: Well, as they are sitting there and they witness everything what is done during the feast and if we do it properly and then we speak about what's to be done. And that's what all the Chiefs are there to be witness the Feast. And if I do anything wrong or give anything out what is not belong to me or what doesn't belong to Gitludahl or in any territory, one of the Chiefs is going to stand up and speak up and say that I am not doing the right thing. If everything is doing the right thing they say they glad they attended and witness the Feast and so on like that. And they all satisfied with what they get.

* * *

Q: And what does the name of *Luu goo'mx* mean when it's translated from Gitksan into English?
A: Well, I take you through it. It's the meaning of it, like if you say it's a grizzly bear, it have six cubs. That's the meaning of the *Luu goo'mx*.

* * *

MR. MULDOE! THERE IS A SMALL RESTAURANT ON KISPIOX RESERVE WHERE YOU CAN BUY HAMBURGERS ISN'T THERE?! AND COKES! AND FRIES!

YOU CAN PROBABLY BUY ICE CREAM THERE TOO!

MAY 19/1988 THE PROVINCE OF B.C. DEFENDS ITSELF.

The Province's theory that Native people are no longer Native if they use white society's fast food joints...

Gitludahl describes some of the small scale logging mills in the territories.

...We wasn't the only one that had a mill around that area, there must be about 20 or more small outfits that having a mill all around the area, all along the Kispiox River and down towards Hazelton.
Q: About how many people from the Village of Kispiox did you employ?
A: I think we employed about 15 or 20, maybe more.

* * *

The Witness: Like, like after quite a few years, a bigger company coming in there and they trying to push everything out of there if they can. And I was supplying the lumber to the Hazelton Sawmill, and shipping some through—Sargant shipped some through the Northern Mill at Smithers. Sargant was handling all the shipping for us. And then all of a sudden, the Hazelton Sawmill said I owed them some money, but then they put in everything like that and other people stepped in and said I owed them money. I don't know just what I owe them. They just wanted to push us out of there and I wasn't the only one. They pushed all the little sawmills right out of the country and they operate the Hazelton sawmill.
Q: And what happened to your equipment?
A: They took all the equipment.

Gitludahl, Cross-examination
by James Mackenzie

Q: And he is the person who's—his name is Delgamuukw, isn't it?
A: Yeah.
Mr. Mackenzie: Yes. I think Your Lordship has the spelling of that one.
The Court: Yes, I've heard it before.
The Witness: Getting pretty familiar with Delgamuukw.
The Court: All right. Before you go on, I've been giving much weighty consideration to these matters and can counsel tell me how they think, or with instructions of course, how is this often used word properly pronounced, is it Gitksan or Gitskan?
Mr. Rush: Gitksan.
The Court: Some people says Gitksan and other people say Gitskan.
Mr. Rush: Yes, I know, and that's not the pronunciation.
The Court: And some say Wet'suwet'en and others say Wet'sew'wetain.

"All of a sudden, the Hazelton sawmill said I owed them some money... They just wanted to push us out of there... They pushed all the little sawmills out of the country."—Gitludahl (Pete Muldoe)

Mr. Rush: It's Wet'suwet'en.

The Court: That's not what Mr. Joseph said. He kept calling it Wet'sew'wetain.

Mr. Mackenzie: That's the name of a berry ground, yes, just northeast of Collins Lake? Yes?

A: It might be quite a ways above Collins Lake. This Collins Lake is just newly named that.

Q: Yes. We're referring—

A: Just because by the person that named that George Collins logged in there, that's why we get this name. They call that lake *Dam Xsi Gwin Ya'a.*

Mr. Mackenzie: Yes.

* * *

Mr. Mackenzie: Okay. Did the Kispiox Band come to you as Gitludahl?

A: Not very often.

Q: Did they come to you to ask you whether they could commit that territory on the reserve to the wood lot licence?

A: Well, all the Chiefs get together and they all agree that they have to cut the logs because no other way they going to get enough money to build that. They have a meeting on that and they all agree that they have to cut the logs to have enough money to build the community centre.

Ax Gwin Desxw (Glen Williams), La<u>x</u> Gibuu Clan, Kitwancool Village by Peter Grant

The Court: Mr. Grant. I make this the hundredth day of evidence in this case. An auspicious occasion should be noticed.

* * *

Judge Allan McEachern decides not to hear bells.

The Court: Are there bells ringing outside or has this case just been going on too long for me? There were bells ringing lower down, but no fire bells ringing out there?

The Registrar: No.

The Court: Well, let's pretend they're not ringing.

* * *

The Witness: ...We have had a very frustrating history with the government agencies that I have had to deal with. Fishery, major profiles have came in around 1977 with undercover operations, and people have been set up and been charged and nets been taken, and it is really frustrating and makes you very angry to see the treatment of our people, especially when we have done this for years and years without even any interruption that we have taken the salmon and we have used it. We have our own conservation laws of how we respect the salmon, and yet, all of a sudden this major force comes in and I have listened to the Chiefs and our Elders that have been harrassed by government departments with respect to Fishery and it makes me—

The Court: Mr. Grant, how can I really be helped by the subjective feelings of the witness? I have no doubt he is expressing true beliefs but how can it be helpful to me?

* * *

The Witness: ...and we want to try and incorporate it in the treatment centre, our own philosophies and our own values of how we want to treat alcohol problems and using the value system that we have.

Q: What does—where did the name *Wilp Si'satxw* come from?

A: *Wilp Si'satxw* is a Gitksan word meaning purification, to clean yourself.

* * *

The Witness: If we had our own land base back,

if we had that, the Chiefs and their Houses would be responsible for providing housing to their own people in their House and dealing with other problems and ensuring that their House members are dealt with and not to be suffering from social and housing problems that we have today. Their resources would be there for them. They would have a good economic return from their territories which is rightfully theirs. That's the solution that we envision. That's the solution that the Chiefs discuss extensively.

Q: And did they discuss that solution in relation to the alcohol problems as well?

A: Yes, they do.

* * *

Ax Gwin Desxw Cross-Examination by Geoff Plant for the Province

Q: Would I correctly be detecting a sense of frustration on your part at what you have felt to be lack of progress from time to time in many of these negotiations?

A: Yes, Mr. Plant. There has been quite a bit of frustration that we are so rich people. We have all this land and yet we are denied the benefit and the use of our land. And we are conscious of that in our minds and the Chiefs tell us that we have all this land the 22,000 square miles and yet the moment we try and do something there is injunctions that come down, the tobacco attack, all those different things come down against us. We are always sub-

"Trains, 110 cars long, every 20 minutes, 24 hrs a day taking resources off the land ... through the reserve."
Leonard Bright

"We have all this land and yet we are denied the benefit and the use of our land. Yes, there is quite a bit of frustration."—Ax Gwin Desxw (Glen Williams)

ject to their policies, their regulations and limitations. Yes, there is quite a bit of frustration.

Ax Gwin Desxw
Cross-Examination by James Macaulay for the Government of Canada

Q: And there is no income tax?

A: That's correct.

Mr. Macaulay: So that a band member who works at Westar has a considerable advantage over the average I.W.A. worker?

Mr. Grant: Well, My Lord, I don't know what the point of it is. It depends on one's perspectives of advantages and disadvantages and what relevance is it to this case as to whether or not the band member has the advantage. He has got the evidence out about the tax exemptions.

The Court: He has an isolated financial advantage.

Mr.Grant: An isolated advantage so long as he's living in intolerable housing conditions this witness has testified to.

Mr. Macaulay: Is that evidence, My Lord?

The Court: I think it is. It is pretty close to intolerable for some.

Gwis Gyen (Stanley Williams)
by Peter Grant
Video-Taped Commissioned Evidence, Gitanmaax

April 11-28, 1988

Q: Mr. Williams, your chief's name is Gwis Gyen?

A: Right.

Q: Are you the head of a House?

A: Right.

Q: What House? What is the name of your House?

A: 'Yax Yagaa Huuwaalp.

Q: What does that name mean?

A: 'Yax Yagaa Huuwaalp means a house hanging off a cliff.

Q: Can you tell us why the name of your House is 'Yax Yagaaa Huuwaalp?

A: That house 'Yax Yagaa Huuwaalp, it's hanging over the cliff.

Q: Where?

A: Gitsegukla.

Q: Is it still there?

A: All the time.

* * *

...My grandfather told me that our people from the ancient times always knew that there was a Creator. This is thousands of years before the white man came, when the Creator made the Earth. In the ancient times when... they had any kind of sufferings, they would build a fire and they would make an offering, and when... the smoke was going up, they would start praying, and they would ask the Creator to help them.

...All the Gitksan people use... a common law between Gitsegukla, Gitwingax, Gitwancool, Kispiox and Gitanmaax. This is like an ancient tree that has grown the roots right deep into the ground. This is the way our law is. It's sunk. This big tree's roots are sunk deep into the ground, and that's how our law is.

The strength of our law is passed on from generation to generation, and each generation makes it stronger, right to this day where I am now. I've taken the name that I have now since I was ten years old and I'm 80 now, and our law was always the same and it's the same today. Every time we put this law into action, it becomes stronger and stronger. Each time our people use our law, they make it stronger, and it still goes on today. We never deserted our Grandfather's seat and we never deserted our land, our territories. It's still the same today. Today the government wants to take all this away from us, and they want to take the laws of our people, of our ancestors, and they want to break our laws today. I don't think they could do this, because it's been passed on from generation to generation and we've had this law for thousands of years.

* * *

...Since the world was created, the Creator separated the different nationalities and gave each one of us a custom to follow, and this is what we did.

* * *

...This is what my Grandfather told me. Do not tell me about a territory that you haven't been on. You have to have the dirt of that territory under the soles of your shoes before you tell me the boundaries of the territory. This is the reason why I'm here today in front of the Court, to tell them what I know about the territories.

* * *

...When a grizzly bear gets into the provisions of another person, then he eats it up, and when the owner comes back, then the grizzly gets mad instead, gets mad at the owner. And that's how the government is treating us today concerning our territories.

* * *

whisper whisper.

On April 21/88 during commissioned evidence Stanley Williams whispered to his interpreter Alice.

I DEMAND TO KNOW WHAT WAS JUST WHISPERED TO THE INTERPRETOR!

Geoff Plant lawyer for the province.

He just said; "This guy is going to put me in a mental institution if he asks me any more stupid questions."

April/88

GWIS GYEN
(Stanley Williams)
Day 111, June 1988

"All the Gitksan people use a common law. This is like an ancient tree that has grown the roots right deep into the ground. This is the way our law is. It's sunk. This big tree's roots are sunk deep into the ground, and that's how our law is."—Gwis Gyen (Stanley Williams)

...When the Queen usually comes, she only goes to Edmonton, to Winnipeg; she never comes here and sees the way ...we are living, our customs, our traditions—she doesn't see these things. And it's not for us to give our land away to her; this is our land, not hers. As long as we live, we will always fight for our land; we will always have our land. We have the laws of our ancestors and *aluugigyet,* and we've always had this law, and we are going to put it into action.

Q: Under the Gitksan law, can you, Gwis Gyen, sell your territory?

A: No, I could not.

* * *

Margaret Alfred (left) and Vicki Russell (right).

Gwis Gyen
Cross-Examination by Geoff
Plant for the Province

Q: You have told us about travelling with a person that you called Sima diiks. Did that person also have the name Sakxum higookx?

A: Yes, he had the name ...we have two names. ...When I die, my white name of Stanley Williams will disappear, but my Chief name, Gwis Gyen, will always be there.

* * *

A: After this Court is over, I would like to ask all the lawyers how they live their lives and what they do, where they came from, and who their Grandfathers were, and their ancestors.

Q: Okay. I'm going to refer you to another territory. Okay?

A: Pretty soon I'm going to get mad.... I would like to hold a Court after this is finished. I would like to hold a Court and use our Gitksan law, and then I'll ask all you lawyers the questions that you've been asking me.

SUBMISSIONS

Vancouver, B.C. October 6, 1989

Mr. Grant: Before my friend proceeds, my lord, I had a couple of matters that I wish to raise with your lordship. First of all, I thought, given that you met this person and spent a day with him, you would want to know that yesterday Mr. Stanley Williams was involved in a traffic accident and he died at 4:00 p.m. yesterday afternoon.

The Court: Well, I'm most disturbed to hear that, and I hope that you will convey my regrets and sympathy to his family.

5 provincial lawyers, 4 federal, 3 native, 1 clerk, 2 translators, 1 stenographer, 1 judge, 1 witness.

BRITISH COLUMBIA SUPREME COURT IN SESSION 1988

GITKSAN WET'SUWET'EN AIR LINES

Say! There aren't any straight lines on this map! Except the roads and clear-cuts of course!

Justice McEachern over flies the territory, June 6 and 7.

Photos by Peter Grant

Above: Chief Justice McEachern overlooking Bear Lake on the eastern boundary of Gitksan territory.

Right: Chief Justice McEachern and Alfred Mitchell standing in ancient "footprints" at Goosly Lake.

June 1988. Neil Sterritt showing Storage Pits to Chief Justice McEachern
at Slamgeesh (Blackwater Lake). Loryl Russell, federal lawyer (at left),
and David Blackwater, Gitksan Chief, looking on.

Niist' Gravehouse at Slamgeesh, with Chief Justice McEachern.

Photos by Peter Grant.

Chapter 4

Two Solitudes:
Expert Witnesses For The Plaintiffs

Knowledge: "The sum of what is known—the body of truth, information, and principles acquired by mankind." That's one definition offered by Webster.

Truth: "...being in accord with fact and reality. A transcendent fundamental and spiritual reality."—Also from Webster.

In the great pursuit of knowledge, humans strive to gain an understanding of the truth. What principles and factors guide us to arrive at the truth? Whose truth determines reality? These questions may seem philosophical, but they are fundamental to the Gitksan and Wet'suwet'en because of the nature of evidence that forms the bulk of our case in *Delgamuukw vs. The Queen*.

Advocating the view of their colonial forbears, the governments of Canada continue to perpetuate the image of the First Nations as "primitive and aimless" by implying that we did not own or manage clearly defined tracts of land. They claim that we only occupied and used the lands during our "wanderings." It was necessary for us to show the courts that we had, and continue to have, a very complex and structured system of governance that has existed for thousands of years. And so, our Chiefs and Elders, historians in their own right, recounted the histories of their Houses in all their detail to "experts" who were suitably qualified in the court's eyes.

The government lawyers were quick to discredit the knowledge of our historians. Since we are oral societies, how was the court to determine our truthfulness? How can the courts believe us when we have nothing *written* to support the recounting of our histories? What Canada was saying was that truth can be truth only if it is written, or proven scientifically to be true. Otherwise it must be discounted as merely "hearsay." It is ironic that when our people are asked to swear to tell the truth, their capacity for truthfulness is ordained by the Christian ethic represented by the Bible—the "Written Word," as I've heard it referred to. Did not its origins spring from the knowledge and experiences of the people of that time? Did it become humankind's truth only after it was in its written form?

As much as oral histories coincide with natural and other significant events over the eons, in the eyes of the western world, especially its courts, the truth of oral history cannot stand on its own. It becomes credible only when substantiated and validated by scientific proof put forward by accredited personalities degreed in western academia.

If our Chiefs and Elders were to be measured or qualified for their knowledge and experience in a parallel university of our society, would their accreditation match or surpass that of the various "—ologists" whom courts rely on to guide their decisions? We will probably never know the answer. Suffice it to say that the truth as the Gitksan and Wet'suwet'en know it to be, is not acceptable to the western courts without the substantiation of degreed experts.

So, in this chapter you will meet the "secondary witnesses" for the Gitksan and Wet'suwet'en people: qualified men and women, eminently respected and internationally renowned in their fields of expertise, who supply scientific data and opinion covering the time through history reflected in our evidence.

Oral history based on intimate knowledge and experience, and scientific history based on rational knowledge and accreditation—two solitudes coming together and applying different shades to the same picture.

—Skanu'u (Ardythe Wilson)

"Of we get into logging and logging practices over the past number of years... well that's getting into a whole new area, an area that that has nothing to do with the territory."

OH REALLY?

GOLDIE

SO FAR IN THE TITLE ACTION THE REGISTRAR ESTIMATES ABOUT 2,000 EXHIBITS.

Peter and Stu-Ball ride the paper bucking horse. Not the Kipiox Rodeo!

THE LAW IS HIS RIGHT

ANY OBJECTIONS?

YES!

ON STRIKE

B.C.G.E.U.

B.C.G.E.U. ON STRIKE

JUSTICE "MERI MOTU", (ALAN McEACHERN), STOPPED THE COURT WORKERS (B.C.G.E.U.) FROM PICKETING THE COURTHOUSES OF B.C. BY WALKING INTO HIS OWN EMPTY COURTROOM AND MAKING HIS OWN MOTION AND GRANTING TO HIMSELF AN INJUNCTION... A RARELY USED LEGAL PROCEDURE KNOWN AS A 'MERI MOTU'... IT PASSED IN THE B.C. COURT OF APPEAL AND NOW SITS BEFORE SUPREME COURT OF CANADA.

original line was drawn with a felt pen - at 6000 to 1 the line represented 2½ miles. first map was an approximation, best we could do then.

Putting questions to Neil that they never asked any of the Chiefs... Questioning authority in Houses and the motivations of witnesses. Making out that Neil is the one who really started this case and not chiefs.

Stuart Rush
de-briefing

Neil explaining overlaps and changes in the map from 1977 declaration and the 1984 court claim. (1977 big line 1984 dotted line.)

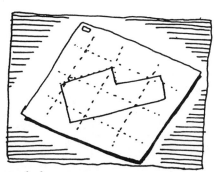

Neil had to create the first maps with the chiefs ...who were unfamiliar with the process of meets and bounds.

Talking about Experts !!!
Why, when they established traplines, there are so many straight lines?
Alfred Joseph

Sometimes I'd like to get up there and slap his face!
The contempt Goldie shows for us ... I hate it!
Who does he think he's talking to, children?...
He's speaking to the aboriginal people here... this little immigrant.

Don W. Kenni

A TIRED PETER GRANT MAKES A POINT AT DE-BRIEFING.

...AND DID SHE APPEAR ON BEHALF OF A NUMBER OF GITKSAN PEOPLE WHO HAD BEEN PERSECUTED FOR BREAKING FISHING BY-LAWS?

PERSECUTED or PROSECUTED, Mr. Goldie?

—Oops! I'm adopting the language of the Plaintiffs, My Lord...

Oct. 13/88 - transcript

Neil J. Sterritt, Cartographer, Cross-Examination by Michael Goldie for the Province

Q: Now, I suggest to you in 1975, that virtually no one knew where the territories were?

A: Well, you are wrong about that. The Hereditary Chiefs know where their territories are, they knew in 1975 where their territories are and where their boundaries are, they knew the geographical features within them. That's not a correct statement, Mr. Goldie.

* * *

Regarding the province's argument that the acceptance of traplines discredits the Chiefs.

A: The Hereditary Chiefs understood from the 1930s—and they have given this information in evidence—that if they didn't register their territories as traplines, that they would lose them, and that the Department of Indian Affairs and the Provincial Wildlife authorities were going to map those properly and they would be registered as traplines and then they would not lose their territories.

* * *

Q: Then the claim that you make here is, in effect, to clarify that the Queen in right of British Columbia and the Queen in right of Canada does not have sovereignty over the Gitksan and Carrier lands; is that correct?

A: The Queen does not have full sovereignty over that land because there is the title of the Gitksan and Wet'suwet'en to be dealt with, and it has never been dealt with to this day.

* * *

Q: Do you know of any of these customs and laws which are in the course of being codified which conflict with any of the the laws of Canada or British Columbia?

A: The laws of the Gitksan, the few that I'm aware of, generally correspond to many of the laws of Canada and other nations. Where I see the variation is in the implementation and the policy. And that's where I see the difference and there is a higher respect for the animals and for the needs of the people within the territory.

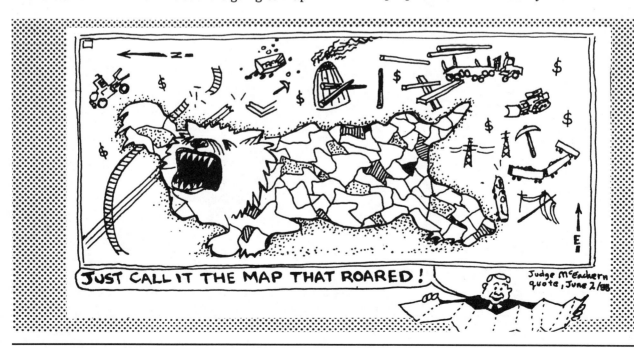

JUST CALL IT THE MAP THAT ROARED!

Judge McEachern quote, June 2/88

NEIL J. STERRITT Jr.
Days 112-143
June, September, October 1988

"The Queen does not have full sovereignty over the land because there is the title of the Gitksan and Wet'suwet'en to be dealt with, and it has never been dealt with to this day."—Neil Sterritt

Rolf W. Mathewes,
Paleobotanist,
by Louise Mandell

Louise Mandell describes to the judge an ancient ada'ox *that the next two witnesses will prove scientifically.*

Ms. Mandell: ...Mary Johnson at that time told the *adaawk* of the men of Mediik, and you will recall that she spoke in part in the *adaawk* at least, about a giant grizzly bear, a giant forest coming down the valley of a creek, and that the forest was torn apart and there were trees uprooted. I am paraphrasing her *adaawk*. And that the bear glared at *T'am Lax Amit*, which she spoke about, and then moved down the bank and entered the water.

And later she spoke about young women who were gathering berries by the lake and that eventually when the men arrived at the lake they found where the women had been berry picking, and the lake had risen considerably, and they felt that their sisters were drowned, and she identified that lake as Seeley Lake.

Now, Your Lordship will be able to refer back to the *adaawk*, and there will be other accounts of it told later in the—or referred to Your Lordship according to the written records of the *adaawk*, but it's on the basis of this *adaawk* that Seeley Lake will be described by Dr. Mathewes.

My Lord, I am seeking to tender Dr. Mathewes as an expert in the field of paleobotany, and in particular pollenanalysis and environmental reconstruction.

* * *

A: Yes, there are a number of possibilities for such clay bands in the lake, but looking at all the evidence that I could find, I would feel very strongly that this clay band was formed by a sudden rise in water level at the time of around 3,380 years ago, which caused mineral matter to be washed into the lake and deposited as part of Clay One.

Q: And is that sudden rise of water level disturbance consistent with a landslide?

A: It would be consistent with a landslide damming the outlet, certainly.

Alan Gottesfeld,
Geomorphologist,
by Louise Mandell

A: Geomorphology is the study of existing land forms and the processes that cause them and ongoing processes on the surface of the earth today.

* * *

Q: And did you also assume that various occurrences may be either ascribed to supernatural events or to extraordinary physical events depending upon the cultural perspective?

A: That's my assumption.

* * *

A: To say at least the composite fan at Chicago Creek is the largest feature and, assuming that the 3580 year event, the 3600 year-old landslide, occupied all or most of the area now covered by younger deposits, it would have been the largest event in the area.

* * *

Ms. Mandell: If you had been standing about three or six kilometres downstream from Seeley Lake, the bottom of Chicago Creek when this landslide event happened, what would you have seen and heard?

* * *

Mr. Willms for British Columbia: My Lord, the one point, and it goes back to what this witness was qualified for, and what he said in his evidence. I don't think he said that he's ever seen a landslide this large...

* * *

The Courts: Well, I am sure Beethoven heard his symphony, although he was stone deaf and he knew what was there, and he could—in words that he can describe...

* * *

The Witness: Well, if you could see the mountain from where you were standing, there would be tremendous noise, overwhelming loud noise, a great cloud of material, swaths of forests being cleared as the debris slide came down across the Chicago creek, I envisioned the debris tarring where lots of water was incorporated and debris, and there would be this great mud- charged mess of material coming down the valley, great rolled wall of brown material, trees tossed around, just a swath of countryside being cleared that would come towards you, I am sure you would be frightened and run away. That's the time where you make sure you are standing up on a good hill or something.

ALLEN S. GOTTESFELD
Days 144-145
October 1988

ROLF W. MATHEWES
Days 143-144
October 1988

Sybille Haeussler,
Forest Ecologist,
by Louise Mandell

Q: I would like to tender Ms. Haeussler as an expert in the area of forest ecology....

* * *

Applying analysis of ecoregion to the claims area, what is significant about the claims area?

A: ...The claims area...is the very location where three broad ecoregions converge, and it's the only place in North America or even the world where those three diffferent very broad vegetation types or ecological units come together.... So you have species such as hemlock and western red cedar that are typically found on the coast. Species from the interior, such as lodgepole pine and trembling aspen, are also very abundant. You also have some northern species, such as the black spruce, reaching their southern limits in that area. The climate is intermediate between all those three areas, and you have this unique mixture of vegetation with a diversity of species that you don't find elsewhere.

Q: You say, "Black huckleberry is the favorite berry for both Indian and non-Indian people whenever it is available. The Gitksan name for black huckleberry means the real, the true berry.... The berries were stored in water or grease rather than being dried and reportedly kept quite well. They are unsuitable for drying, presumably because of their extreme juiciness and the large seed."

Is it accepted as a method of studying fire ecology to investigate the human use of fire in an area?

AT A TIME WHEN WE ARE EXPERIENCING BUDGET PROBLEMS AND SMALLER STAFF THAN LAST SESSION, BOTH THE PROVINCE AND THE FEDS ARE PUTTING MORE PRESSURE ON, ASKING FOR MORE DOCUMENTS AND DISCLOSURES... TRYING TO TAX THE RESOURCES THEY KNOW ARE DWINDLING. ITS ALMOST THE SAME STRATEGY THEY USED IN AUSTRALIAS LEGAL TRIALS.

Peter Grant in de-briefing

A: Oh, yeah. In large parts of the world, humans are the main ignition source of fires.... Historically, ecologists have tended to include aboriginal fires as part of the natural fire regime.... When they talk about the fire history of the boreal forest, they don't say it is only lightning fires.

Q: All right. At page 29 of your report, you say that: "It is impossible to generalize about the type of burning regime (i.e., frequency, intensity and size of burn) that could be used to maximize berry crops. Frequent light fire might be ideal for some species, while more intense on intervals of, say, 10 to 30 years might be more appropriate for others. Because recovery from fire can take many years, a pattern of prescribed burning that creates a mosaic of small stands at various stages of recovery, will normally be more efficient than one that creates large burns of uniform age."

And then you say: "A natural fire cycle of 150 to 300 or more years has been replaced in many areas by a logging rotation on the order of 70 to 200 years.... If fire suppression policies have been respondible for preventing periodic burning of certain Gitksan and Wet'suwet'en berry patches, then it is very likely that they have caused a decline in the crop production of those berry patches."

Where is everybody?

over here!

HAZELTON

VANCOUVER

TRIAL REOPENS SEPT. 12/1988 1300 km. from where it can be seen to be done. Expenses have shrunken the size of the chiefs Vancouver offices and staff.

Nov. 15, 88

Dora Wilson (Yaagalahl), Alfred Joseph (Gisdaywa) and Homer Muldoe (Galistump x) in court daily for three years.

Sylvia L. Albright, Ethnoarchaeologist, by Stuart Rush

The Court: Mr. Rush, I think I'm going to need a definition of ethnoarchaeology.

* * *

The Witness: Ethnographic observations on cultural behavior of the aboriginal group of people living in a specific area with archaeological evidence from the same area, of understanding the past occupation of that same area.

* * *

Mr. Rush: And what is a hearth?

A: A hearth consists of fire-cracked rock, sometimes referred to as gore-altered rock, that cracks from heat, carbon-sustained soil, quite often very greasy black bits of charcoal, so that chunks of the charcoal are taken as samples for dating.

* * *

A: In the Kitselas Canyon area there are again several hundred pits have been recorded by Coupland and discussed by Coupland in connection with his work at the Paul Mason site. And this Kitselas Canyon was also a large population centre. And given the nature of the canyon setting there, deposits have been preserved in that canyon which exhibit occupation over the last 5,000 years...

...The clustering of archaeological sites in the vicinity of major fish camps and villages which are still being used and occupied today suggests that these have been significant village locations and fishing areas for centuries if not millenia....

* * *

A: The intensification of salmon production and storage of large quantities of dried salmon resources for winter use or later use for purposes of trade is an indication of very sophisticated technology.

...For processing salmon in terms of drying requires drying racks and smokehouses. It also involves organization of people to be able to carry out those activities in that salmon resources are not an abundant resource. They are very restricted in time and place...

* * *

A: *Dawdzep* is a Gitksan term for a fortress or a fortified site. There are three well known *dawdzep* or fortress sites in the Gitksan territories...

* * *

A: ...He refers to the Kitwanga Fort as being part of a much larger framework of intertribal trade as well as warfare which dates back as early as the first millenia B.C. or that would be 3,000

In 1898, in the Upper Skeena country, Johnny Muldoe was digging a hole for a house-post on the flat just below the Hagwilget Canyon of the Bulkley River and, four feet down, under a capping stone, he found 35 stone clubs cached together. He handed them over to Mr. A.W. Vowell, Superintendent of Indian Affairs for British Columbia, who happened to be visiting Hazelton at the time, and they became part of Mr. Vowell's private collection in Victoria ... some of them, at least, found their way into the Museum of the American Indian in New York. The clubs from the Hagwilget cache, and others from the same vicinity which are in the same style, are among the most singular images from our 30 centuries of stone sculpture.

...One of the most curious things about the stone clubs is that they are not so much functional weapons as they are images of weapons. They are either stone replicas of functional clubs, or metaphors in stone of what "club" might also mean. When ordinary weapons were required, clubs of wood, antler, and bone were presumably preferred. Sometimes, judging from the images, these were inset with stone-striking blades. Stone, that is to say, was really more important as a medium for metaphoric messages than as a material for practical weapons. Needless to say, the imagery, often as not, is phallic.

Tsimshian myths make the occasional mention of stone clubs, and these are usually magic clubs. They are capable, for example, of killing enemies by turning their entire villages upside-down. Another tradition of the Hazelton area may be a clue to the Hagwilget cache. It tells of an old woman who gathered up the weapons of the slain after a war and cached them away, and then was killed herself.

—Wilson Duff, *Images Stone, B.C.* (Hancock House, 1975.)

years.

...The radiocarbon dates appear to confirm interpretation of the site stratigraphy and suggest that Moricetown Canyon has been occupied fairly continuously for over 5,000 years...

...This is the earliest date recovered so far from the central interior of British Columbia....

* * *

B.P. stands for Before Present.

A: The features themselves, the post features indicate a large structure there. The size of the features and the alignment of the post features indicate quite a substantial house structure at the site, and we have the date of 5660 B.P. and another one at 4700 B.P. But the earliest one at 5660 for the post mould, for that post. And so we have people using large structures, living and using large structures at that site at that time.

* * *

The Witness: A large cache of stone clubs has been found at Hagwilget Canyon. They are similar in form to clubs found at sites in the Prince Rupert Harbor and at Kitselas, dated to more than 2,000 years ago...

Heather Harris, by Peter Grant

Mr. Grant: My Lord, Miss Harris is tendered as an expert witness on Gitksan kinship and social structure, including as part of that the research formatting and development genealogies.

* * *

The Court: Sorry, what is social structure again?

The Witness: Major institution and organizing principles of a society.

...Matrilineality is a system of kinship whereby people are related through women; patrilineal is a sytem whereby they are related through men; and bilaterality is a system whereby people within a kin group are related through either men or women.

* * *

A: ...People with whom you are related by blood are called consanguineal kin and the other major category are affinal kin which are people to whom you are related by marriage.

Q: And is there any other category of kin relationship?

A: Yes. There can be classificatory kin. ...Commonly, wherever clan systems are used, when a person is travelling and they are from a member of, say, the Wolf Clan, and they are travelling to

---

𝔍𝔫 𝔱𝔥𝔢 𝔖𝔲𝔭𝔯𝔢𝔪𝔢 𝔠𝔬𝔲𝔯𝔱 𝔬𝔣 𝔅𝔯𝔦𝔱𝔦𝔰𝔥 𝔠𝔬𝔩𝔲𝔪𝔟𝔦𝔞

(BEFORE THE HONOURABLE THE CHIEF JUSTICE)

Layout from cover page on all transcript.

M. Goldie Q.C. (Queens Counsel)

Proceedings At Trial

---

another place, they will be welcomed and taken care of by members.

* * *

Q: ...How many Elders did you interview?

A: Over 200 people.

Q: And you were referring this morning to the fact that you read some of Barbeau?

A: Yes.

Q: As part of your research for this. How many of the *adaawk* or oral history of Barbeau did you read in that of that work?

A: I would say over four hundred.

Heather Harris, Cross-Examination by Marvyn Koenigsberg, for Canada

Lawyer Marvyn Koenigsberg suggests to the judge that Heather is a race traitor.

Q: It is commonly described in the literature as a problem which can flow from participant observation?

A: Some people consider it a problem and others consider it an advantage.

Q: Yes. What it means is that you become so involved in the culture that you lose your objectivity, that's what's described as "going native?"

A: Objectivity is relative.

Q: Yes, it is, isn't it.

A: Yes. For either culture.

* * *

Heather Harris, by Peter Grant

Describing the problems with using academically created forms with the Elders.

Q: And what was the difficulty with using the form?

A: I found that structured interviews are just problematic with Gitksan Elders. It's hard to keep them on one topic, you have to be very patient, because it would be considered outrageously rude to demand that they stop speaking about one topic and return immediately to the topic at hand which, when you have a structured format like this, you are attempting to elicit precisely this, this and this

---

"The symbol in geneology for a man is △, the symbol for women is ○, if someone is dead the anthropological standard is to use a slash △̸ – I found that this insulted the memory of loved ones – so we began to use ⊙ △."

Jan 16/89

question as found on the form...

* * *

A: This is very early in the game for the Gitksan where English last names were concerned, and you'll notice that they don't play the game by the rules, in that a whole House...you might have noticed in *Delgamuukw* House in the early days everybody was called Johnson. Matrilineally related kin called themself Johnson, so they don't precisely follow the rules...

* * *

A: ...when someone like Mary Johnson says "my grandmother" or "great great grandmother," that can mean a huge number of relatives, and this is why I have to go back to tracing the relationships very clearly...

* * *

ARENT YOU AFRAID OF GOING "NATIVE"?

Koenigsburg for Govt. of Canada –

The province makes a point of describing to the judge the possibility that the Gitksan have a class system.

Q: That's *Simiget* and *Laxgiget:* Is that Chiefs and commoners?
A: Yes, but they're ranks, not classes.

Jim Kari, Linguist, by Louise Mandell

The Court: I take it your evidence is that the Gitksan are not Athabaskan, or are they?

The Witness: No. The Gitksan language is a Tsimshianic language…it is not at all classifiable as an Athabaskan language…. The Tsimshian has been postulated to be related to languages down in Oregon and Washington and in Central California.

The Court: But different areas from the ones you described yesterday?

The Witness: … Carrier [Wet'suwet'en] does turn out to be a Sekani origin name for the Stewart Lake people…. The Sekani called the Stewart Lake people Carrier, and they didn't call the Babine people the same way they call the Stewart Lake people. But through folk usage in British Columbia history for a hundred years or so, Babine-Wet'suwet'en people have been called Carrier. Morice 1925 is very interesting to read, because he strenuously objects that Babine are not Carrier, and they are their own people. It's a serious mistake… to start calling these guys Carrier….

Now, Morice's positions have vacillated on this, but he was sensitive to the distinct differences of what he called Babine. But in the modern context…it's not easy, I tell you. You go in and you don't know these folks, and you want to work with the language, and it's not easy. And what are you going to call the language? We've had discussions in the community, and when the Gitksan-Carrier Council changed its name to Gitksan-Wet'suwet'en, that was a sincere attempt to redefine this in their own language. They have their own name for themselves and for the name of their council.

…Jenness sounds extremely deprecatory of their language skills in terms of Athabaskan knowledge of Gitksan. If certain Elders are good at Gitksan today in 1989, they were certainly just as knowledgeable of Gitksan in 1922 or '24, and so …he's not doing linguistic work; he's doing ethnographic work, and he's making judgment calls about language skills….

The sophisticated dialogue that took place even as recently as yesterday with Dora and Alfred and me over Gitksan and Athabaskan etymologies bears out the fact that Wet'suwet'en speakers do know Gitksan language very intimately. So I could say I've got counter-evidence to Jennis 1943, very sophisticated etymologies.

THE JUDGE DECIDES WHAT WEIGHS WHAT, WITNESSES AND FACTS.

Richard Overstall Gitksan-Wet'suwet'en researcher listens to lawyers at debriefing describe weight.

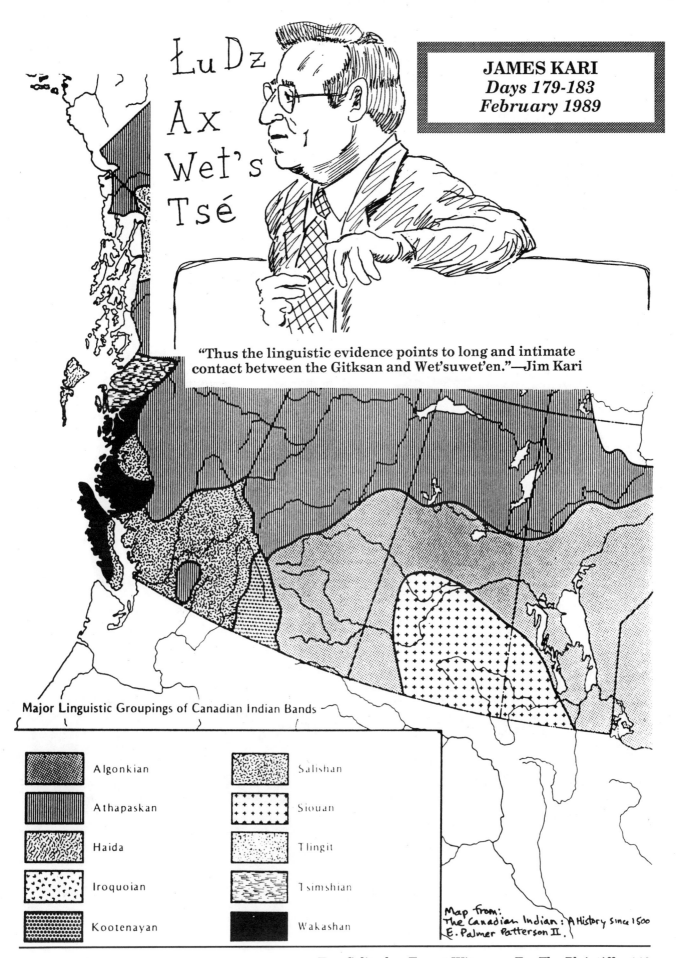

Łu Dz
Ax
Wet's
Tsé

"Thus the linguistic evidence points to long and intimate contact between the Gitksan and Wet'suwet'en."—Jim Kari

Major Linguistic Groupings of Canadian Indian Bands

Algonkian

Athapaskan

Haida

Iroquoian

Kootenayan

Salishan

Siouan

Tlingit

Tsimshian

Wakashan

Map from:
The Canadian Indian: A History since 1500
E. Palmer Patterson II.

Richard Daly, Ethnologist, by Peter Grant

Mr. Grant: All right. And I intend to qualify Dr. Daly in the following areas: As an ethnologist or social anthropologist, who is giving opinions in the field of social and cultural anthropology.

* * *

...I like the term ethnology, because it deals with the study of culture and society and social structure against a historical and comparative background...

* * *

The Court: Do you like Emily Carr paintings?
A: I do. I don't think she understood the clan system very well though.

* * *

Richard Daly describes the anthropologists' desire to live within and participate in a culture.

A: ...It's like the Holy Grail in the sense of anthropology. Everybody is trying to find a way to engage in some participant observation. It's the getting in touch with another culture first hand. It's part of your existential period. Part of your training.

* * *

Q: What does the word tribe come from?
A: It comes from a Latin word from the Roman times, tribua. It means the people who are identifying a political group with the land it occupies.

* * *

A: ...So you may have Chiefs and commoners, but they are all part of the same family. And it's not as though you have a whole class of have-nots and a whole class of haves, because that kinship link creates a possibility of moving up or moving down.

* * *

The Court: ...I have never had to deal with a 700- page report before and I think it is almost unmanageable. I haven't taken the time to read it and I have to rely on counsel to highlight the parts that bear special attention...

* * *

Q: ...There is archaeological evidence of the inscription of crests on material objects along the Skeena System for at least the last two and a half millennia.

* * *

Q: ...Aboriginal Australian rights to property ownership are validated in ways similar to those found among the Gitksan and Wet'suwet'en through crests, narratives and songs that have to do with the way the ancestors came to walk the land....

* * *

A: ...it is a feature of tribes and bands, you don't have a police force, you have a moral force and you have the effects of gossip and possibilities of ostracism. The constant pressure on people to follow the rules, it is common knowledge in the nature of tribal societies.

* * *

Q: When you refer to witchcraft, it implies to me in our perspective a negative aspect. Is that how shamanism or the use of psychic powers is usually considered?
A: No, power is power. It's like electricity or fire. Used in one way it's beneficial, and used in a different way or uncontrolled it's dangerous. It's the same attitude towards many, many phenomena, that if they're kept in control they're of use to people and if they're not, they can be dangerous.
The Court: Sounds like judges.

* * *

A: ...It's a give-and-take relationship, a reciprocal relationship. You give to the land, you take from the land. You eat from the land, and ultimately you feed the land with your bones.

* * *

Q: And you describe many of the things that you actually saw yourself?
A: Not just saw, I actually was given a lot of items from the land which I enjoyed. Jars of moose broth and canned moosemeat and berries, spring salmon, smoked salmon and so on.

* * *

A: ...In Gitksan and Wet'suwet'en cultures, to be talked about is not a sign of honor but rather of shame....
Q: ...The feast is not an old, fragile, family heirloom, and the Gitksan are not a nostalgic, backward looking people. They are proud of their heritage and yet practical in anticipating their future in the developing high-tech world. The Feast accomodates wage work, technological change and various residential and educational changes, yet its basic reciprocal nature remains constant."
Raising a crest pole is a testament to the present prosperity of a House and its political fortunes in the community. In the past, a whole generation of leaders, the Chief and counsellor Chiefs, would throw its total resources into the pole-raising.

"It's a give-and-take relationship, a reciprocal relationship. You give to the land, you take from the land. You eat from the land and, ultimately, you feed the land with your bones."—Richard Daly

Years of outstanding House business would be settled and witnessed by the greater community. The pole would stand for two or three generations, a monument not only to the predecessor being commemorated, but also to the industriousness of the generation that raised the pole. The same ethic prevails today. Today, as well as in the past, the raising of a pole and the associated Feasting is the crowning event in the cycle of Feasts a Chief can be expected to host during his lifetime. This feast incorporates the main activities and transactions found in less elaborate Feasts into a complex settlement of accounts, both spiritually, materially and socially, on behalf of a whole generation of Chiefs of the host group.

* * *

The Court: ...I think that whatever the aboriginal rights are, they spring in part from the social order as well as the occupation, and a system of laws might, which seem to be part of a social order, that could form the basis for an aboriginal right of an amalgam of aboriginal rights...

FIRST WHITE TRADER WAS THE HUDSON BAY'S BILLY BROWN, BABINE LAKE 1822. DEPICTED HERE IS THE PROVINCE'S LAWYER WILLMS WHO IS HAVING A HARD TIME REMAINING COMFORTABLE ATOP THE PROVINCE'S DEFENCE IN 1989. ALSO SHOWN ARE THE RIVER BOATS THE GITKSAN USED TO TRADE AMONGST INDIAN NATIONS UP AND DOWN THE SKEENA RIVER SYSTEM - SOME 200 miles. ACROSS THE RIVER IS A FANCIFUL DEPICTION OF ONE OF THE MANY VILLAGES USED SEASONALLY BY BOTH THE WET'SUWET'EN AND THE GITKSAN PEOPLE.

AFTER DR. DALY EXPLAINED THE WETSUWET'EN xet'atii, THE HUNTING PREPARATION CEREMONY, MCEACHERN SAID:

"BUT MY UNCLE NEVER DID THAT BEFORE HUNTING AND HE ALWAYS GOT A DEER!"

—DON'T SPEAK HEATHEN!

SLAP!

residential school

The Durieu system in anthropology is an idea of Father Durieu that the sedentary effect of church and school should be used to make Indians change their ways and become good Christian farmers.

"THE MATRILINEAL SYSTEM IS NOT CRUMBLING, THE PATRILINEAL TRAP LINE REGISTRATION IS LIKE A ROCK IN THE MIDDLE OF THE RIVER... THE CULTURE, LIKE WATER TRIES TO GO AROUND THAT ROCK."
Richard Daly

"THE QUALITY OF BERRIES TO THE CHIEFS, IS LIKE WINE TO A CONNOISSEUR."

Then a man would shimmy out on the pole & secure it to the next.

HEE, HEE
PSST!
BLAH, BLAH
GIGGLE
GIGGLE
HEH, HEH!

I'm sorry your lordship but I was distracted from the question by the racist comments coming from the lawyers for the province.

THE PROVINCE DOES THIS TO EVERY WITNESS.

LOOKING AT A PHOTO OF A PRE-CONTACT BRIDGE ON THE GREASE TRAIL.

Antonia Mills, Anthropologist, by Stuart Rush

Q: And you indicate that you have a Ph.D from Harvard University obtained in 1982. Was that in the field of anthropology?

A: That's right.

* * *

A: Oh, it was over 15 Feasts. They were at Moricetown, one at Gitanmaax, one at Kitwanga, one at Kispiox. The Hagwilget Feasts tend to take place in Moricetown.

Q: What was the importance, if any, to you of attending these Feasts?

A: I really wanted to document and learn how Feasts take place and what they are, what is done at a Feast and to see the variety, by looking at not just a single Feast or a few, but the whole range of Feasts that took place while I was there.

* * *

A: You may note also that I did not take notes at the Gitksan Feast that I attended because I had not been authorized by the Gitksan Chiefs to do so...

* * *

A: The Wet'suwet'en perceive themselves as having been in situ in the location where they are found now since the very earliest times.

The Court: What do you understand that to mean? What do you understand them to understand that means?

A: I understand them to mean that they have been there for such a very long period of time that this is basically their homeland. This is their homeland.

Q: And is there a village to which the Wet'suwet'en people trace their origins?

A: Yes, there is. They call it Dizkle. It is called Dizkle.

* * *

A: The oral traditions of the Wet'suwet'en is called *Kungax*. There are stories which are recited by people who are considered validated to recite them. *Kungax* also has other meanings, however. It breaks down into several words. The *kun* means spirit or spirit power.

Q: That's K-u-n, is it?

A: Yes, the first part, and the *gax* added on means also the trail of song or trail of power, so there are several senses in which the word is used. It also refers to the enactment of crests or by the Wet'suwet'en.

* * *

A: The *Kungax* of the Wet'suwet'en portray their perception of their history and of their acquisition of crests and titles, their relations with other people, their wars and events that took place with other peoples.

* * *

A: I draw significance from the fact that the warring nature of the Wet'suwet'en, as they perceive themselves, and the neighboring peoples, is changed by inviting the people who have been their adversaries to a Feast, and the Feast then succeeds in making peace with these people, who then settle down with this village.

* * *

The Court: ...But when you have a story that starts with a woman hiding in the ground and digging down in the ground a paralyzed person, still alive, that she digs him up and brings him back to life and he becomes a powerful Chief, I recognize the significance of the story being told over and over again, but does it really help you to determine anything more than the fact that the people have been there for a long time?...

* * *

A: ...It's saying this man is very special, he is extraordinary, he is not like the ordinary person who could not be buried in the ground and survive.

The Court: I don't find it strange at all because I think you will find the same thing in every culture.

A: That's true.

* * *

A: Some people have oral traditions that recount the beginning of a clan in a particular event, natural or supernatural. The Wet'suwet'en *Kungax* are noteworthy for always assuming that clans exist.

Q: What's noteworthy about that?

A: That means that the clans were the very elemental, earliest features in the social organization of these people...

* * *

Q: ...What is interesting and outstanding about the Gitksan Wet'suwet'en contact is that the two people have co-existed next to each other, intermarried and borrowed and learned from each other and yet retained their separate languages and cultures and maintained essentially peaceful relations with each other over what appears to be thousands of years..."

* * *

A: ...Archaeology provides us with a portrayal of the antiquity of the occupation of this area, and the stone clubs found at Hagwilget bespeaks another kind of communication between these people.

Q: And what type of communication was that?

A: It's basically a sexual interchange of bespeaking marriages between these people.

3,000 yr. Club found near Tse Kya (Hagwilget)

105
**Stone Club:
Death-Bringer**

Length: 18"
Courtesy of the Museum of the American Indian,
Heye Foundation, New York.
12/3273

This masterpiece among clubs has the diamond-
shaped blade of many of the clubs found in the
Hagwilget cache, and a strange human head on the
handle which might be interpreted as representing
death. According to the museum records, it was
found on the same site as the cache ("Spring, 1922,
under two-foot cedar stump near Two-Mile Creek;
old Gitksan village site, Bulkley Canyon, 4 miles
from Hazelton.") References: Dockstader, 1962, P1.
4; Duff, 1963, p. 7 and Fig. 3a.
    Wilson Duff, *Images Stone B.C.*

"The Gitksan and Wet'suwet'en people have co-existed next to
each other, intermarried and borrowed and learned from each
other, and yet retained their separate languages and cultures
and maintained essentially peaceful relations with each other
over what appears to be thousands of years."—Antonia Mills

Skip Ray, Fur Trade Historian, Cross-Examination by James Macaulay for Canada

During cross-examination of Skip Ray, Macaulay reads the diaries of many "explorers"... Here he reads about Horetsky's visit to Gitksan country in 1869. Rocher-De Boule is the mountain near Hazelton.

Mr. Macaulay: ..."Finally on Friday, the 4th of June, 1869, at the moment that the sun disappeared behind the "coast range," the first missionary arrived in front of Rocher-DeBoule."

...And then in the middle of the page he says: "Rocher-DeBoule is a village in the style of those of the coast. The lodges are large and of planks of cedar; the poles that support them are carved and represent monstrous human caricatures. In front of the lodge of each Chief stands a large and very high pole. It is the trunk of a tree on which are carved the emblems of their families. One sees there numerous figures of bears, of crows, of owls, of toads, etc.

This village is like a great savage market, where every summer the Indians of the coast and those of the interior meet to trade. The Atna, the Simshean, the Naaska bring their products of European history, groceries and dry goods, and receive in exchange the furs of beaver, of marten, of fox, of bear, etc."

Then he goes on to describe the part liquor played, and then an incident.

"Not later than last autumn, the savages had a dispute, they took their rifles and dispute became a veritable battle. Three men from Rocher-DeBoule were killed stone dead, there were numerous wounded; but how many were there dead on the side of the Simshean? One knows nothing of that.

The Witness: Did you read the rest of this report?

Q: Oh, yes, I read it. Do you want to point something out about it?

A: The very interesting thing, that opening comment about the village of Hagwilget there was a comment there about—here: "On our left, deep down in the hollow, we could see several Indian huts of wretched construction, partially lighted up by the fitful glare of their fires, while the dismal chants and "rattling" of the medicine man were heard as they performed their heathenish rites over the departing spirit of some relatives, laid low by the ravages of an epedemic then rife amongst them."

He says the guy unfortunately mislabelled his camera a cholera box.

Q: Yes.

A: And then: "After the revered gentlemen's departure, however, it most unfortunately happened that a species of cholera broke out among the native Hazeltonians; the origin of which they most illogically attributed to the 'one eyed devil' in the lantern." In the 19th century, I am not sure if you are familiar, but apart from warfare these natives were ravaged time after time by disease...

* * *

During his cross-examining, James Macaulay for Canada repeatedly tried to imply that the Gitksan were a savage, blood thirsty people...incapable of controlling themselves.

Q: ...Do you say that the violence that we have read about in Downey and later, originated in the fur trade and in the foreign influence?

A: ...The level of violence increases after 1830, Yes. However, the thing that, I object to, the way a lot of people do Native history, is that every time one Native gets killed it's described as a war. We don't describe murders in our society, as a war, as pointed out to me the other day, so all violence does not equate war.

Q: But where you have a reciprocal killing system, a murder leads to another and retaliation after that and so on, until there is a peace treaty cobbled together; is that right?

William Brown was the first white trader in Gitksan country.

A: ...We have at least several instances in Brown's cases where these things were solved peaceably through a Feast, which is one of the institutions they had to establish peace.

...The Chiefs held in highest esteem were the peace Chiefs, not the war Chiefs, and not these guys who were described as inclined to violence. They were not held in regard.

...I think we have to be careful of just seeing revenge as a phenomenon of Indians. It sort of falls, to my mind, into the stereotypical view of Indians as a bunch of bloodthirsty savages and I just don't buy it.

* * *

The case where an armed party trapped an adversary in his lodge. Rather than kill him they accepted payment for wrongs and left. Macauley says he had a good bunker, that's why they left.

Hudson's Bay Company Flag
at Tse Kyawet'en Feast
(Hagwilget)

"I do not subscribe to the bloodthirsty
savagery of Native people, nor the
noble savage. I don't subscribe to
either. I see Native people as people.
They have the same problems that
other peoples have around the world
and in different points in time."
—Skip Ray

Q: They couldn't have stopped in the bunker forever. They accepted the payment and that's the point, isn't it?

A: Well, that's how that one was resolved. …That's a common way of resolving them. My point is that your thesis is that once a blood feud starts it never stops.

* * *

Q: I put it to you, Dr. Ray, that's really the point of the cross-examination, or one of the points anyhow, that is a very fragile system and it was interrupted by such things as a single killing… Do you agree that the reciprocal killing system had that effect?

A: My point would be that societies generally value peace, that's both within groups and between groups; that their systems for sustaining peace break down from time to time are easy enough to prove. And if you wanted to use the European example, just remember the period we're talking about is close to the Napoleanic Wars, right?

Q: Yes.

A: A lot more people got killed in those. And would you not say that those European societies valued peace as well?

Q: I'm not saying European societies valued peace, Dr. Ray—

A: Well, would you say that the European societies had equally fragile systems? No human society has been able to sustain peace both in itself and between itself.

A: …It seems that your thesis is that these people had no way of maintaining peace and order and that all they did was kill each other.

* * *

Mr. Macaulay: That is a demonstration of a warlike nature of the Gitksan…

Mr. Macaulay: Isn't that the source of the violence …that the endemic violence was based on a fair degree of truculence?

* * *

The court cartoonist loses his decorum and puts one word into the transcript. The judge looks up, Macaulay stops. After a silence, he continues.

Q: …But I'm putting that to you to ask you whether you agree that there was a certain excitability and ferocity that led to the whole village…

A Voice: SHAME!

Mr. Macaulay: …taking up arms rather than individuals

A: …It's a very stereotypical view of Native people and I think it's long out of order. It is after all the 20th century, not the 19th.

* * *

The Witness: …And my only point was I do not subscribe to the bloodthirsty savagery of Native people, nor the noble savage. I don't subscribe to either. I see Native people as people. They have the same problems that other peoples have around the world and in different points in time. That is the main point of my report. Nothing more; nothing less.

* * *

The Witness: I would submit to you that if this whole country of what's now Canada was constantly in a state of war—because that was the native condition—the Bay men couldn't have stayed out of it. They would have been drawn into it and deaths would have been much higher than in fact were the case. You can count on, I think, two hands all the deaths of the Bay men at Indian hands, probably from the time the company was founded.

It seems to me your underlying assumption is we are dealing with people who were sort of out of control or nearly out of control all the time, and I don't see that in the record.

* * *

The Witness: What I object to is the suggestion that the only way violence was ever resolved was by more violence. That's the thesis and I don't accept the thesis.

Mr. Macaulay: And I don't know whose thesis that is, my Lord, but the witness took it that way.

A: But you were talking about blood-feuding, never-ending blood-feuding.

The Court: I'm not sure where blood-feuding crept into it, but the suggestion was a retalitory syndrome.

Mr. Macaulay: Reciprocal.

A: So you are saying you don't accept the thesis that blood-feuding was the way—

Q: Well, I don't have to tell you, witness, what I'm accepting or not accepting.

A: Well, that's what I was reacting to, if you are saying "no" then we are in agreement, that's all.

Leonard Bright's new license plate.

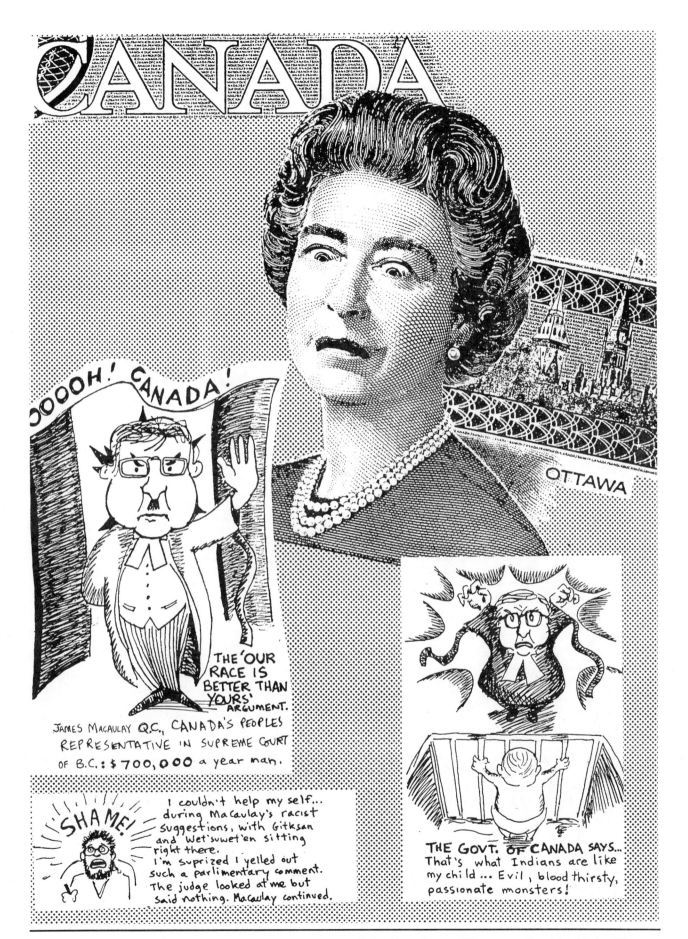

Mike Morrell, Fishery Biologist, by Peter Grant

After Mike Morrell's long qualification arguments the Judge decides he could not speak about Gitksan culture—only about fish. It makes his evidence narrow compared to what he could have shared.

Q: Now, what did you do with respect to the analysis of fish catch with respect to the Gitksan and Wet'suwet'en fishery?

A: The areas covered varied from year to year. The technique, in general, involved making observations on the amount of fishing efforts.

* * *

A: Okay. For the bulk of the study the major areas were as defined in this report what we called the Lower Skeena, which is the Skeena within the territory downstream of the confluence of the Bulkley River, essentially downstream of Hazelton, the Upper Skeena, which is the Skeena above Hazelton, and the Bulkley River.

Q: Okay. Go on with what you did.

A: Okay. In the study we're discussing now, the fish management study, the fisheries that we looked at were the gillnet fisheries in the two sub-areas of the Skeena, and the gaff, dipnet and a few other pieces of gear.

* * *

A: The principle technique is gillnetting with fixed nets, nets that are attached to shore. They're also called set nets as opposed to drift gillnets or gillnets used in all of the tidal fisheries of British Columbia, tidal gillnet fisheries.

* * *

Q: Now, in just taking that first sample of week 15 the 33 nets and the average catch of chinook was 5.75?

A: That's right.

* * *

ALL THIS TALK ABOUT FISH HAS MADE ME HUNGRY!
Alfred Joesph

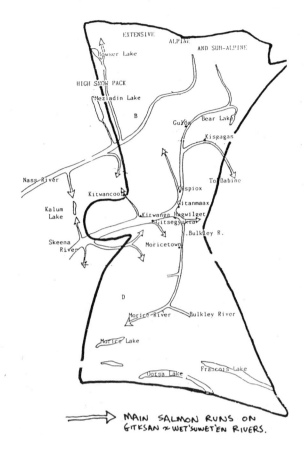

MAIN SALMON RUNS ON GITKSAN & WET'SUWET'EN RIVERS.

A: ...Chronologically as you go through the season, the pink salmon run follows the sockeye run. ...Indicating that although there are sockeye around, my interpretation of this is that people are reducing their fishing effort as the sockeye run wanes and the pink salmon increases.

...The sockeye is the priniciple species of interest, pink salmon are of lesser interest.

* * *

A: ...I came to appreciate different fishing strategies that people were using, different purposes that they had in fishing ranging from catching fish solely for immediate consumption and distribution to supplying organized preserving operations, smoking, canning, etc....

A: ...That is very hard to generalize about but there is that the fishing itself is decentralized, it is widespread; that the units of production if you will are family units operating independantly of each other; that fish are never concentrated at one point after they are caught as they frequently are in industrial fisheries as when a number of catcher vessels deliver to a central processing location.

* * *

A: I think it's extremely unlikely that the weirs would be fished in such a way as to impede the passage of the majority of the fish that were trying to pass them. It is consistent with my under-

MIKE MORRELL
Days 206-209
March 1989

"I came to appreciate different strategies that people were using, different purposes that they had in fishing, ranging from catching fish solely for immediate consumption and distribution to supplying organized preserving operations—smoking, canning, etc."—Mike Morrell

standing of how weirs are fished. It could be most imprudent of the people fishing the weirs since the future impact of it would be obvious to them of preventing the fish from reaching their spawning grounds.

* * *

A: —The Chief felt that the fishery at the coast was impacting on the Babine Fishery, that the fish were becoming less abundant, but that before the advent of that fishery there had not been problems with abundance.

* * *

A: ...So fishing is always intermittent and is

keyed to the ability of the people running the smokehouse to handle the fish, to butcher the fish and prepare them for smoking.

A: I would estimate that we have recorded about 230 different gillnet sites, and there may be an average of three or four people involved at each site. That puts us in the neighborhood of a thousand people. At Moricetown Canyon in a given year there might be 150 different individuals who would not all be the same from one year to the next. So 250 to 300 people over the years that I have been involved would seem reasonable to me. So 1,300 seems to me a ballpark estimate of the numbers of people who have fished in the five years that I have been collecting data.

Hugh Brody,
Anthropologist/Film-maker,
by Michael Jackson

The Witness: ...Newcomers, sure of their superior knowledge, understanding and rights, do as they think fit, encourage others to do likewise, and call upon the forces of Canadian law and order if too directly thwarted and opposed.

...According to white interpretations of events, the villages that make up most of the 45 square miles represent the conclusion of a historical process (unless the reserve is viewed as a step before a full and final assimilation, at which time even reserve lands would be things that the Indian past).

* * *

The Court: ...Does it matter if, from the time of contact, circa 1800 A.D., that they have been treated badly or they have been treated well? Does it make a difference?

* * *

Mr. Jackson: ...I am thinking, for example, in relation to the province's argument regarding the establishment of reserves. It is our submission that understanding the cultural context in which that took place will enable Your Lordship to make a conclusion, a legal conclusion.

* * *

The Court: ...that settlers in governments have tended to see Native peoples through unclear or distorting lenses. Seems to me to be highly questionable relevance.... As I said a moment ago, they may view each other from completely irrational bases. They probably do. Most people do view each other from an irrational basis. Again what difference does it make?

Mr. Jackson: I think it does make a difference, My Lord, in terms of understanding events which have taken place which are relied upon by my friends as evidence of loss or acquiescence in the loss of rights. And I will—

The Court: Well, I don't recall at the moment whether acquiescence is an issue. I suppose it is—

* * *

A: ...The word "Indian" is the beginning of a misconception. It places in a single category a whole range of diverse cultures.

* * *

Allan McEachern describes his theory of history.

The Court: Well, is it not the function of the anthropologists to tell us about ourselves and about other societies.

Mr. Goldie: I said irrelevent to this litigation, My Lord. It would be a very interesting and perhaps educational process if Mr. Brody told us about ourselves and held up a mirror to us, but what has that got to do with this litigation?

The Court: I simply don't know. ...At one time I thought that Mr. Jackson was going to develop some kind of a conspiratorial theory of history, which I had always thought to be a fallacy. I think the accidental theory is far more accurate.

* * *

A: ...They thought that the people should be thrifty, especially people who are, in a way poor. They should save their possessions and resources and should not waste them by burning them and by giving them away. The missionaries were also very disturbed by the power the *halyt* or shaman had at the Feast. And the Feast tended to be a place where shamanistic power was reaffirmed and accepted.

* * *

A: ...Indian agent Loring refers in his reports and papers to the irritating custom the people have of going from village to village, and reports on one striking occassion, I believe in 1901, that he has stopped a boat load of people setting off to go to a Feast and has arrested one of the the principals, on the grounds that he doesn't want this moving about. And he makes this clear in his reports.

"IT IS COMMON BELIEF, AN ASSUMPTION OF THE POLITICAL LEFT AND RIGHT THAT THEY ARE AT A LOWER EVOLUTIONARY LEVEL - THAT THEY WOULD EVENTUALLY PROGRESS TO LIVE LIKE US IN TOWNS CITIES ETC... THIS..."

WHAT DOES THIS GO TO MR. JACKSON?

"JUSTICE DAVEY IN THE NISHGA TRIAL FELL INTO THE TRAP OF ETHNO CENTRICITY - THAT INDIANS WERE LOWER ON THE EVOLUTIONARY SCALE. ASSUMPTIONS."

"I CHECK MY ASSUMPTIONS AT THE DOOR."

← PROVINCE'S GOLDIE.

GOLDIE'S BIG BAG

DOOR

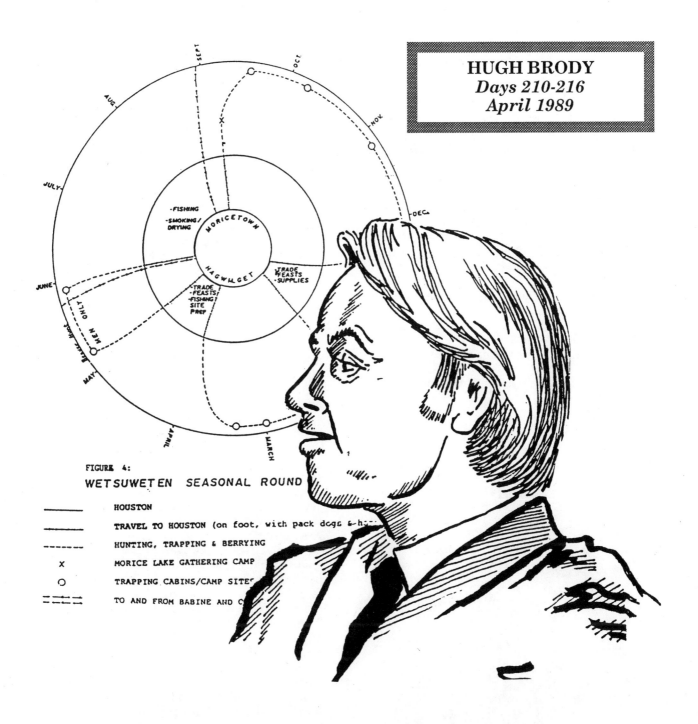

FIGURE 4:

WETSUWETEN SEASONAL ROUND

——————— HOUSTON

——————— TRAVEL TO HOUSTON (on foot, with pack dogs & h...

- - - - - - - HUNTING, TRAPPING & BERRYING

X   MORICE LAKE GATHERING CAMP

O   TRAPPING CABINS/CAMP SITES

═══════ TO AND FROM BABINE AND C...

"Kisgagas is a haunting place for an archeologist/anthropologist because there is so much evidence of continuous life and living at that spot. It is replete with Gitksan memory and nostalgia. I must say ...it is a place that has a living tissue today... there is still salmon being dip-netted, children play on the rocks, cabins are occupied, especially at key hunting and fishing periods."—Hugh Brody

Marvin George, Cartographer, by Stuart Rush

Q: Why did you stamp "Draft Copy" in two places on the map?

A: It was the understanding that all the maps would be draft until the time that they were extensively reviewed with the hereditary Chiefs.... And I had color coded the different areas to differentiate between the different clans.

Q: Are those the 1:50,000, 1:100,000 scaled maps and other scale maps that you referred us to earlier?

A: Yes. Yes, they would be.... And I also had...prepared ahead of time...a description based on those draft maps, and I had already grouped the diffferent geographical features under lakes, rivers, creeks, mountain areas, and identified the Indian name that we already had, plus the English name that was associated with that particular geographical feature on the maps.

Q: And then what did you do with that information?

A: What I did then was, with the assistance of

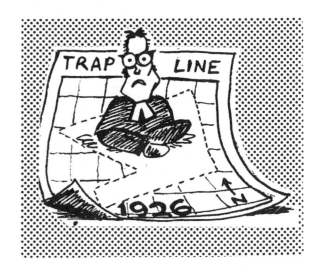

the interpreter, to describe the boundary as we had understood it to be, as plotted on those draft maps. And we had systematically drawn around the external boundary of that particular area, and I had identified the geographical features which were previously identified by them and by other people.

Q: I take it that you are describing what occurred at an interview with a Hereditary Chief?

A: Yes. This would be the first meeting that we would have had with them regarding the affidavits and the identification of the territories.

Q: Okay. And then would you just explain what you said to them in a typical interview with a Hereditary Chief?

A: What we were trying to define was the external boundaries of the Hereditary Chiefs, and we made it a point that they understood that they were not talking about traplines. When we referred to territory, we also referred to the territory as *yenta*.... *Yenta* means the hunting territory, to differentiate between that and trapline.... When we had picked up Martha Brown at Glen Vowell and we were driving up the Kispiox Road, we made a point to pick a spot that we could identify on the maps. And the spot that we chose was the turn-off into Kispiox Village, which would be right beside the band office there on the road. We identified that as our zero point, and we tripped the mileage indicator at that time to zero. And as we were driving up the road, Martha would say, "Oh, this particular place is so and so," and we would identify what kilometer point it was on, and identify what feature she was describing to us.

200+ year old territorial marker carved into a living tree. Gaal's House.

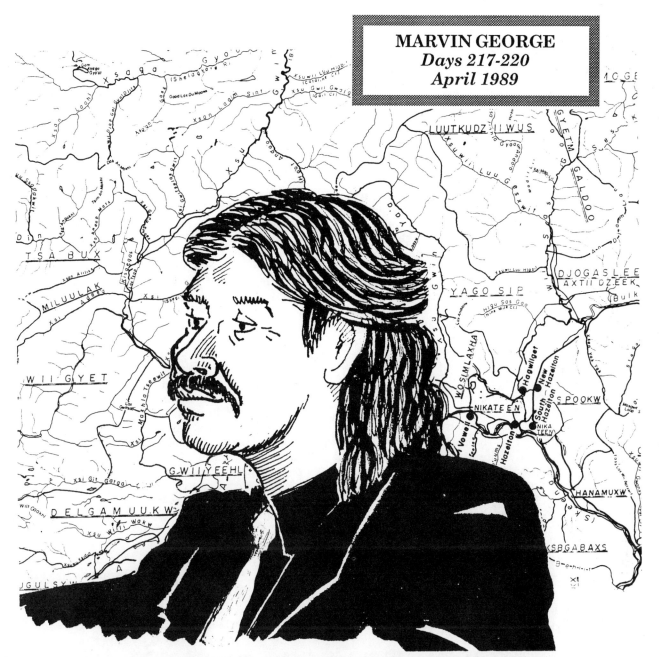

"I had already grouped the diffferent geographical features under lakes, rivers, creeks, mountain areas, and identified the Indian name that we already had, plus the English name that was associated with that particular geographical feature on the maps." —Marvin George

PROCEEDINGS

The Court: By my count, today is the 217th day of this trial. I have heard the evidence of 31 witnesses, whose evidence comprises over 16,000 pages of transcript. Well over 4,000 exhibits have been filed, and there are many more to come.... The case is one of overwhelming importance. At stake in the action is title to over 20,000 square miles of priceless unalienated land in the Skeena and-Bulkley Watersheds, and the judgment in this case will be the first comprehensive judgment on non-treaty aboriginal rights since the inclusive Calder case in 1974. There are other serious issues in the case, additional to the title of the land I have just mentioned. At least five other similar actions are pending in this Court awaiting judgment in this case. I doubt if a more important case has ever been tried in the courts of this province.

Robert Galois,
Historical Geographer,
by Murray Adams

Mr. Adams: My Lord, the Plaintiffs' next witness is Dr. Robert Galois. He is a historical geographer, as was Dr. Ray, and in some sense is going to pick up the story where Dr. Ray left off. And he has produced an opinion report. Its focus is on Gitksan and Wet'suwet'en protest and resistance activities and Indian encounters with non-Indian society, and with that focus he covers a somewhat longer period. He begins at 1850 and goes until 1927:

"European penetration of new lands was not a penetration of unoccupied or untouched environments. The frequent conflict situations which developed are a clear indication of the widespread distribution of Natives and of their attachment to and exploitation of particular areas."

"...The historian is necessarily selective. The belief in a hard core of historical facts existing objectively and independently of the interpretation of the historian is a preposterous fallacy, but one which it is very hard to eradicate."

Q: On page six of your opinion report, you say that: "An examination of Hudson's Bay Company records indicates that the white economy and society maintained only a marginal and indirect presence in the upper Skeena area from the 1820s through to the end of the 1850s." When was the Hudson's Bay post at Hazelton established?

A: 1866. It was closed in 1868.

The Court: The Hudson's Bay post at Hazelton?

A: Well, "Aquilgate" is the correct designation in the Hudson's Bay Company records. There is some uncertainty as to its precise location.

The Witness: With a resident population of less than one hundred in the mid-1890s, whites depended upon Indian participation for the success of most economic activities.

* * *

"The basic feature of protest is the component of opposition to the actions of some other party; in the present context, Gitksan and Wet'suwet'en opposition to white actions is viewed as unacceptable."

"...The Gitksan and Wet'suwet'en responded in a number of ways to the white pressures but, in the end, the most efffective tactic was simply to continue to operate the system. Such persistence, in the face of powerful white hostility was an important dimension of protest."

"...The principle change in the form of Gitksan protests concerned the use of white intermediaries. On a number of occasions, at Kitsegukla in 1872 for example, the Gitksan used third parties to give their protests written form. Such documents were shaped by whites, but their substance reflects Gitksan values and institutions."

"...In part the disputes that arose between whites and Indians in the upper Skeena region were a product of the mutual lack of understanding. Sometimes whites became embroiled in intra-Indian conflicts: this may well have happened at Kispiox in 1874; it certainly happened in 1888. Some conflicts, though, reflected white transgressions against Gitksan norms or laws. In the 1880s, primarily as a result of gold mining on Lorne Creek, the question of competition for access to land and resources was brought to the fore."

- KIDNAP THE CHILDREN.
- MOVE THEM FROM HOME.
- TEACH SELF-HATRED.
- DENY LANGUAGE.
- DENY SPIRIT.
- DENY NURTURING.
- TEACH NO HISTORY.
- TEACH WHITE.
- SEND THE CHILDREN HOME WHEN THEY ARE ADULTS.

Excerpt From The Opening Statement of The Chiefs

The Gitksan and the Wet'suwet'en Chiefs have seen parts of their territory destroyed. This will only increase as large corporations build faster, more efficient, computer-operated sawmills which will increase the rate at which the trees are turned into lumber and exported out of the Gitksan and Wet'suwet'en territory. The Gitksan and Wet'suwet'en Hereditary Chiefs have watched their land being stripped bare. They have seen the destruction of fishing sites and spawning grounds and the extinction of salmon stocks. They have protested and resisted. Whenever possible they have enforced their own laws. They have continually insisted on their recognition as peoples with authority over the territory in which they have exercised stewardship for many thousands of years.

"Missionaries told the Indians the only way to get land was to purchase, find or steal it... that the B.C. government were thieves."—Macaulay cross-examination.

What do you think Mr. Macaulay (Govt. of Canada) is saying? (Posted at the coffee machine.)

1. Sleeping Giant?—I'll show them sleeping!

2. Zzz... Mph! Huh? O.K., Marvyn, help me out of this one!

3. Hey! The Gitksan and Wet'suwet'en *ties* to the land *are* strong!

4. I like it as it is—blank!

5. Turn me loose: I'll return your land!

6. What's this in my mouth?

7. I give up!

8. The G & W may wander around on the land, but we're the ones with the real tie$.

9. That's how the West will win.

10. What a joke! The G-W say they have ties to the land...

11. I am not taking this lying down!

BARBARA LANE
Days 228-231
May 1989

Barb Lane, Ethnohistorian, Re-Examination by Stuart Rush

"Ethnohistorians, like biochemists, understand that their subjects require diverse approaches."

* * *

The Court: Dr. Lane, on page 7...which Mr. Rush read to you, it says: "Both kinds of analysis are indispensable to any well-reasoned judgment regarding what the policy actually was at any given time." I'm sure—well, I'm not sure about anything anymore. Does your discipline recognize that very often the world moves on ad hocery and not reasonable policy?"
The Witness: Yes.

* * *

Province's Mr. Goldie: The focus of her study is not the culture of the people of the United Kingdom or the culture of the people of Canada or the culture of the people of the Colony of British Columbia or Vancouver Island; her focus is in the culture of the Native peoples, but she wishes to address Your Lordship in terms of the documentary records of those other societies.
The Court: With regard to Mr. Goldie's second principle submission, I have the view, as I have expressed before with respect to Dr. Ray and Mr. Morrison, then there was someone else, Galois, that while the witness can explain why they think these documents are relevant, they cannot interpret the documents. That, it seems to me, in the Court of Law is the exclusive province of the judge.

* * *

The Court: I am not sure, Mr. Rush, that you are able to persuade me that you can now deter-mine what somebody's policy was 100 years ago or even last year. I have seen enough of life to know that very often what people later come along and say was obviously policy, was nothing more than accident, and I think we are into a very, very slippery piece of ground if we are trying to determine not just what happened, but the policy behind it....

Where Judge McEachern gets mad at the experts.

I think there have to be serious limits put on the scope of this kind of evidence. The Court has come very close to surrendering its authority to experts, and I am determined that that must not be allowed to happen. Experts have gone far too far in many cases. What is happening is deplorable, in the sense of the way experts are being used to change the face of litigation, and I don't think it's a healthy change, and I am quite determined to see it doesn't go much further than it has.
The Witness: As I recall, I was asked to explore the documentary record to identify those written documents which appeared to shed light on policy or lack of policy regarding Indian title in the area now known as British Columbia, and I understand that task to include the time frame from the first British presence in this area. And I date that period from Captain Cook's arrival here in 1778. I perhaps neglected to say in the first sentence that I understood the task to be Imperial policy and later Colonial policy and later Dominion policy with respect to Native people in what is now British Columbia.

Susan M. Marsden, Cultural Anthropologist, by Peter Grant

The Witness: That was the beginning of my understanding of the Feast, when I realized that the giving out of gifts was in payment for services, and when I received money and objects, that I was being paid to witness events.

Q: You then set out, at the bottom of page four, as part of your research, the sources that you went to, and you refer to Elders from Kispiox, Kitsegukla, Kitwanga, Kiwancool and Hazelton, and you list the UBC Museum of Anthropology and Department of Anthropology and the Department of Ethology at Victoria and the National Museum of Canada, as well as others, Gitksan Association and the School of Art. Did you go to all of these sources in developing this material?

A: Yes.

Q: Would this chart be referring specifically to the Fireweed, or would it be referring to—

A: It's only graphing here the Fireweed Wilnat'ahl from Temlaham.

Mr. Grant: Now, if we go back to Exhibit 1043, that's that chart you did of the Fireweed. This is this ancient history chart, my Lord.

Q: How long did it take you in terms of your analysis of the *adaawk*?

A: Well, in the case of the Fireweed, their *adaawk* contained a lot of information that allowed me to chronologize them alone, and then I found it far more difficult with the other clans, and that was when I started to use the Duff files to help put things in order. And I did that process over the four years that I worked with the Tribal Council.

Q: Did you do that full time?

A: Yes, I did.

* * *

A: When I first moved among the Gitksan people, I was told by them that the people, the things the white people call stories are not stories, they are history.

A: ...Boas' transcriber of oral histories—his name was Tate—felt that he had to clean them up, he had to take out references that would offend white people and make them acceptable to Christian thinking, and I don't use those in the same way as I use the Barbeau-Beynon *adaawk*.

* * *

A: They didn't have an A.D./B.C. dating system. They didn't use numbers to reflect time. They had other ways of reflecting time....

Q: ...There's no measured time in historics?

A: Not in the way we measure time, no.

Q: But isn't it the case that in your report, you have purported to review oral histories to give a 10,000-year history of the Gitksan?

A: Yes.

SUSAN MARSDEN
Days 232-236
June 1989

Ancient times – the arrival about 10,000 years B.P.

Robert M. Atkinson, District Manager, Department of Indian Affairs for the Northwest, Cross-Examination by Geoff Plant for the Province

Mr. Grant: ...So since May 11, 1987, when the last amendment was obtained, the late David Gunanoot, Chief Nii Kyap, has died and Gerald Gunanoot now holds that name, and that amendment is made. Lelt, Fred Johnson, has died, and Lloyd Ryan has taken that name. Martha Brown, the late Kliiyem Lax Haa, has died and Eva Sampson has taken that name. George Naziel, the former Madeek, has died and James Brown has taken that name. Johnny Mack, the former Klo Um Khun, has died and Patrick Pierre has taken that name. Sylvester Williams, the late Hagwilnegh, has died and Ron Mitchell has taken his name. Joe Wright, the late Xsgogimlahxa, has died and Vernon Milton has taken that name. And Magnus Turner, the holder of the name Wiigyet from Kitsegukla, has died and Roy Wesley has succeeded to that name.

The Chiefs decide to put in this witness at the end of the Canadian Government Department of Indian Affairs witnesses.

Q: In Paragraph 2 of your Affidavit, I think it's in the third sentence, you say that you became knowledgeable about the traditional laws of the Coastal Tsimshian, Nisga'a and Haida, which includes succession based on matrilineality. Then you say in Paragraph 3, "I was aware that both the Gitksan and Wet'suwet'en had similar rules of succession on a matrilineal basis." Now, you're not trained as a lawyer, are you, Mr. Atkinson?

A: No.

Q: You're not trained as an anthropologist, either?

A: No.

PEOPLE OF ALL RACES AND MIXES NEED TO LOOK INTO THE MIRROR OF HISTORY AND UNDERSTAND WHO THEY ARE, WHO THEY WERE, WHERE THEY CAME FROM, AND HOW THEY FIT IN... AND WHERE. — THEN FROM THERE THEY CAN SEE WHAT CAN BE DONE TO CHANGE THE WORLD, THEIR OWN COMMUNITY, BUILD ON STRENGTHS, RIGHT WRONGS.

Q: Is it fair to say that you have got what might be called a layman's knowledge of the customs and practices of the Indians of, I guess firstly, those serviced in the North Coast district, and then secondly, in the Hazelton district?

A: Yes. I would call it an informed layman's opinion, though.

* * *

A: We refused to accept expenses for things like headstones and whatnot, because the community at large had very clearly told us to keep our nose out of that; that was the business of the traditional system, and it would be handled through the traditional system. We were chastised a couple of times by Band Councils.

Q: For interfering?

A: For interfering in the local custom.

* * *

Q: Tribal Council is establishing a resource centre through which they are amassing a great wealth of information as part of their overall objective to achieve just resolution of land claims and aboriginal rights issues of the Gitksan and Carrier [Wet'suwet'en] people.

* * *

Where the Government of Canada uses the Chief's Witness to include three more contentious estate files. This is the way we do business.

Mr. Macaulay: Now, I think that exhausts all the questions I have of you, Mr. Atkinson. My Lord, I have prepared a small binder that augments the documents.... And I propose filing this binder as the next exhibit. It has three tabs; they are documents that come from three estate files.... And, in my submission, they put the documents which are exhibited to Mr. Atkinson's Affidavit in a larger context. I have got copies.

The Court: Have you seen these, Mr. Rush?

Mr. Rush: No, I haven't seen them, My Lord, and I would like to take a moment to reflect on what my view is on this.

The Court: All right. Thank you. Well, you can hand it in, but we won't mark it until we hear from Mr. Rush. Mr. Rush wants to look at the documents.

Mr. Plant: Yes, that's fine.

The Court: We won't mark it yet.

"The whites, when they came to the territories, they had to live in tents before they lived in skyscrapers in Vancouver. They don't have to keep living in tents to prove they have a culture. You don't expect them to not change with the times—it's the same with us."—Yaga'lahl (Dora Wilson)

Chapter 5

Pioneers, Perfiders,
And Cultural Ghouls:
Expert Witnesses
For British Columbia

In this chapter of our history, you will witness how government lawyers, no longer able to deny our continuous existence on our territories over thousands of years, attempt to prove that, passively and without resistance, we accepted their "superior" civilization and all its "comforts." This was their argument of *acquiesence*.

With thousands of documents, maps and business records, the Province marched government agents, former politicians, and history "experts" into the witness box to prove that we willingly accepted the jurisdiction and technology of their society. It was well noted by our people that these "experts" were mostly government bureaucrats who, for the most part, worked outside of our system and outside our territories. Other witnesses called by the Province included "pioneers," guide outfitters and other settlers in our territories who would testify that, in the few years they had been living and profiting from the land, they saw no evidence of Gitksan and Wet'suwet'en people on that land. Our Chiefs and Elders quietly shook their heads and agreed that the towering stone figure of Lady Justice standing in the foyer of the British Columbia Law Courts was not the only one wearing a blindfold.

The most desperate evidence issued from the Province was that elicited from the only anthropological "expert" they called to the witness box. Consulting with a "secret informer" whose identity the Province refused to make known, she claimed that the Gitksan and Wet'suwet'en, contrary to our oral histories, did not organize ourselves into our complex system of governance until the advent of the European fur trade—meaning, I gather, that in the time of my great, great, great, grandmother when the first white man stumbled out of the forest sick, hungry and poorly clothed, we were unorganized, unstructured and primitive. It further implies that, within a matter of ten years, we were firmly structured in our Clans, Houses and territories to accommodate the influx of fur traders. As much as we purport to a strength of spirit and determination, such a feat proclaimed by this anthropologist would cast us as being a people of extraordinary, remarkable and superhuman abilities! Of course, we would not object too strenuously to her praise! With the nature of her testimony, it is small wonder that her "secret informant" was reluctant to reveal his or her identity.

—Skanu'u (Ardythe Wilson)

Excerpts from the Province's Statement of Defence...
...simplified

IN THE SUPREME COURT OF BRITISH COLUMBIA

BETWEEN:

DELGAMUUKW, also known as KEN MULDOE,
suing on his own behalf and on behalf of
all the members of the HOUSE OF DELGAM
UUKW and others *79 others*

Each chief representing a house of 50-100 people.

PLAINTIFFS

WHAT! WE Are the defendants?

AND:

HER MAJESTY THE QUEEN IN RIGHT OF THE
PROVINCE OF BRITISH COLUMBIA and
THE ATTORNEY GENERAL OF CANADA

THAT'S ME!

And I represent all you citizens of the colony, including, of course, British Columbia!

DEFENDANTS

FURTHER AMENDED STATEMENT OF DEFENCE
OF THE DEFENDANT HER MAJESTY THE QUEEN
IN RIGHT OF THE PROVINCE OF BRITISH COLUMBIA
TO THE AMENDED STATEMENT OF CLAIM FILED
MAY 11, 1987.

1.   This Defendant denies that each of the Plaintiffs named

in paragraphs 1 to 49D of the Further Amended Statement of Claim

dated May 11, 1987 / / (and hereinafter all references to

paragraph numbers are, except where otherwise stated, to those in

the said Further Amended Statement of Claim) holds the respective

position which he or she is therein alleged to hold, and says

that the holding of any such position confers no rights known to

the law on the holder.

What this first paragraph of defence means is that none of the named plaintiffs are chiefs... and even if they were, it wouldn't matter anyway.

Mike Goldie, Q.C. Head Lawyer for the province of B.C.

5.   This Defendant denies that the Plaintiffs referred to in paragraph 53 are the hereditary Chiefs of the Wet'suwet'en and are descendants of the hereditary Wet'suwet'en Chiefs.

TRANSLATION → "You aren't a Chief and neither was your Granny"

6.   In answer to paragraph 54 this Defendant denies that the Wet'suwet'en together share in common any territory, language, laws, spirituality, culture, economy or authority.

THAT'S RIGHT FOLKS! FOR YOUR PROVINCES DEFENCE WE HAVE CHOSEN TO TAKE A PAGE FROM B.C.'s RACIST HISTORY AND DENY THAT INDIANS EVEN EXIST!... THAT IS, THEY HAVE NO LAND, NO LANGUAGE, NO LAWS, NO SPIRITUALITY, NO CULTURE, NO ECONOMY, NO AUTHORITY.

13.   In further answer to paragraphs 56, 59, 60 and 61 this Defendant says that, if the Plaintiffs or any of them, either singly or in combination, or their ancestors singly or in any combination, exercised jurisdiction over the Territory or any part or parts thereof, whether against other aboriginal peoples or at all the right so to do was extinguished when complete dominion over the territory was taken by the United Kingdom of Great Britain and Ireland.

WHAT THIS MEANS IS THAT WHEN WE TOOK OVER AS A COLONIZER - INDIAN RIGHTS WERE EXTINGUISHED.

RIGHTS PSSSSSSSSSSSsssss

CENTER OF UNIVERSE ← ENGLAND

16.   In further answer to paragraph 65 this Defendant says
that the Royal Proclamation does not confer upon the Plaintiffs
ownership or jurisdiction over the Territory; that the Plaintiffs
have no right at all to have the Territory reserved to the
benefit of the Plaintiffs, and that the Plaintiffs have no
aboriginal title, ownership, jurisdiction or relationship to
either the Imperial or Federal Crown of a character that is
entitled to the recognition alleged.

28.   In answer to paragraph 75 this Defendant says that, if
this Defendant has alienated any lands within the territory to
other persons, She has not done so wrongfully, and denies that
the effect of the said alienation has been the appropriation or
use of any lands of the Plaintiffs within the Territory by this
Defendant or other persons relying on this Defendant's exercise
of jurisdiction over the said lands.

33A.   The title of the Crown to the lands of what is now the Province of British Columbia is not now and never has been burdened or excluded by aboriginal right, title, ownership or jurisdiction but if it was, that burden was discharged by the voluntary acts of the Crown in setting aside particular tracts of land as reserves for the use and benefit of Indians.

NOBODY HAS EVER RULED THIS LAND EXCEPT US... BUT IF YOU DID THEN IT DOESN'T MATTER BECAUSE WE MADE YOU RESERVATIONS. RESERVATIONS TO A DINNER OF OUR CRUMBS.

39(b)... The Plaintiffs and their ancestors having knowledge of the said exercise of sovereign jurisdiction have on many occasions too numerous to particularize acquiesced in this Defendant's sovereign jurisdiction by seeking and receiving benefits, licences, grants and protection from Her. By delaying the commencement of this action the Plaintiffs and their ancestors have obtained the benefits of such licences, grants and protection and the benefits of expenditures of public funds by this Defendant. In the circumstances the Plaintiffs have delayed unreasonably in advancing their claims and this Defendant says that the Plaintiffs are barred and estopped by their laches, acquiescence and delay from asserting the rights claimed by them against this Defendant.

SORRY! YOU TOOK TOO LONG.

EVEN IF YOU RAN THE PLACE BEFORE, YOU LET US STAY AND BULLY YOU AROUND... SO THAT MEANS YOU ACCEPT US... BESIDES YOU TOOK TOO LONG, AND WE GAVE YOU A FEW TOKEN DOLLARS FROM THE BILLIONS IN RESOURCES EXTRACTED FROM YOUR OWN LAND.

WHEREFORE this Defendant submits that the action against her should be dismissed.

COUNTERCLAIM

42. This Defendant repeats the allegations set forth in the above Statement of Defence.

43. WHEREFORE this Defendant claims:

1. A declaration that the Plaintiffs have no right, title or interest in and to the Territory, the resources thereon, thereunder or thereover;

WE WANT THE COURT TO RULE THAT THESE PEOPLE HAVE NO INTEREST IN THEIR HOME LANDS.

2. Alternatively, a declaration that the Plaintiffs' cause of action, if any, in respect of their alleged aboriginal title, right or interest in and to the Territory and the resources thereof, thereunder or thereover is for compensation from Her Majesty the Queen in right of Canada;

AND IF THEY HAVE ANY RIGHTS AT ALL IT ISN'T OUR PROBLEM - IT'S CANADA'S!

AND BELIEVE ME, OUR COSTS ARE TEN TIMES WHAT THE CHIEFS HAVE SPENT.

CHEAP!

3. Costs.

THATS ME!

YUCK!

Solicitor for the Defendant, HER MAJESTY THE QUEEN IN RIGHT OF THE PROVINCE OF BRITISH COLUMBIA.

THIS FURTHER AMENDED STATEMENT OF DEFENCE AND COUNTERCLAIM is filed by D.M.M. Goldie, Q.C., of the firm of Messrs. Russell & DuMoulin, whose office address is at 1700 - 1075 West Georgia Street, Vancouver, B.C. V6E 3G2 (Telephone: 688-3411).
Ref.: ATT-2253 (DMMG/jmp)

The famous MacMillan Bloedel building!

Opening By Michael Goldie For The Province of British Columbia

The Court:: All right. Well, Mr. Rush, I must say that from time to time I have been reminded of Napoleon's musings on the opening of the second day of the Battle of Waterloo when he wondered if the enemy would ever close—would ever show their backs. I am sure your friends are wondering if you and your friends would ever show your backs, but you have reached that stage without literally fitting the description, I'm sure. It is good that we have at least reached this milestone. Mr. Goldie, do you want to start?

Mr. Goldie: Yes, my lord. My lord, I do not propose opening the Defendant's case at any length. And that's not because of the fact that the Plaintiffs' case still has a number of loose ends. It is because I don't think there is any doubt about anyone's mind here as to what the issues in the case are all about ….

I need not enlarge upon the difference between a claim of ownership and jurisdiction which, if it's successful to the degree contemplated in the prayer for relief, would remove substantially all, if not all, control of the lands and its resources in the claims area from the Province and vest that control in the Plaintiffs.

…There are a number of other lawsuits awaiting the outcome of the case, and the sooner your lordship is enabled to consider the evidence and to hear counsels' final submissions, the better….

I want to conclude by making a comment about some of the statements made by Plaintiffs' counsel in their opening, and some of the opinion evidence tendered in the case so far. I'm referring to evidence which calls in question what I will call the honor of the Crown, and that's a phrase that your lordship has seen, and it relates not only to the Crown or the executive government of the Colony and then the Province of British Columbia, but also in right of Canada and by extension the Imperial Crown. And in its broadest terms, the issue that… has been raised is whether the Indian peoples of this Province have been treated fairly.

…The policy of the Colony of British Columbia towards Native people was in its time, and even now when viewed from the perspective of the late 20th Century, enlightened and humane. The governments of the United Kingdom and of the Colony were resolved to avoid a policy similar to that pursued in the United States….

The next point that the colony of British Columbia recognized was that humanity required that lands used and occupied by the Indians be protected and preserved from them. And those—those are virtually—it's a paraphrase of the words Governor Douglas used.

The Court:: From them or for them?

Mr. Goldie: Preserved for them.

…And I will ask your lordship to reject what I will call the conspiracy theory of history which appears to have been reached by the Plaintiffs in support of the far-reaching claims of present-day ownership and jurisdiction.

My lord, that is as much as I propose saying by way of an opening, and subject to your lordship's direction, I'll call the first witness.

The Court:: All right.

Mr. Goldie: Dr. Steciw.

"When you have no basis for an argument, abuse the plaintiff."—Cicero (about 75 BC)

Igor Steciw, Medical Doctor and Guide Outfitter, Examination by Michael Goldie for the Province

Q: Dr. Steciw, you're a medical doctor practicing in Smithers, where you have lived since 1967?
A: Yes.

* * *

Q: Now, I'm instructed that in 1969 or 1970 you purchased a half interest in a small guide outfitting area. Would you tell the Court how this came about and the nature of what a guide outfitting area is?
A: Okay. This came about because since I was a young boy, I was always interested in the out-of-doors and hunting, fishing....

Q: I take it that the name "guide outfitting" sufficiently describes the nature of the business that's carried on?
A: Yes.

* * *

Q: —the game that was being sought?
A: Mountain goat, grizzly bear, moose, black bear, essentially.

Q: And what time of year would you take people in there for the purpose of hunting?
A: The beginning of September until probably the end of September, some such time.

* * *

Where Mike Goldie asks Dr. Steciw if he knows Goohlaht (Lucy Namox), a Wet'suwet'en Chief.

A: I actually think I know her, but I'm not dead sure. You see, your Honor, I take care of a lot of the Native people in Smithers, and when I'm on call for other doctors and so forth, a lot of these names run, you know, into each other. I'm fairly sure I know Lucy, Lucy Namox.

* * *

The beginning of Goldie's questions regarding the in- visibility of Native people on the territory.

DR. IGOR STECIW
Days 250-252
July 1989

A: On the old Suskwa Road, which is sort of parallel to the Bulkley River, I think one or maybe two occasions at the most, right on the road I think, as I recall, one or maybe even two cars there were some Native people, one or two people, in.

Q: And did you see any hunting by Indian or Native peoples?
A: No.

* * *

Q: Now, I want you to give his lordship an estimate of the size of the area as you bought it before the first addition to it?
A: Approximately 4,000 square miles.

* * *

A: I took two American hunters, for goat only, hunting into Kuldo'o Lake. We flew in there with a Beaver, made camp, and hunted.

...I also flew in a jet boat, an aluminum 20-foot jet boat with motor, jet—a mercury motor with jet attachment—and I explored the river with these two men down the stream.

The Court:: The Skeena River?
A: Downstream approximately eight miles.

Q: ...Now, I want to ask you while you were doing any of that, whether you observed any signs of human activity other than your own?
A: No present activity whatsoever.

* * *

Q: Were you at either Slamgeesh or Chipmunk again in that year—'79?
A: Yes....
Q: Again, any signs of use by Native peoples?
A: Nobody was around, sir.
Q: All right.

A: No sign.

Q: All right.... Any sign of Indian presence [in 1980]?

A: No.

Q: ...You cut trails in that area [Chipmunk Creek] in 1979.... Well, now, any sign of activity of Native or other people?

A: No.... We hunted...down the Skeena, Foster Creek, up in the headwaters and the valleys there along the Skeena.

Q: And any evidence at all of Native use or any use of those areas apart from what you've testified to?

A: No, not any Native use.

* * *

Mr. Rush: He said he saw people with hard hats on....

A: From what I understand, these were railroad people, like engineers in hard hats. They were white people, that's all.

Q: Well, did you see in 1984 any sign of Native activity?

A: No, sir.

Q: ...Did you see any sign of Native activity, or did you run into any Native people in the Swan Lake area?

A: No, I didn't.

* * *

Q: I now want to revert to your airplane.

A: Okay.

Q: In 1986, did you acquire a new type of airplane?

A: Yes, I did.... There are a number of very, very small lakes. I wanted to get more of a short take-off and landing potential.

Q: ...Now, Doctor, you've described fairly extensive, I will call it reconnaissance.

A: Mm-hmmm.

* * *

Could it be that the good doctor wasn't just flying American hunters around, but doing military reconnaissance for the Province?

Igor Steciw, Cross-Examination by Stuart Rush

Q: Those two boats you have hidden because you don't want people to find out where they are and to use them?

A: Fair enough.

Q: And I suggest to you that if you have got them hidden, you expect people to be there.

* * *

Q: Now, you told the Court that in 1986... you phoned David Blackwater, or I took you to mean David Blackwater, to buy his trapline.

A: ...I asked him if I could buy it from him, and he said no. And I said, you know, "Well, gosh, you know, you are not using it. What do you want it for?" And whoever it was that was on the phone said, "Well, we are not using it, but, you know, it's like money in the bank; you just like to kind of keep it there."

* * *

Q: If I tell you that these photographs were taken in September of 1986, it would indicate Indian activity at Slamgeesh Lake, wouldn't it?

A: Well, it would indicate their presence as pictured on the photograph.

Q: But I think your point is that there wasn't any presence of Indians in the area either.

* * *

Q: ...In terms of human activity below the forest cover, when you're flying over it, you cannot see that activity beneath the forest cover?

A: In most cases, this is correct.

* * *

Stuart Rush refers to a Letter to the Editor written by Dr. Steciw.

Q: In 1983, Dr. Steciw, you described the Gitksan- Wet'suwet'en court claim for the ownership of river waters and fish passing through reserves as a frivolous and arrogant claim?

A: Okay....

Q: Your statement about that case at that time is also your view of this case at this time?

A: Let me think about that. No. Although...I told you in principle I think that all Crown lands belong to everybody, all citizens of British Columbia, and they should belong so equally, and we should have... equality of laws; we're all living in a country with equal opportunity. Isn't this the hallmark of any democracy? Instead of saying that a certain group, whether it's white or Native or any racial group or interest group, owns it all—on what basis? And that's my personal view. And, if I may say this, this has not in any case altered any observations or anything I have told you here, under oath or otherwise. ...I would side with the Crown in this case as a personal opinion—as a personal feeling, rather.

Barbara L. Peden, Guide-Outfitter, by James Mackenzie for the Province

Q: Mrs. Peden, I understand that you were born in Lloydminster, Alberta?

A: Yes, I was.

Q: And you and your family subsequently moved to British Columbia?

A: Yes.

Q: ...Did any Native person ever assert title over property in your presence?

A: No.

* * *

JIM P. TOUROND
Days 254-255
July 1989

BARBARA L. PEDEN
Days 254-255
July 1989

Where Barb Peden shows her distaste for her neighbor

Q: What sort of house, if any, does Bill Sholtie have?

A: He has a good-sized house. It's a government-built house that they built for the Natives, and he has power there.

Q: Have you ever been to that house?

A: Yes.

Q: And do you have any knowledge about what Bill Sholtie does as an occupation?

A: Doesn't do very much of anything.

Q: Do you have any knowledge whether Mr. Bill Sholtie hunts?

A: I have never seen him hunting.

Q: ...And when he is outside his house, what have you seen him doing, generally speaking?

A: Well, he tries to grow a little garden, and he tries to fix up his house, and he's fencing his area right now, so he's been building a fence all summer.

Barbara L. Peden, Cross-Examination by Stuart Rush

Where Stuart Rush points out that Barb Peden was on the land for two months out of three years.

Q: I take it that your statement about not seeing any Indian trappers west of Francois Lake applies to the 1980s?

A: Not really. It's just about any time I was up the road.

Q: ...All right. In 1986, Mrs. Peden, my count is 30 days; in 1987, 24; and in 1988, six. And I've simply gone through and counted the number of days it appears that you personally were guiding in those years.

A: Okay.

* * *

Q: Let me suggest to you that the reason that you fly in is that it's easier to get your clients and your equipment into where you're going to start the hunt?

A: Well, it's about the only way to get in there.

Q: Well, presumably you could have walked?

A: Yes, if your hunters would walk that far.

Q: Well, that's the point. They wouldn't, would they?

A: No.

* * *

A: The Hollands were just Hollands. I don't know any first names.

Q: Of the people that I've shown you, you can't recognize any of those people?

A: No.

Q: ...Well, Mrs. Peden, you said that since 1960 you hadn't seen any of the Seymours or the Hollands around. If you don't know their names and you can't recognize them, how do you know you hadn't seen them around?

A: Well, I have seen very few Natives in the area. Let's put it that way.

Q: And that's the way you would tell us that you hadn't seen them around, is it?

A: Right.

James P. Tourond, Guide-Outfitter, by James Mackenzie for the Province

The third witness, James Tourond, is Barb Peden's son by a previous marriage.

Q: And what proportion of the meat that you were eating in your house would have been wild game meat?

A: I would say probably 95 percent or more was wild meat ofsome sort.

* * *

Where Goldie gets James to use his boyhood friend to imply that the Natives don't speak their own language. Were they just being polite?

Q: Now, I would like to speak about the years when you were attending high school in Burns Lake. Were there Native students attending the high school in Burns Lake?

A: Yes, there were.

Q: Did you know any of those people?

A: Yes. One of my good friends that I chummed around with while in high school was Native.

Q: And what was his name?

A: Simon Brown.

Q: ...Did you hear the Browns speaking among themselves in Native languages?

A: Very rarely. Whenever I was present they would speak English amongst themselves. Every once in a while there would be the odd Native word spoken.

Q: Did the Browns ever advise you of their Indian names?

A: No, they did not.

* * *

Q: Have you seen non-Native people hunting?

A: Yes. Lots of non-Native people hunting....

On one occasion I have seen a Native person hunting....

I saw the two Native people removing the insides of a cow moose, and I went up to have a look at it while they were in the process. They assured me that they had a sustenance permit to carry this out.

Q: Was that cow moose pregnant?

A: Yes, she was.

Q: And what were the Native people taking from the inside of the cow moose?

A: The sack that holds the foetus was removed from the insides of the animal and set aside.

* * *

The Court: At the moment, it seems to me that these two persons, who have been described as Natives, may have come from Vancouver Island, for example, and unless the evidence is brought home to the Plaintiffs, it's wholly unadmissible, is it not?

* * *

A: The white people who have killed moose, of course, remove the insides, and some do and some don't remove the heart and the liver of the animal. But I've never seen any of them remove the area that I was talking about previously.

Q: You are speaking about the foetus?

A: That's correct.

* * *

Q: Where else have you seen Native people within the land claims area?

A: Oh, I've seen a lot of Native people in Burns Lake, some in Topley, Houston, Smithers, Hazelton, Kitwanga, Fort Babine, Babine.

Q: Yes, you are outside the land claims area now.

A: Oh. Sorry.

* * *

Q: Have you ever learned the names of Houses or Clans?

A: No. I've just heard of them through the Court here.

Why lawyers wear black...

JUSTICE DIED

Cyril M. Shelford, Pioneer Politician, by Chuck Willms for the Province

Q: Now, did Jimmy Andrews or Matthew Sam tell you about their reaction and the reaction of the Native people to the coming of the white settlers?

A: Certainly, both of them told us that they were very pleased to get their hands on fishnets and rifles.

Q: For the obvious reasons?

A: It was easier to hunt game and catch fish.

* * *

Q: You said earlier that you served with the Canadian Army between 1939 and 1945 in Europe, and you were in Italy, France and up to Holland.

A: Yeah. I was a sergeant of the gun crew.

Q: Did you have Native Indians on that crew?

A: Yes. I had Ray and Fred Prince from Fort St. James. They were excellent people to be with, and they went pretty well all through Sicily and Italy with me and on into the rest of Europe.

Q: Do you know how they came to be in the Canadian Army?

A: They were like the rest of us; they volunteered, and there was quite a number of Native Indians in the Canadian Armed Forces, and I must say they did very well. They were the same as everyone else. We didn't look on them as Indians or others; we just used to look on them as sunburned Canadians, because we were also sunburned when we got into Italy....

When I came back from overseas, they had a returning men's dance in Burns Lake, and I took a couple of young ladies to the dance with me, and when we got to the door, there was Moses David, who served with the Canadian Forces. He lived in the Burns Lake District, and they stopped him from going in because he was a Native Indian.

Q: Who did that?

A: The people at the door that were putting on the function for the returned men. And I had had a couple of drinks before I went and was quite upset about it, and said that if they didn't allow him in, we would wreck the place. So it was not the smartest thing to say, I guess. Anyway, it worked, and they let him in....

* * *

Q: Were there, in your first election, Native Indians that were part of the electorate?

A: Oh, yes. They had only just recently got the right to vote, and like all people in a democracy when they first get something like that, they value it a great deal. Of course, we have had it so long we don't value it like we should....

First People in B.C. were given the right to vote provincially in 1947. Across Canada, the federal vote was given in 1960!

Cyril M. Shelford, Cross-Examination by Peter Grant

Q: Now, did Jimmy Andrews speak any language other than English?

A: Yes, he spoke his own language because he'd speak to his wife and family most times in his own language, but he'd always speak to us in English because he knew we didn't know their language.

* * *

Q: You were taught about the use of certain trees such as balsam pitch for medicine; is that right?

A: Yes. That was from my dad's experience in Alaska when he had blood poisoning up the Tanaha River when he was trapping and several hundred miles from a doctor, and it's a very effective bit of medicine.

Dr. A.L.Farley, Historical Cartographer, by Michael Goldie for the Province

NORTH EAST DRAINAGE

The Province sets out to prove that King George III's Royal Proclamation—which sets out British policy to deal fairly with sovereign Indian Nations—never applied to B.C.... because he didn't know we existed.

ALBERT L. FARLEY
Days 267-273
September 1989

Mr. Goldie: I propose calling this morning Dr. A. L. Farley, who will be the first of two witnesses called in respect of the Royal Proclamation issue.

...It is the position of the province with respect to the Royal Proclamation that it never applied to what is now British Columbia or to the Native peoples in it and, alternatively, if it did, the rights granted have been extinguished.

...The area drained by rivers which flow from the west and the northwest into the sea, and that's almost a quotation from the Royal Proclamation, will be identified and the evidence will identify the most northerly of the sources of those rivers. The central portion of the continent, to the west and to the south of the Great Lakes, is drained by the Mississippi River system, and the Mississippi flows in a southerly direction into the Gulf of Mexico.

...After dealing with the determination of certain watershed points, Dr. Farley says, and I quote:

"It is inconceivable, however, that the framers of the Proclamation in 1763 could have had access to more than a very rudimentary knowledge of this rather remote area."

The Witness: To set this in perspective, one could say that before the publication of the narrative associated with Cook's third and last voyage, publication dated 1784, before that, even the coastline of what is now British Columbia was remote from the known world.

A.L.Farley, Cross-Examination by Stuart Rush

Oops! Stuart Rush discovers a King's map with B.C.'s coastline on it. Dr. Farley decided not to include it in his brief.

Q: Now, Dr. Farley, can you agree with me that this is a Thomas Jefferys map of 1761?
A: Yes....
Q: Now, if you look, Dr. Farley, the title is "A Map of the Discoveries Made by the Russians on the Northwest Coast of America?"
A: Yes. ...I have seen the Jefferys map before.
Q: You did not include it in your folio?
A: No.
Q: Is there any reason you did not?
A: It seemed to me that the Muller map was the first derivative from the Russian information, and that was the appropriate one to include.
Q: Clearly here Thomas Jefferys, as Geographer for the King—I think you've agreed that he was—is stating there is a northwest coast of America?
A: It is portrayed on the map, yes.
Q: It's also stated in the cartouche?
A: Yes, in the title box.

When I think what my people did to the Beothuk in Newfoundland, I'm ashamed. I cry deep inside, I cry. When you talk to people today, they don't know, they say,"look at all the money we give the Indians". Don't they know, this country was built, created, out of the resources from the pockets of the Indian people of this country... It's not fair, some justice must be done.

—Unidentified gentleman, Robson Square Conference, Vancouver, 1989.

F. M. Greenwood, Legal Historian, by Mr. Goldie for the Province

King George had to make a Proclamation because, at the time, he was losing the battle for Canada to Chief Pontiac on the St. Lawrence River.

A: Then the supplementary report goes on to recommend the immediate issuance of a Proclamation by the King dealing with Indian matters on the North American frontier…. They justified this recommendation on the basis of:

"On Account of the late Complaints of the Indians, and the actual Disturbances in Consequence."

And that refers to, I believe, the initial stages of Pontiac's rebellion.

The Court:: What was the year of Pontiac's rebellion?

A: It's May 1763. July gets very serious, but it looks like the northwest is going to be taken out of the British Empire. There's a British victory in August 1763 that's quite significant, but the unrest goes on until the autumn of 1764.

Cross-Examination by Stuart Rush

Q: Now, one of those pamphlets that you reviewed was the Benjamin Franklin pamphlet?

A: Yes, the so-called Canada pamphlet.

Q: And that pamphlet was published in the colonies?

A: No, published in London, England, in 1760.

Q: Do I take it then that Benjamin Franklin, from your review of those pamphlets, was one of those who supported the view of western expansion as a positive value?

A: He was the only one. That's up to the Proclamation date.

Benjamin Franklin is used to show that the British wanted to expand west. Dr. Greenwood feels that the King wasn't thinking of expansion.

Q: Now, can you identify, Dr. Greenwood, that this is a statement of account rendered to Macaulay McColl [Canada] in care of Russell & DuMoulin [Province]… and it indicates at the bottom comments "re: *Delgamuukw and the Queen* 50 percent share" …and this refers to the 50/50 split arrangement [between the Province and Canada]?

A: Yes.

Q: …Now, Dr. Greenwood, I understand that your billing rate for services provided to the Defendants here was at the beginning in the amount of $250 per day?

A: That's correct.

Q: And that subsequent to that, your rate was increased to $350 per diem?

A: That's correct.

That's one expensive witness! But Canada and the Province split him 50/50. Besides, Mr. Goldie's law firm gets paid approximately $2,000 per day…!

FRANK M. GREENWOOD
Days 274-279
October 1989

D.R. Williams, Popular Writer, by Michael Goldie for the Province

Mr. Goldie: My lord, I tender Mr. Williams as a person called to undertake research directed to the imposition and acceptance of law and order in British Columbia with a particular reference to the land claim area in this case, to evaluate the results of such research and to express conclusions with respect thereto.

Cross-Examination by Murray Adams

Q: There's the book listed, *Trap-Line Outlaw Simon Peter Gun-a-noot*, 1982, reprinted 1988. And in fact, you've made some additions in 1988, did you not?

A: Yes.

Q: And I suggest to you that that's the only thing you've written, apart from your summary of opinion for this case, that deals with the land claims territory specifically?

A: Yes.

Q: And would it be fair to describe the *Trap-Line Outlaw* book as a popular history?

A: If by popular you mean non-academic, yes.

* * *

Q: And what do you need to know about the people in order to evaluate them?

A: Whether they are trustworthy, whether they are observant, whether they have an axe to grind.

Q: ...You will agree with me that you can be highly observant, but not be knowledgeable about what you are observing?

A: I'm sure that could be the case, yes.

* * *

Q: And is it your view that Indian people in the north country are pretty much the same from place to place?

A: ...I don't think there is a great deal of difference amongst the northern people in that respect.

* * *

Q: All right. If you look at the cover page of Exhibit 1173, your summary of opinion... that calls itself "Imposition and Acceptance of Law and Order Within the Claim Area." Can you explain to me, please, what you understood "law and order" to be?

A: I took that to mean generally the administration of justice according to the judicial system of the country—of the province.

* * *

Q: And your report was going to be about the imposition of law on Indians, correct?

A: Yes, the imposition of law and order within the claim area, and the reaction and response of the Indians to it.

Q: Then how is it that you decided to make only passing reference in your report to the potlatch law?

A: Well, I really can't say how it is, but it's what I did or what I did not do.

* * *

Q: Okay. The next word I want to take up with you is "acceptance." What did you mean by acceptance. What were you looking for?

A: I was asked to consider the reaction—what was the phrase used? The response, reaction and amenability of the Native people within the claim area. That has translated itself into the shorthand of the word "acceptance."

Q: Well, every response wouldn't be acceptance, would it?

A: Of course not.

Q: And every reaction wouldn't be acceptance?

A: No. But in weighing the totality of the sources, it was my view that there was an acceptance.

* * *

Q: What about instances of just not obeying the law? Is that opposition?

A: Of course. But I did not run across any evidence of widespread disobedience or civil disobedience or anything of that sort—very little of it, in fact.

* * *

Q: And that's a letter that appears to be dated August 6th, I think it was, 1910? ...And Ashdown Green, as his initials indicate, was a surveyor?

A: Yes.

Q: ...All right. He gets to Kitwanga on the 8th, and then in the third paragraph on the first page

NATIVE PEOPLE HAVE BECOME THE FOOD THAT FEEDS OUR GLUTTONOUS JUSTICE SYSTEM.

Hereditary Chiefs Convention. 88

says:

"Although I did not know it at the time, I have encountered at the hands of Indians a passive obstruction of my work that continued until I left."

* * *

Q: Okay, this appears to be Mr. Green, the surveyor ... and it's dated August 27, 1911, at Prince Rupert.... And he says:

"I have the honor to report my return from the Kispiox and Skeena Valleys and my arrival at Prince Rupert.

"I regret to say that the Indians at the former places were unanimous in refusing to have any reserves defined for them; their claim that the whole country belonged to them and that they would not accept anything less, was a repetition of the argument advanced by the Indians at Andimaul last year."

Q: Yes.

A: ...Research never ends on a particular subject. There are always new materials that come forward. One hopes that they won't scuttle the original enterprise.

Q: And you don't think that enterprise has been scuttled by new material, do you?

A: No, but new materials have come forward.

Sheila P. Robinson, Provincial Researcher, Cross-Examination by Peter Grant

Sheila Robinson starts off on a bad foot, academically. She had originally claimed to have written a Master's thesis, but...

A: I'd like to make a qualification or a correction there. I didn't write a Master's thesis in the North American sense of a Master's thesis. That's a major paper that was associated with one of the courses.... I would say that the major academic work I've done, apart from my dissertation, is one of the reports I did for the Echo Creek site for Parks Canada.

Q: ...Okay. You are a member of the Underwater Archaeological Society of British Columbia. Now, this is a private society, isn't it? It's not yet considered a professional association, is it?

A: Oh, I'm sorry. I wasn't clear on the distinction you were making. It's a group of people who are interested in the shipwrecks of the Province and other archaeological sites that are submerged.

* * *

Q: Well, we can say that your work in this case...is in opposition to the Native claims?

A: Yes.

Q: We can say that your work in *Sparrow* was in opposition to the Native claims?

A: Yes.

Q: And the third—there's three times in which you've been involved in Native claims—the third is Kwakiutl?

A: Yes.

Where Robinson wonders whether a magazine subscription gives her membership to an academic association!

Q: You know the Canadian Ethnological Society?

A: I know of it.

Q: You know of it. You're not a member of that?

A: No, unless my subscription to *Anthropologica* entitles me to membership. I'm not sure on that detail.

* * *

Q: And you haven't prepared any referenced articles or books on any of the reports related to your dissertation or opinion report?

A: No, I have not.

HER ONLY PROFESSIONAL ASSOC. IS WITH THE UNRECOGNIZED··· UNDERWATER ARCHAEOLOGICAL ASSOC.

Sheila P. Robinson, by Chuck Willms

The Witness: The clear picture emerging from available data is that, up to the 1860s, peoples of the Northwest Coast were living in a constant "state of war."

* * *

A: "In my research I have discovered no conclusive evidence that suggests that, prior to the advent of European influence in the claim area, the Gitksan and Wet'suwet'en lineages and families identified ownership rights to large and precisely defined tracts of hunting territories."

* * *

A: Well, there seems to be generally a recognition that the coastal people were more complex, had more elaborate ceremony, had more intricate crests, titles, and privilege attributes in their cultures, and that these were sought after by the interior people with whom they traded, and the general understanding from cultural, ecological theory is that more complex societies tend to dominate and influence less complex ones, and that there's generally a pattern of dominance-subordination that's expressed in terms of superior and inferior.

* * *

Q: "Kobrinsky's viewpoint is important for two reasons.... European influence was a major factor in disrupting "traditional" Native lifestyles before direct contact between Indians and Europeans occurred. Second... Kobrinsky asserts that precise delineation of territorial boundaries relating to the

allocation of rights to fine-fur species was a by-product of the fur trade."

Sheila P. Robinson, Cross-Examination by Peter Grant

Q: And that's what you understood your task was to be, to develop the argument in support of your proposition of your theory?
A: Yes.
Q: And that's what you did?
A: Oh, to the extent I was able to.

* * *

Q: "Dr. Kobrinsky was not in a good position to analyze the Wet'suwet'en Feast" ...Dr. Mills is, I think, relying on his thesis for what she knows, when she says:
"He went to Babine Lake. He found that the major centre of Feast was at Moricetown. Not knowing those people, he stood outside the door uncomfortably at one Feast, but he never attended any Feasts."

Does that refresh your memory about what he reported on his field work?
A: No, it does not.

Proceedings

The Province has a "secret" anthropologist helping them. That person's name remains a secret. What are they worried about?

The Court: Can you identify by description who prepared the document?
Mr. Willms: Well, My Lord, the identity of the person is something that's also privileged. Now, I'll

---

hand it up to Your Lordship....

The Court: I can imagine consultants sitting around a table with masks over their heads. Well, all right....

* * *

The Court: What if a person—not this witness, I'm sure, but in the position of this witness—says, "This is another one of those specious claims being put forward by the Indians in British Columbia, about which there are far too many?"

Mr. Grant: I would like to see that.

The Court: Would it not then become a relevant document going in as a bias, perhaps even prejudice?

CULTURAL GHOUL...?

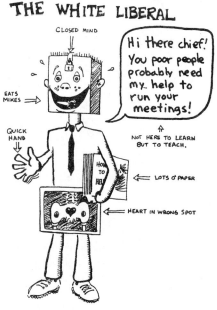

During her evidence, the gallery was full of academics barely containing their disbelief.

Sheila P. Robinson, Cross-Examination by Peter Grant

Q: Then you say:
"In a nutshell, I will be investigating any leads suggesting that the Gitksan and Wet'suwet'en Indians' socio-economies were undergoing changes in the protohistoric (just before direct European contact) and early post-contact periods as a result of indirect or direct European stimulus."

Now, that is, in a nutshell, what were you doing?
A: Yes.

* * *

Q: "So it seems that we will be able to marshall an army of support, although I have yet to see really convincing demonstration of proto-historic changes."

That's what you were doing—you were marshalling the army of support for your argument, weren't you? Those are your words, not mine, doctor.

A: Well, it's perhaps a casual phrasing and, if anything, it reflects my naiveté about this whole

litigation process, or I might have been tighter with my words or my phrasing. But, yes, an army of support—I imagine them out there like shelves of books.

The Court: Well, shall we adjourn 'till 2:00 o'clock?

Mr. Grant: Certainly, My Lord. Time is marching on.

* * *

Q: So I take it that you are going to be available in a week's time, are you?

A: I guess I'll have to be.

The Court: Well, if you were going to the Club Med somewhere, I would think you might give it some priority.

The Witness: No, My Lord, I don't have any plans for such elaborate things.

SPECIES SEQUESTOR...

THE WHITE LIBERAL

CLOSED MIND

Hi there chief! You poor people probably need my help to run your meetings!

EATS MIKES →

QUICK HAND →

NOT HERE TO LEARN BUT TO TEACH.

HOW TO HELP

← LOTS O' PAPER

← HEART IN WRONG SPOT

Chapter 6

The Paper Elephant:
Expert Witnesses For Canada

Although the conduct of the Province in protecting its interest in what they perceive to be their jurisdiction should have prepared us, our people were nevertheless appalled at the tactics of the federal lawyers. Having accepted our Declaration in 1977, the federal government was not in a position to deny our title and rights to the land. They would, however, make every attempt to limit the scope of that title and those rights. Working hand-in-pocket with their provincial counterparts, the federal lawyers also set out to prove our acquiescence.

The first indication as to what lengths the Government of Canada would go to support its provincial brother in the cross-examination of our witnesses was the unearthing of estate files and records of the parents and grandparents of each of our Chiefs and Elders who took the stand. The emotional battery suffered by our witnesses and their families was caused not only by the base infringement of the privacy and memory of their ancestors, but by the blatant abuse of responsibility on the part of the Department of Indian Affairs for supplying the personal and private documents of the long-deceased family members. In a relationship claimed to be based on confidentiality and trust, the Department of Indian Affairs abused that relationship throughout the course of the trial by supplying selective documents, records and Indian Agents to their government's lawyers.

One of the many rules of court is that when a plaintiff or defendant is ready to present its arguments, copies of evidence and exhibits must be provided to the other parties. At the onset of the federal argument, a U-Haul truck pulled up and deposited a roomful of colonial permits, documents and records at the offices of our lawyers. When the federal lawyers stated that their case would be based mainly on documents, we had no idea how the federal government would thunderously live up to the nickname we had attached to it—"the Paper Elephant."

—Skanu'u (Ardythe Wilson)

UNDERLYING TITLE

The Government of Canada has this idea that Native peoples may have lived *on* the land, but the Canadian Government owns *beneath* the surface—UNDERLYING TITLE...

Opening by James Macaulay for the Government of Canada, Vancouver, November 21, 1989

Mr. Macaulay: I do not intend to argue my case, but only to outline some positions that will be taken on behalf of the Attorney General of Canada, and I will make observations on what we consider to be the principal issues.

First, the matter of the claim for ownership and jurisdiction. We will submit in argument that that claim is unsupportable by the law and by the facts that have been adduced in evidence up to now. It is essentially a claim for provincial status, as I understand it; it is a claim that the Plaintiffs own not just in fee simple, but have some sort of sovereignty over 22,000 square miles of territory that they say was occupied by them and governed by them before sovereignty was acquired by Great Britain. It challenges that very sovereignty. It only challenges that sovereignty in respect of provincial jurisdiction in this case. But the gravamen of the claim is that it applies to both jurisdictions. I can't see how it would apply to one and not the other.

I submit that the important issue before Your Lordship and the issue on which we will make most of our submissions has to do with the matter of use and occupation of those territories comprised in the claim area. It's been a topic that's almost as old as the Colony....

I can't think of a more important issue, and it's time it was decided. It is sometimes said that British Columbia denies that there is any such thing, but that's, I think, an exaggeration, to be fair to British Columbia. I noted with some interest some remarks made by my learned friend, Mr. Goldie, in his opening address on July 10th last.... He is talking about the Colony, and the Colony's position regarding this matter. He says:

"What was recognized and protected was an interest of the Native peoples of British Columbia in their occupied village sites and where they had adopted an agrarian way of life, as in the southern interior, cultivated fields and as much land as they could till and enjoy the rights of was required for their support, together with the free exercise of fishing the lakes and rivers and hunting over all unoccupied Crown lands in the Colony."

Your Lordship will recall from the evidence you've already heard that Sir James Douglas addressed large gatherings of Indians at Cayoosh and elsewhere in just those words.... Canada has always acknowledged these aboriginal rights. But we will submit at the proper time and in argument, a definition for Your Lordship's consideration that will be broader, or perhaps more precise, than the words used by Sir James Douglas and echoed by Mr. Goldie in his able opening....

* * *

Macaulay delivers
Canada's opening...
CANADA DAY   Nov. 21/89

Mr. Macaulay: ...I hadn't said much about missionaries, but our material will cover that, and we will be making submissions about missionaries and their effect. We will be submitting that the missionaries were really the originators of the idea of the comprehensive claim sounding very much like the ownership and jurisdiction claim being made today, in addition to the other effects that Your Lordship has heard about.

* * *

Macaulay refers to the Province's position that if they lose the case, Canada pays. Are they fighting over last place?

Mr. Macaulay: ...We are aware that the Province is trying to construe historical material in such a fashion that it will escape any liability for any finding that Your Lordship may have to make.

Terry D. Turnbull, Fisheries Officer, Smithers by Marvyn Koenigsberg for Canada

Q: Could you describe what the general duties of a Fisheries Officer are?

A: Well, we work in the field of what we call habitat, which is businesses or people who wish to do environmental projects that might affect water quality or cause deleterious effects to fish habitat. These projects are generally referred to agencies in the Provincial Government, and they refer them to us for comments in areas that might affect salmon. We work on counting fish, spawning fish in the various streams. We patrol sports fisheries. We patrol Indian food fisheries.

Q: Okay. And in your patrol and jurisdiction in relation to the Indian food fishery, what kind of regulations do you enforce or look after?

A: We issue licences for Indian food fisheries, and there are certain sections of the British Columbia fishery, general regulations regarding Indian food fisheries.

Q: And how do you patrol the districts, just generally?

A: We travel by truck, by boat, and by helicopter.

Q: All right. Could you describe briefly the relationship between what you do under the Fisheries Act, which is Federal legislation, and the Provincial jurisdiction?

A: The Provincial jurisdiction in fish manages fresh water species, such as rainbow trout, steel-head, cutthroat trout and other lake species, and Federal fishery officers participate in the management of salmon.

* * *

The Government of Canada submits a car-load of paper. Can permits and paper tip the scales of justice?

The Court: Your friend didn't say that. He said you shouldn't descend to such details. You can describe what he does, what he sees, but there is no reason to become enmeshed in a minutiae of regulations.

Ms. Koenigsberg: Yes. And, My Lord, the difficulty is, of course, you don't know yet, and it hasn't been explained yet, what the purpose of putting this document in is to the witness....

The Court: Oh, all right, yes, all right, yes, all right. 70?

A: Yes, 70 is from Smithers.

Ms. Koenigsberg: It's from Smithers, and it's another report kept in the usual and ordinary course of business, to your knowledge?

A: Yes.

Q: And you could say the same for tab 74?

A: Yes.

Q: And the same for tab 85?

A: Yes.

Q: And the same for tab 89?

A: Yes.

Q: And the same for tab 90?

A: Yes.

Q: And 93?

A: Yes.

Q: And 104, that's on page 11?

A: Yes.

Q: And 110?

A: Yes.

Q: And 113?

A: Yes.

Q: And 115?

A: Yes.

Q: And 116?

A: Yes.

Q: And 120?

A: Yes.

Q: And 122?

A: Yes.

Q: 126?

A: Yes.

Q: 127?

A: Yes.

Q: 130?

A: Yes.

Q: 133?

A: Yes.

Q: 134A?

THE HAZELTON SENTINEL, Thursday, September 3, 1987

Armed feds net man, 82, in river raid

Eighty-two year old George Jackson watched helplessly as eight or nine federal fisheries officers wearing revolvers took his sockeye net and the fish he had caught. He told them, "I really want to spit in your face but there are too many of you."

All his long life George Jackson has fished for food for his family. His fishing grounds below the Kitsegukla Reserve have to supply five families related to his wife Maria, who is 75, and six individuals on his side of the family.

The fisheries officers come in large numbers on these raids. They carry sidearms, and are said to wear bullet proof vests. There is helicopter surveillance, and they swoop in fast river boats. The actions against Natives have become more heavy-handed, more frequent over the years. It is a bizarre, tragic story.

A: Yes.
Q: 137?
A: Yes.
Q: 139?
A: Yes.
Q: 140?
A: Yes.

Peter T. Woloshyn, Fisheries Officer, Hazelton, by Marvyn Koenigsberg for Canada

Q: Mr. Woloshyn, you are a Fisheries Officer?
A: Yes, I am.
Q: And you are stationed in Hazelton, the sub-district of Hazelton?
A: Yes.
Q: How long has the Hazelton office been operational, to your knowledge?
A: Since 1978.
Q: If I put Volume One of the fisheries reports collection in front of you, if you look in the index, you have a much shorter job than Mr. Turnbull. Tab 136, I believe, is the correct one.... And is that document kept in the usual and ordinary course of business in Hazelton at this time?
A: Yes, it is.
Q: And Tab 141?
A: Yes.
Q: And tab 145?
A: Yes.
Q: And Tab 148?
A: Yes.

* * *

The Court: How many of these witnesses are you going to call, Fisheries Officers?
Ms. Koenigsberg: This is it, I believe.

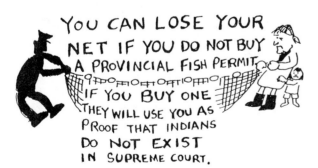

YOU CAN LOSE YOUR NET IF YOU DO NOT BUY A PROVINCIAL FISH PERMIT. IF YOU BUY ONE THEY WILL USE YOU AS PROOF THAT INDIANS DO NOT EXIST IN SUPREME COURT.

Peter T. Woloshyn, Cross-Examination by Stanley Guenther (Plaintiffs' Lawyer)

Mr. Guenther: The Province has pleaded that the rights of the Plaintiffs here are reduced, diminished or extinguished by, amongst others, the administrative actions pursuant to not only Provincial legislation, but Federal legislation, presumably relating to the actions of the people like Mr. Woloshyn, in exercising his fisheries powers. Now, if in fact when one examines his actual actions and dealings with the local Indian people, his actions do not disclose support for the proposition pleaded by the Province, then that is relevant, with respect.

The Court: What you ask may have some relevance, particularly to the argument of the Province. I am not in a position to decide whether it will or not. I think I have to take the easy way out, which is to allow you to proceed, if you wish to do so. But I think I will be very decisive about this and say we will do that at 2:00.

* * *

Mr. Guenther: Did you ever encounter, Mr. Woloshyn, resistance of any sort from any individual Indian fishermen as to the acceptance of food fish licenses?
A: Yes.
Q: ...Let me put a specific instance. In 1978, just after you started, did not the Glen Vowell and Gitsegukla bands specifically say they would not accept food fish licenses?
A: I would have to check back in my files, but there were some in early 1978 that refused, yes.
Q: Your response to their refusal was simply that, rather than providing the fish food licences, a person was simply to mail them out to them; is that correct?
A: It seems that was the thought at that time.
Q: Were you instructed toward the outset of your involvement in about 1978 to attempt to co-operatively manage the fishery in the area?
A: I've always attempted to act that way.
Q: Was that on instructions, or is that your own view of things?
A: I would say both.

* * *

Q: Is it fair to say, Mr. Woloshyn, that at various times from 1978 to 1981, resistance to acceptance of food fish licence was expressed by almost every band within your subdistrict at different times?
A: Yes.

TERRY D. TURNBULL
Day 300
November 1989

Michelle said more than 30 nets had been seized by Federal Fisheries officers in the area this year alone. "But the river is why we settled here many centuries ago. All our villages are near the river which we have always used for travel and for food. They are trying to take away our liveli-hood. It is just like emptying out our fridge when they take our nets and fish. But we are not going to go away. We will run our own fishery in our own way, as we always have done."

Meanwhile, for 82-year old George Jackson and his wife Maria, the seizure of their net will mean hardship this winter. They use surplus fish to trade for moose meat which they can no longer hunt themselves, or berries which they can no longer gather.

"What will you live on?" *The Sentinel* asked George Jackson. He shrugged. "Air," he said.
—*The Hazelton Sentinel*, 1987

PETER T. WOLOSHYN
Day 300
November 1989

NOW WE AIM TO REALLY EXTINGUISH YOU!

Cammo cap

FISHY COP

un washed

infra red binocs

Snub nose bullets

bullet proof vest

FED

JERK

police special

KILL

repeater shot gun

FISHERY OFFICERS IN B.C. USE
- HUEY HELOCOPTERS
- JET BOATS
- FOUR x FOURS
- DOGS
- REPEATER SHOT-GUNS
- UNPRECEDENTED POWERS OF SEIZURE AND ENTRANCE.

Submissions by Geoff Plant

About the age-old reluctance of colonialism against being a defendant.

Mr. Plant: Your Lordship has to bear in mind that the Attorney-General of Canada is the reluctant Defendant here.

The Court: I have never known a Defendant yet who wasn't reluctant.

Ms. Koenigsberg: Even more reluctant.

The Court: All right.

Mr. Plant: Even more reluctant Defendant. How about the second most reluctant Defendant? At any rate, we had to apply to bring them into this action.... We got much better guidance from Mr. Macaulay when he said yesterday, in his opening, "Canada has always acknowledged these rights, these aboriginal rights."

...The Province's position is, if anything, consistently the opposite.

Submission by Peter Grant: On Entering People's Wills and Estates as Evidence During Indian Agent McIntyre's Evidence for Canada

The Court: It does nothing more than allow them to show what the Indians did.

Mr. Grant: But this witness can describe what the Indians did. The tendering of the Wills and the Estate files is not necessary for that. The witnesses were cross-examined as to what they did. They were cross-examined.... The impact of tendering over 200 Wills, I say, is not necessary, and in this place, confidentiality and the fiduciary obligation should be given precedence.

The Court: Well, it may be that in the common course of events in a case like this, there would be an admission and it wouldn't be necessary to put in 200 Wills. But I don't see much sign of admissions

THE INDIAN AFFAIRS MINISTER AND THE D.I.A. HAVE BETRAYED THEIR TRUST AND GIVEN ME CONFIDENTIAL FILES, WILLS, & ESTATES WHICH I WILL NOW INTRODUCE AS PUBLIC EVIDENCE IN THE NAME OF CANADA.

THAT'S AN OUTRAGE!

IT MAY WELL BE, BUT I'VE GOT TO LET HIM DO IT.

BANG!

Macaulay (Head of Defence, Govt. of Canada)

Grant (For the Plaintiffs the Hereditary Chiefs)

McEachern (Chief Justice, Supreme Court of B.C.)

being made in this case. It seems to me to be relevant, if such is the case, that 200 Plaintiffs have purported to dispose of property that is said to be communal. But I don't know if that's the case or not, and it seems to me that it would be relevant if the evidence showed that.

Mr. Grant: Well, My Lord, I submit that the Federal Crown in its particular position and its statutory power under the *Indian Act* is taking advantage of that to the detriment of the very beneficiaries it's supposed to be giving. The statutory power and authority of the Federal Crown with respect to Indian estates is ongoing and you have, I believe, tendered here, the estate of Albert Tait and others who died immediately before the trial started. In other words, the Plaintiffs, the Indian people, have no way out of this situation, and the Federal Crown can continue to take advantage.

The Judge assumes the jurisdiction to okay dirty tricks...

The Court: And where is my jurisdiction to say to a party who is tendering relevant evidence, "No, you can't do that because it's a dirty trick?" And I don't say it is, but that's what you are saying it is."

Mr. Grant: I say it's more than even a dirty trick....And I say, My Lord, that the effect of allowing the Crown to do this in this manner is to allow them to take advantage of their fiduciary relationship to the Plaintiffs to the detriment of the Plaintiffs, allow them to collect data, collect the information, and to use it in any manner they see fit.

...Mr. Justice Dickson described that fiduciary relationship on page 501 of the *Guerin* case; he says that:

"...The hallmark of a fiduciary relation is that the relative legal positions are such that one party is at the mercy of the other's discretion."

The Federal Crown here is stepping over the

Every Native Nation in a relationship with Canada now knows that the government will use the Department of Indian Affairs against them in court.

bound, and they should not be allowed to utilize their trust responsibility regarding Indian estates in the way that they are doing here. I may say, My Lord, that of course if the Federal Crown wasn't ordered in, I don't think the Province could even get access....

The Court: I am sorry, Mr. Grant; I am against you on this one. I do not think I have much choice. And it is not for me to characterize the decision of Crown to use this or not use this. That is their decision, and there may be a political price somewhere else to pay, but that is not my concern.

Mr. Grant: I may say then, My Lord, that I ask that all of these documents coming out of these estate files be dealt with as you directed with respect to Exhibit 13, that these documents not be generally public documents. And that, I would submit, would be some minimal protection to the parties.

The Court: Well, I have some misgivings about that, Mr. Grant. My experience is that you only get in trouble when you do that. But I'll hear what your friends say about that. Perhaps it's not their concern; perhaps it's my concern about maintaining the principle of open proceedings. I haven't the slightest doubt that if the representatives of the media knew that I was even thinking of making such an order, they would be here with counsel and making submissions about the collapse of Western Civilization if any such thing was to be countenanced.

Mr. Macaulay: May I continue with Mr. McIntyre's evidence, My Lord?

The Court: Well, I think I have to rule on your friend's request.

Mr. Macaulay: Oh. Yes.

The Court: I think that I will make an order that the Will material be protected from public examination until I have seen some of it and have had a chance to assess the true nature of the information.

Indian agent (retired), Mr. Boys—a Provincial witness—is cross-examined by Stuart Rush during his commissioned evidence held in a Victoria hotel.

Ray McIntyre, Federal Indian Agent, by James Macaulay for Canada

Mr. Macaulay: We will be calling another Indian agent.... That is a Mr. Ray McIntyre. Mr. McIntyre had a long career with Department of Indian Affairs from 1956 to 1982.... He will describe his duties as superintendent of the Burns Lake agency....

* * *

About taking Native children to Residential School.

Mr. McIntyre: With increasing emphasis and determination that Indian children should receive a formal education, it obviously took them off the trapline.

Q: And what effect did that have on trapping?

A: It denied Indian children an opportunity to learn trapping, because they obviously couldn't attend school and trap at the same time—particularly those children who were required to attend an Indian residential school. And I don't know what else I can say.

* * *

Q: Did you learn about the destruction of the fur habitat from Band members?

A: I heard many, many complaints from Band members who had earlier been out trapping, and who were discovering, as they are still discovering, that clearcut logging—logging of any kind, for that matter—is detrimental to fur habitat.

Ray McIntyre, Cross-Examination by Peter Grant

Q: You didn't attend such a potlatch in Lake Babine, you have indicated to Mr. Macaulay?

A: No.

Q: Although invited. But did you attend any such Feasting or potlatching in Burns Lake?

A: No.

* * *

Q: Did you ever advise people who came to you about making a Will that the making of the Will could or would possibly jeopardize their rights?

A: No.

Q: Did you ever perceive that that was a possibility at the time you advised them?

A: No, and I don't perceive it now, really.

Q: When you said that you advised "when we were aware of people having assets of substance, we would encourage them to make Wills," were you considering at that time such assets as their Chiefly names?

A: No, because I wasn't aware of their Chiefly names.

Q: Regalia, traditional regalia?

A: I wasn't aware of their possession of this by any of the people who I dealt with.

...I didn't feel it to be my prerogative as the government person to venture at all into things of a cultural or traditional nature. That was ...an area that I felt it wise to stay out of.

Ray McIntyre, Re-examination by James Macaulay for Canada, Exam by Court

The Court: Mr. McIntyre, in view of your wide experience in this geographical area, how would you rate the seriousness of the various problems facing the Native people in the claim area?

Surveyor's map of Hagwilget reserve, circa. 1890.

RAY M. McINTYRE
Days 303-305
November 1989

"The biggest problem facing these people today is
one of lack of economic opportunity... if they had an
improved economic circumstance, many of their
social problems might be lessened."—Ray McIntyre

A: In my view, Your Lordship, I would say that the biggest problem facing these people today is one of lack of economic opportunity, and I think if they had an improved economic circumstance, many of their social problems might be lessened.

Chapter 7

The Arguments

Three years, one month and nineteen days after they uttered the first words that set the Gitksan and Wet'suwet'en on a journey through the Halls of Canadian Justice, Delgamuukw and Gisdaywa, accompanied by a small delegation of fellow Chiefs, sat in the spacious, air-conditioned gallery of courtroom 55 of the B.C. Law Courts. Delgamuukw vs. The Queen was in its final day in the Supreme Court of British Columbia.

What thoughts must go through the minds of the participants at this moment? As I cast my thoughts back to those years leading up to 1984 when our Statement of Claim was first filed, I couldn't help but be a little saddened that the warriors who guided and strengthened us to fulfill a part of their bold journey were not sitting in the courtroom this day. I know that should I give voice to my thoughts, I will be reminded that those many grandmothers and grandfathers may have joined their breaths to those who have gone on before, but their spirit permeates our lives and our land... the very reason we now sit in this room.

The principal plaintiff for the Gitksan, Delgamuukw, is an example. Albert Tait was the Del-gamuukw who walked into the court registry, Statement of Claim in hand, in 1984. Ken Muldoe, nephew to Albert, was the Delgamuukw who delivered the opening statement in 1987. Earl Muldoe, brother to Ken, is the Delgamuukw who stands to make the closing statement on behalf of the Gitksan Chiefs in June, 1990. There have been generations of Delgamuukws, just as there will be generations more of Gitksan and Wet'suwet'en people who will embrace and nurture every hereditary name that exists in our Houses.

This chapter of history highlights the last phase of the trial process at the Supreme Court of B.C. level—the presentation of final legal arguments, the reply by the Gitksan and Wet'suwet'en and the

closing comments of the Gitksan and Wet'suwet'en, the Province of B.C., the Government of Canada, and Chief Justice McEachern.

Throughout the course of the trial, the positions of the provincial and federal governments, separately and in support of one another, remained firm. The policy for the treatment of "their" Indians, claims the Province of B.C., has been a humane and enlightened one. Besides, they continue, it's only at the insistence and under the influence of missionaries that these Indians are taking these actions. They would never be capable of doing it otherwise. Even from a distance, it is obvious that the policies of the B.C. Society for the Prevention of Cruelty to Animals for the treatment of animals, is a more humane and enlightened one than that ever upheld by the governments of British Columbia for the First Nations of this province. The government of Canada did not have to exert itself very much throughout the three years of trial. It was very careful in its arguments not to offend or put at risk its relationship with the

Province of B.C.. It's fine to want to retain your identity, they seemed to be telling us, but don't expect us to accept any but our own version of what an "Indian" should be—obedient little hunters, fishers, gatherers of berries and makers of handicrafts who don't have adequate comprehension of land ownership or government and should be content with the largesse of the province for protecting their interests by setting up reservations. The actions of the Crown and its agents to eliminate, deceive, disregard and reject our existence cannot be denied. We have proven our continued existence and jurisdiction on the land. We have proven, contrary to their arguments, that our societies and cultures are viable and thriving.

The Gitksan and Wet'suwet'en have put colonialism on trial. The decision rests in the hands of one man. Will it be a conspiracy of the cloth? An empty land, an empty culture? Or will it finally be honor, law and justice?

—**Skanu'u (Ardythe Wilson)**

Chiefs' closing argument begins

The federal government was accused last week in B.C. Supreme Court of rendering the Constitution meaningless by refusing to recognize the Gitksan-Wet'suwet'en land claim.

Acting on behalf of the hereditary chiefs of the two tribes, Vancouver lawyer Stewart Rush said Ottawa "makes a mockery" of the guarantees to aboriginal peoples under the Constitution.

"This case is about the honor of the Crown because for the first time a court will scrutinize that honor publicly," Rush told presiding Chief Justice Allan McEachern.

by John Young
The Interior News

sands of years gives them rights to and jurisdiction over the land.

Much of last week's argument involved the presentation of archaeological, linguistic and anthropological evidence to support that claim.

Because nothing is written of the tribe's history, oral traditions known as Adaawk were cited as proof of occupation.

Provincial claims that Indians in B.C. were treated "humanely and with an enlightened spirit," from colonial times to present are not supported by the facts, Rush said.

The policy towards Indians was "built on denial and deceit," he said, involving a deliberate attempt to keep natives ignorant of true motives.

"There was a scheme of misinformation...which led to a denial of aboriginal title, a confinement of the land rights and impoverishment of the people."

Introduction to the Plaintiffs' Argument

In this case the Defendants have stood on the historical injustices done to the Plaintiffs and their ancestors as the basis for their defences. This is fully evident from their pleadings, their openings, evidence and argument, all of which deny the existence of the Gitksan and Wet'suwet'en as distinct societies and assert that the Crown, by the force of law or otherwise, can simply steal their land.

In his opening to the Province's case, Mr. Goldie clearly stated that the position of the Provincial Defendant in this litigation was that the reserve-making policy in the colonial era, and later by the Province, was a humane and enlightened one, even when judged by standards of today. This is the justification of the land thief who comes to Court seeking ownership of your house, when he first arrived as a guest, but decided to stay, and after being told to leave, confines you to a cupboard in the basement and then tells you that the house isn't yours any more because he has occupied it for 100 years and you are happy in the cellar.

The Province's position would be dismissable if it weren't dressed up in the discourse of the Courtroom and the pretensions of the Provincial Crown. This Reserve Policy was illegal if it was intended (as argued after the fact) to deal with or extinguish the aboriginal title of the Plaintiffs' ancestors. Mary Johnson spoke for all of the Gitksan and Wet'suwet'en when she described the effect of being confined to the "humane" reserves spoken of by the Province:

"So the way I feel about it is, we are fenced in, the Indians; they just put a fence around us like they did to the pigs or animals. And we can't go out on our territory and do some farming or anything on the outside. So I am hoping and praying that the

Queen will know what they did to us in the olden days when they took away our inheritance."

In fact the policy towards Indians was built on denial and deceit. In the hands of Joseph Trutch, the colony suppressed its obligation to deal with the title of the Indian people of the Province. Officials in the colonial executive purposely lied about the Colony's policy toward Indians. There was a scheme of misinformation, perpetuated by Trutch and Governor Musgrave, which led to a denial of aboriginal title, a confinement of the land rights and impoverishment of the people. Neither the Colony nor the Province has dealt with the Indians honorably or justly. Any such claim is a perversion of history.

...Trutch's Reserve Policy was to cut off land from the Douglas Reserves, reducing even more what little the Indian people had. The aboriginal right to title to the land was, for him, forever to be deferred. What was done was to deny the Indian title; what was said was the Reserve Policy was "fair." Given the extensive denials of

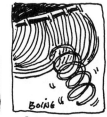

GOLDIE... can't stay put (Gertie Watson idea.)

Your lardship! BOING!
I PROTEST! BOING!
YEOW! BOING!
BOING

FRONT VIEW ... SIDE VIEW ... BACK VIEW ... BOTTOM

the Province in this litigation and the position advanced in its opening, this continues to be the Province's stance today. It is as unjust, dishonorable and illegal today as it was in 1972.

* * *

Without saying so directly, Canada takes the position that extinguishment of the Gitksan and Wet'suwet'en rights and title has already occurred, having been brought about by acts taken or authorized by the Province in respect of the Plaintiffs' land since union. This is the creeping-erosion-of-your-rights-while-I- stand-idly-by argument. What is inexplicable is that, by taking this position, Canada not only disregards its Constitutional duty to protect Indian land, but also stands on its failure to protect as a legal basis for arguing that extinguishment or diminishment has occurred by the unlawful acts of the Province. Federal-Provincial regulations are clearly more important to the Federal government than Constitutional obligations to the Indian nations. Canada says further that Indians have some rights, but they don't amount to much; in fact, they are barely worth talking about.

After sitting through 250 trial days listening to the Hereditary Chiefs, after hearing the wealth of cultural and economic evidence in the historical record, and after being an administrative presence with Constitutional responsibilities to administer

MICHAEL JACKSON DELIVERS AN ADDRESS ON COLONIAL HISTORY.

Indian affairs in the Territory and throughout this country since the turn of the century, all that Canada can see of the Gitksan and Wet'suwet'en is their pre-1900 hunting, trapping, fishing and berry-picking activities. At its core, this is a racist position deliberately blind or refusing to give value to the way of life of the people. It makes a mockery out of the guarantees in Section 35. What the Federal Government says is that it created an empty box for the Indians in Section 35, and the Constitution doesn't really mean anything.

* * *

Only six years after Union, at a time when there were fewer than a dozen non-Indian residents in the whole of the Gitksan and Wet'suwet'en Territory, and virtually no law which had direct impact on the lives of the Gitksan and Wet'suwet'en residents, the highest official in the Government of Canada with responsibility for Indian Affairs: (a) recognized aboriginal title in the Indian people of British Columbia; (b) stated without qualification that aboriginal title had to be extinguished before public lands could be dealt with; and (c) acknowledged that no bilateral agreement between Canada and B.C. could remove the aboriginal rights held by the Indian people, including the ancestors of the Plaintiffs. One hundred and twelve years later, Canada asks this Court to ignore the Crown obligations as expressed by Mills, just as they have ignored the Gitksan and Wet'suwet'en people over the century. Is that just? Is that the honor of Canada?

Take the Federal and Provincial defences at their highest. The Province recognized an "humane" Reserve Policy. The Federal Government was duty-bound to protect the aboriginal people in their village sites, berry grounds and cultivated fields. Then how do they explain to Johnny David, Basil Michell, Emma Michell and other Wet'suwet'en people their forcible eviction from their homes, to replace their ancient ownership there with rights of non-Indian settlers? How

"Mr. JACKSON! DO NOT COMPARE THE PEOPLE OF BRITISH COLUMBIA WITH THE SPANISH"... SI!

WHY DO YOU COMPARE THE GITKSAN AND WET'SUWET'EN WITH 'ODIOUS' KING JOHN?

APRIL 4/1990

A CLASS FROM KISPIOX ELEMENTARY SCHOOL SITS IN THE JURY BOX TO LISTEN TO ARGUMENT.

do the Provincial and Federal Governments answer Basil? When asked how he felt when his family was forced to leave Barrett Lake and after the family home was burned to the ground, Mr. Michell said:

"Even though we were young, we were really hurt by what was done to us. Our people had cleared the land, and white people just moved in and chased us off the land. We weren't happy about it. The white people that worked for the govern-

THE JUDGE CONSIDERS KING GEORGE III'S ROYAL PROCLAMATION OF 1763.

APRIL 7/90

ment just went home after we were chased off our land, and we were left to die, because we had to live in tents at 60 below weather. It wasn't right, what they did to us."

The Federal and Provincial Governments cannot explain to Basil Michell by what principle he was forced off his land. And there is no explanation for it in the extinguishment defences of the Defendants. Because, in fact, their defences on extinguishment are made up. They are rationalizations after the fact, created to justify their position in the case. The extinguishment defences have little, if anything, to do with what was really going on or being said by the governments in the Colony or the Province. The defences have air-brushed the real history. They are couched in the language of fair play, but they deny the existence of the Gitksan and Wet'suwet'en and their right to exist in their homeland as their ancestors have done for thousands of years. The governments have no obligations, according to them, except to keep the Gitksan and Wet'suwet'en confined to reserves and to proceed with the pace of development for the benefit of the non-Indian economy and the governments. I ask you to juxtapose these made-up defences with the richness of the evidence of the way of life of the Gitksan and Wet'suwet'en people which you heard in this case. Their identity and land-based culture have survived.

* * *

The Indians went to the British courts before the patriation of the Constitution, fearing that the Crown would not act honorably towards them upon patriation. In refusing to grant the declarations sought, Lord Denning said that Section 35 of the *Constitution Act* would provide the necessary protection. In *The Queen v. The Secretary of State for Foreign and Commonwealth Affairs* [1981], he said:

"There is nothing, so far as I can see, to warrant any distrust by the Indians of the government of Canada. But, in case there should be, the discussion in this case will strengthen their hand so as to enable them to withstand any onslaught. They will be able to say that their rights and freedoms have been guaranteed to them by the Crown—originally by the Crown in respect of the United Kingdom, now by the Crown in respect of Canada—but, in any case, by the Crown. No Parliament should do anything to lessen the worth of these guarantees. *They should be honored by the Crown in respect of Canada "so long as the sun rises and the river flows." That promise must never be broken.*

The Constitution of Canada guarantees the rights of the Plaintiffs. Those rights are embedded in history. They must be respected by the Crown, whether Provincial or Federal. Consider now what Stanley Williams said in testimony about how he perceives the treatment of the Gitksan by the government:

"When a grizzly bear gets into the provisions of another person, then he eats it up; when the owner comes back, the grizzly gets mad instead, gets mad at the owner. And that's how the government is treating us today concerning our territories." The far-reaching denials of the Defendants, coupled with the negation of the Defendants' historical obligation to the Gitksan and Wet'suwet'en, show without doubt that the Plaintiffs can expect no just and honorable treatment at the hands of the Governments. It is for this reason that the Plaintiffs now turn to Your Lordship's Court for protection in order to enforce the obligations of the Crown and to safeguard the aboriginal rights of the Plain-

tiffs.

I will now turn to our outline of argument. Here, I will set out the propositions, in order of presentation, which we will urge upon the Court.

Excerpts from The Province's Argument

The opinions of Dr. Mills and Dr. Daly ignore or misinterpret the historic, linguistic or archaeological evidence respecting where people lived in the prehistoric past and deserve no weight. It appears clear from the contracts signed by the experts for the Plaintiffs that they were ready to "present the Native Canadian viewpoint when called upon to interpret the cultural historical record." ...The best that can be said about the Plaintiffs' anthropologists is that they were "advocates" for the Plaintiffs in "presenting the Plaintiffs' viewpoint".

* * *

Clan membership is even less helpful as a way of identifying the membership of the society of Gitksan. A Clan is not a corporate body. Clan membership is a way of lining people up at Feasts, of determining who is host and who is guest, and it is a way of organizing a rule of incest.

* * *

—Section 52 of the Constitution Act, 1982 provides: "The Constitution of Canada is the supreme law of Canada, and any law that is inconsistent with the provisions of the Constitution is, to the extent of the inconsistency, of no force and effect."

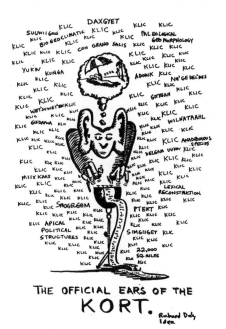

THE OFFICIAL EARS OF THE
KORT.

In light of Section 52 of the *Constitution Act, 1982* and the cited provisions of the *Charter of Rights and Freedoms*, it is submitted this Court has no power to grant the declarations sought in Part I of the Plaintiffs' Prayer for Relief.

...Patriarchal society claims that matrilineal descent is sexist...the lower and middle classes will probably get a laugh out of this note from the upper class—.

The alleged law of matrilineal devolution of property contravenes Section 15(1) of the *Charter of Rights* since it constitutes discrimination based on sex.

Further, there is no place in Canada for a class system of government. It is discriminatory.

* * *

An insult to the ancient laws— comparing them to the despotic English King John's.

On the evidence, the Feast system is so intrusive

into the personal lives of those who participate in the system that its imposition on all Gitksan and Wet'suwet'en would constitute the most punitive interference with freedom of association imaginable.

The alleged laws of the Plaintiffs are, at least in the respects discussed above, as odious as the conduct of King John which led to the Magna Carta.

In summary, the Plaintiffs' alleged laws discriminate on the basis of sex, and create a two-tiered class structure, both of which violate Section 15 of the *Charter of Rights and Freedoms.* The

Plaintiffs' alleged laws constitute an egregious interference with an individual's freedom of movement, including the right to choose one's occupation and where to pursue it and, therefore, violate an individual's liberty and interests. In addition, the alleged laws interfere with an individual's right to engage in family, employment and social relations as he or she may see fit and therefore violate an individual's freedom of association.

THE DEFENDANT province wants you to forget HOUSES, forget CLANS... the only way to see the people is as bands and reserves. we say it is the only 'natural' way to see them.

MR. NATURAL →

- RESERVES
- BANDS

WAIT! Can't the two things - reserves and land claims stand together? Can't they say, "well we are not going to be listened to at this time, so we'll take the reserves while we can and still advance claims." !?

MCEACHERN
MAY 22/1990

Indians never had title, province's lawyer says

Vancouver Sun July 14, 1989

By LARRY STILL

An Indian land claim to more than 50,000 square kilometres of northwestern B.C. is based on an erroneous view of history, according to a lawyer for the provincial government.

Mike Goldie said the claim by the Gitksan-Wet'suwet'en Tribal Council wrongly asserts the Indians were given title to the land prior to 1871, when British Columbia joined Canada.

Contrary to statements by the claimants' lawyers, Goldie said the province does not contend the Indians waived title to the land. It says the Indians never had title in the first place.

"What will be submitted is that there never was in British Columbia prior to July of 1871 any concept of native title ... analagous to ownership and jurisdiction," he said.

Goldie dismissed the concept of aboriginal title as he delivered his opening address for the provincial Crown at the B.C. Supreme Court trial of the land claim.

Described by Chief Justice Allan McEachern as the most important aboriginal land claim trial ever undertaken in Canada, the hearing began in May 1987 and has already consumed 244 trial days.

The Indians' lawyers, who closed their case late last week, relied in part on the Royal Proclamation of 1763 but also said the Indians have title by reason of their centuries-long occupation of the land.

Goldie acknowledged in his opening statement the claim for ownership and jurisdiction, if successful, would vest control of the land and its resources in the Indians.

Saying the province rejects the claim, Goldie noted the Colony of British Columbia never made land cession treaties with Indians — and exclusive authority to do so passed to the federal government in 1871.

The lawyer said all that was recognized prior to union was an interest of the native peoples in their occupied villages and cultivated fields, as well as their fishing and hunting rights.

> ❝I will ask your lordship to reject what I will call the conspiracy theory of history, which appears to have been adopted by the (claimants) in support of the far-reaching claims of present day ownership and jurisdiction.❞
>
> — Mike Goldie

Goldie said colonial governors recognized that Indians should be treated no differently from the white population, except with regard to their village occupancy and hunting rights.

He noted Gov. Sir Anthony Musgrave in 1870 said native Indians should be recognized as "British subjects under the same protection and titled to the same privileges and incurring the same liabilities as the white population."

In short, they were not given specific title to land.

Although he agreed Indians were subject to certain administrative exceptions, such as prohibitive liquor laws, Goldie said: "Whatever one may think of these exceptions (they) were wholly inconsistent with a claim of ownership and jurisdiction" in respect to land.

Goldie told McEachern some of the opinion evidence tendered by the claimants' lawyers "called into question the honor of the Crown" regarding the treatment of native Indians.

"In its broadest terms, the issue that is raised is whether the Indian peoples of this province have been treated fairly," Goldie said.

He said the defence case, which is expected to conclude in December, will support the conclusion B.C. is far from being the only jurisdiction in Canada not to have recognized aboriginal title.

"I will ask your lordship to reject what I will call the conspiracy theory of history, which appears to have been adopted by the (claimants) in support of the far-reaching claims of present day ownership and jurisdiction."

The trial continues.

IF A TREE FALLS IN THE FOREST — AND THE CROWN DOESN'T HEAR IT... IT DOESN'T EXIST.

178 COLONIALISM ON TRIAL

Gitksan-Wet'suwet'en Bulletin, August 1990

Report on the Conclusion of the Court Case

The legal team for the Gitksan and Wet'suwet'en Hereditary Chiefs said that after the Chiefs' argument, the arguments of the Province and the Federal Government and our reply, their unanimous feeling was that the argument and the case ended on a very positive note. We believe we were successful in showing how the big principles of acknowledgement and protection of aboriginal rights applied to the Gitksan and Wet'suwet'en and how there was no basis for the extinguishment arguments thrown up by the governments.

Gisdaywa and Delgamukuw closed the Chiefs' submissions on May 14th with concluding comments on behalf of all of the Hereditary Chiefs. For this (and for the following) week, the Vancouver courtroom was full of Chiefs and other Gitksan and Wet'suwet'en people who travelled to Vancouver to support the closing of our case and to bear witness to the Province's argument.

The Province started its argument on May 14th and concluded on June 12th. The Province's argument centred on the absence of colonial recognition of aboriginal title pre-1871, implied extinguishment of aboriginal rights before and after union with Canada, and provincial discharge of its legal obligations to the Indian people by Canada by the acceptance of the McKenna-McBride recommendations on reserve allocations.

The Province also made arguments that the Chiefs had not shown that the Gitksan and Wet'suwet'en were distinct societies, that they did not have exclusive possession of their land because of the overlaps, that they did not own the specific House territories claimed to be owned by them, and that they did not have the long history in the Territory claimed. The Province also challenged the oral histories and the territories. They argued that the Gitksan and Wet'suwet'en House territories were developed after the arrival of the Europeans in response to the fur trade.

We answered all these arguments both in our main argument and in our reply. Two recent cases of the Supreme Court of Canada, *Sioui* and *Sparrow*, helped us a great deal. In these cases the Court held that government recognition of aboriginal rights was not necessary for there to be such rights, and that clear and plain legislative intention is necessary before aboriginal title could be extinguished. We argued that both in the common law and by virtue of the Royal Proclamation of 1763, the aboriginal rights to ownership and jurisdiction pre-existed the assertion of sovereignty and did not

CUSTERS LAST WORDS...

"MY SIOUXS ARE KILLING ME!"

Alfred Joesph

depend on any act of the colonial or Imperial government.

We also argued that in order to extinguish the title to the land and jurisdiction of the Chiefs and Houses, there must be a clear and plain legislative intention by the colonial, Imperial or Federal Government; and there never was.

The Federal Government's argument started on June 13th and lasted for ten days. Much to their discredit, they accepted most of the Province's argument. They also emphasized the "frozen rights" theory of aboriginal title; i.e., Native people only have those rights today which they had as traditional rights at the time of the coming of the Europeans and no more, despite the changes which have occurred in their communities. This argument is a non-starter. The *Sparrow* Court rejected this theory. It is plainly illogical.

The Federal Government also tried to make a case on the basis of the Loring documents that the whole of the Gitksan and Wet'suwet'en societies were assimilated between 1891 and 1915. Once again there are many factors against this—the Feast, the language, the names, the poles, and the territories....

When the trial ended, the Judge, of course, reserved his judgment. He did not say when he would give his decision. We believe, however, that it will take about nine months. We expect that he will not give a judgment before the end of February, 1991.

—From a report by Peter Grant

Maas Gaak (Don Ryan) on Self-Government

There is no government in this country that can grant us self-government, and that is the premise that we have started from in our planning, and that is the premise we keep in mind in our negotiations for self-government.

Self-government has been within our people for thousands of years and it will not go away. We will continue to practice and develop means of interaction with ourselves and others. With this in mind, Canada cannot dictate to the Gitksan and Wet'suwet'en what type of government they must practice.

The Federal Government has brought a number of conditions to the bargaining table. It says:

- We must surrender our land.
- We must be reserve-based.
- We must have a constitution.

We want the Federal Government to drop all its

THE PROVINCE'S LAWYERS HAVE THIS IDEA THAT NATIVES WANDERED AIMLESSLY IN THE BUSH.

WE SAY THE MISSIONARIES INCITED THE INDIANS!

THEY ACQUIESCED!

THEY WERE EXTINGUISHED!

interest in our lands. We want the programs the Federal Government administers on our behalf turned over to us. Because we are not creating a third-party interest, we see no need to surrender our land.

The Federal Government's assumption that our system of self- government has to be reserve-based has got to go. Our notion of self-government is not confined to reserves, but covers the whole scope of our territories. We must keep our jurisdiction over our territories.

The Federal Government has said it is up to us to define what type of model of self-government we want, and when we tell them what we want, they say, "You can't do that." They tell us our system must be reserve-based, but they are unable to tell us what they mean by reserve.

It is important for people to understand what we are trying to do. We are trying to keep what is rightfully ours, our resource base, because it is vital to our survival, spiritually and economically.

Blockades and Roadblocks

Because the Provincial Government has repeatedly refused to hold just and fair discussions concerning aboriginal title and its implications, and because the recently released recommendations of The Premier's Council on Native Affairs have not gone far enough in addressing the issue of title, the Gitksan and Wet'suwet'en have erected a number of roadblocks and informational blockades to draw attention to B.C. Premier William Vander Zalm's unwillingness to deal with the Indian land question in a fair and just manner.

—from *Gitksan & Wet'suwet'en Bulletin*, August 1990

Closing Statement of the Chiefs by Gisdaywa (Alfred Joseph) Delgamuukw (Earl Muldoe) Yaga'lahl (Dora Wilson) Maas Gaak (Don Ryan), May 14, 1990

LOOK, THERE'S A SPARROW IN COURT!

JUNE 1990

THE SPARROW DECISION BY THE SUPREME COURT OF CANADA RECOGNIZES ABORIGONAL FISHING RIGHTS AND CAUSES QUITE A STIR IN COURT.

We, the Gitksan and Wet'suwet'en people, are in the Court to state the truth of the ownership and jurisdiction we exercise over our territories. Three years have passed since we made our opening statements to this Court. At that time, you did not know who Delgamuukw and Gisdaywa were. Now, this Court knows I am Gisdaywa, a Wet'suwet'en Chief who has responsibility for the House of Kaiyexwaniits of the Gitdumden. I have explained how my House holds the Biiwenii Ben territory and had the privilege of showing it to you. Long ago my ancestors encountered the spirit of that land and accepted the responsibility to care for it. In return, the land has fed the House members and those whom the Chiefs permitted to harvest its resources. Those who have obeyed the laws of respect and balance have prospered there.

I am Delgamuukw, the third since this trial started. I also have obligations to my House and the territories of my House. You have heard oral histories of the Gitksan and Wet'suwet'en that tell of the many groups that migrated into our territories. Many stayed, contributing to our culture, acknowledging the authority of our Chiefs and obeying our laws.

Of all these groups, only the Europeans failed to recognize our ownership and jurisdiction. This Court now has an opportunity to redress this situation.

We, the Hereditary Chiefs, decided against wearing blankets and regalia in this courtroom because we believe that our authority would not be respected by the government lawyers. Under our

EUROPEANS ARGUING THE COMMON LAWS OF TRESPASS IN THE ENGLISH COURT... ON STOLEN LAND.

law, respect for people and for their territory requires compensation.

We, the Gitksan and Wet'suwet'en, must be compensated for loss of the land's present integrity and for the loss of economic rents.

We ask that the Court not only acknowledge our ownership and jurisdiction over the land, but restore it to a form adequate for Nature to heal in terms of restoration. We would like to see clearcuts and plantations returned to forests; contaminated rivers and lakes returned to their original pristine states; reservoirs of drowned forests returned to living lakes, and diverted rivers to life-sustaining flows.

We realize that the true financial value of this compensation for restoration would bankrupt both the Federal and Provincial governments. Compensation must remain an ongoing obligation of the Federal and Provincial governments "until our hearts are satisfied."

However, this compensation should not be viewed by this Court as an alternative to the acknowledgement of our ownership and jurisdiction of our land. We do not want financial compensation without the recognition of our authority over our territories.

We are asking you to make declarations on Gitksan and Wet'suwet'en aboriginal title. We, the Gitksan and Wet'suwet'en people, own our lands.

I will identify those areas where the powers of the Province and the Federal governments need to be restrained in order for us to exercise our responsibilities under aboriginal title.

First, we the Chiefs must have our authority recognized in order to exercise our responsibility to protect the land for the future, and to conserve resources. We must have the power to manage all

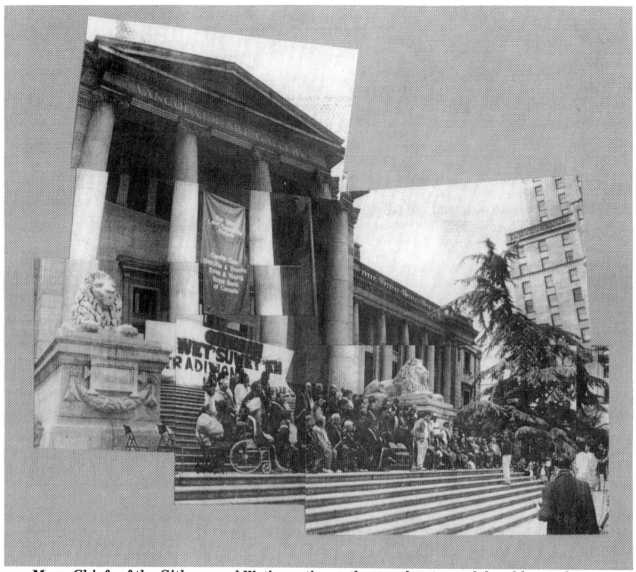

Many Chiefs of the Gitksan and Wet'suwet'en gather on the steps of the old courthouse in Vancouver.

human activity that brings change to the land, air or water on all of our territories.

Second, to enable each House to provide for its members and all those living in their territory, the Chiefs must have control over the local economy by managing natural resource allocations. This would include licensing, leasing and permitting. As well, royalties and taxation payments from resource use on our territories must be paid to us.

It is not our intention to exert any powers over the non-Gitksan and Wet'suwet'en people living in our territories. Fee-simple lands held by third parties as of October 1984, would be exempt from this resource allocation. We see the pulling back of these central government powers as being the minimum required to restore not only individual self-reliance, but also community self-reliance. We have presented you with ample evidence of the

effects on our land resulting from government resource management. We have also given evidence of the effect that centralized economic management and government welfare has had on our people. The government's system does not work. We, the Hereditary Chiefs, believe we can change the situation under our laws and practices through our authority.

Our system of government is as powerful today and will be as powerful tomorrow, as it was one hundred or ten thousand years ago. You have heard both ancient and modern histories tell of how our system has remained relevant through the evolving ecological, cultural and economic circumstances in which our people have found themselves. To say we disobey our laws and ignore our Chiefs' authority because we change a piece of technology or use our land in a different way, is a desperate

Gitksan, Wet'suwet'en, and supporters from other Nations watch the proceedings.

argument.

This case, then, is about learning from the past so we can repair the present and pass on a healthier land to our grandchildren. It is not about retrieving frozen rights from a Nineteenth Century ice-box.

Our aboriginal title is found in common law and takes precedence over the Provincial Crown. We do not have to, and will not, surrender our aboriginal title in order to be recognized by the Federal government. We are self-governing.

However, we see a layering of responsibilities among the Gitksan and Wet'suwet'en, the Federal government, and the Provincial government being resolved in an ongoing series of negotiations. Given the strong imperative for the Gitksan and Wet'suwet'en, British Columbia and Canada to have social and economic activities continue throughout our territories, consensus on the neces-

sary political and administrative framework must be found.

We are asking this Court to properly apply common law. We want a declaration of recognition and affirmation of our continued ownership and jurisdiction. We will not surrender or diminish our title and rights. We do not request a "right" to use and occupy the land, and we refuse extended Reserve lands. We will decide what our future relationship will be with Canada and British Columbia on this basis.

We ask nothing more than what should have occurred prior to Confederation and prior to this Province entering Confederation. We are here to right the wrongs that have been occurring for over one hundred years. This Court has the power to recognize and affirm Gitksan and Wet'suwet'en ownership and jurisdiction.

Closing Remarks by Stuart Rush

My lord, if I may say these closing words on behalf of the Gitksan and Wet'suwet'en people and my co-counsel. This has been a long and difficult trial for both the bench and the bar. The hectic schedule that we've all been under in order to complete the argument by today's date is one testimonial to that fact. The duration and the difficulty of the trial obviously speaks to the importance of the Court's decision to the Gitksan and Wet'suwet'en people and to the people of the Province as a whole. There are large questions of principle which have been placed before your lordship for decision and it will take all of the Court's strength to deal with these. And I might add it will take a good deal of the Court's strength to carry some of the volumes from the office to home.

On behalf of the Gitksan and Wet'suwet'en people, my lord, and my counsel I would like to thank you for your care and your patience in dealing with the many ups and downs over the course of this trial and especially at times the testiness of counsel. I wish to add that there are many Hereditary Chiefs, 15 of whom were named as Plaintiffs, who could not be here today as they had passed on during the course of this trial. Their absence has been a hardship for the community and a loss to the case. Notwithstanding that, my lord, the people have persevered and as your lordship is well aware despite the fact that the Court case is far and long away from their community have had Chiefs in the courtroom throughout the duration of the trial. On their behalf, on behalf of my co-counsel, I'd like to thank the Court and as well the staff and the court reporters for their role in the trial.

Closing Remarks by Michael Goldie

My lord, may I on behalf of my colleagues associate myself with the remarks that my friend Mr. Rush has made with respect to your lordship's consideration of the problems that have come before you and his acknowledgement of the role in which the Court staff and the court reporters have played. And I do so on behalf of myself and my colleagues. I add one further observation, my lord, and it has to do with the nature of the burden which your lordship has assumed. As you have remarked on a number of times this is a case that is somewhat precedented in its size and in the complexity and number of issues which have been placed before the Court. I would hope that your lordship would not hesitate to seek the assistance of counsel as you develop your thinking on the matter, if you come across matters which appear to you to be a problem I'm sure that all counsel would respond very willingly to any requests for further assistance.

Closing Remarks by James Macaulay

My lord, may I join in with the remarks of my friend Mr. Rush and Mr. Goldie. We are grateful to your lordship for putting up with us for so long and I think it should be noted that despite the strains of a contest of this magnitude and this length that at no time, although there were a few sharp exchanges, was there ever any true unpleasantness in Court of a kind that is occasionally seen in some hotly contested litigation. It's a great credit to my friends for the Plaintiffs and for the Province as well as my own associates. Thank you, my lord.

Closing Remarks by the Court

Thank you, Mr. Macaulay. The judgment of course will be reserved. I've wondered for some time what one could possibly say when one reaches this stage and what counsel have said and with which I respectfully agree that this has been a long trial. ...One cannot look at the record of this trial, that is the physical manifestation of the record of

this trial, without recognizing the incredible effort and expenditure of energy and time that has gone into the research and preparation for this case, and for that and for all the other efforts of counsel I am most grateful. ...I think that we will all have to prepare ourselves for a long siege. I will have more to do than you will for the next little while, but I have no doubt that what I say will not be the last word.

I have thought of what I should say at this time. I'm reminded of Cromwell's admonition to the rump Parliament which might more properly be said by counsel to me, which was, that you have sat here too long. In the name of God go. And I am going to accept that suggestion. I think counsel could perhaps think of Martin Luther King's famous "I'm free at last, I'm free at last, I'm free at last. Thank God Almighty I am free at last." But I think the more appropriate analogy might be to the reference to the syndrome sometimes known as the Stockholm Syndrome which is where the hostage falls in love with his captors. And I have said from time to time that I have been a captor or a prisoner here, that there have been things happen which I could

not avoid and things had to be dealt with which could not be dealt with in anything but an arbitrary way and I had been a captive in the circumstances of this case.

...I think that it is probably the safe course in a time like this for a judge to say as little as possible. I have probably said quite enough. ...I wish again to express my sincere appreciation to our court reporters. I have already said, and I do not think I can improve on what I said to them privately, is that I have often been reported before but I have never been reported so well. I wish also to express my appreciation to Sharon Ritchie, who was the clerk for approximately the first half of the trial, and to Sue Thomson for the balance, without whose marvelous assistance we would have been in a terrible state of confusion about the exhibits, which fortunately is not one of the problems we've had in this case and I am grateful to both of them for their very outstanding service to the Court. I wish you all a well-deserved respite from this case, that is until Factums are required, and I thank you all and wish you a restful summer. Thank you. We will now adjourn.

Chapter 8

The Decision

Reasons for Judgment
of the Honorable Chief Justice Allan McEachern, March 8, 1991

The judgment in this case:

(1) The action against Canada is dismissed.

(2) The plaintiffs' claims for ownership and jurisdiction over the territory, and for aboriginal rights in the territory are dismissed.

(3) The plaintiffs, on behalf of the Gitksan and Wet'suwet'en people described in the Statement of Claim (except the Gitksan people of the Houses of Kitwancool Chiefs), are entitled to a Declaration that, subject to the general law of the province, they have a continuing legal right to use unoccupied or vacant Crown land in the territory for aboriginal sustenance purposes...

(4) The plaintiffs' claims for damages are dismissed.

(5) The Counterclaim of the province is dismissed.

(6) In view of all the circumstances of this case, including the importance of the issues, the variable resources of the parties, the financial arrangments which have been made for the conduct of this case (from which I have been largely insulated), and the divided success each party has achieved, there will not be any order for costs.

Excerpts from the Judgment

Introduction

I am sure that the plaintiffs understand that although the aboriginal laws which they recognize could be relevant on some issues, I must decide this case only according to what they call "the white man's law..."

* * *

As I am not a Royal Commission, and as I have no staff to assist me, it will not be possible to mention all of the evidence which took so long to adduce, or to analze all of the exhibits and experts' reports which were admitted into evidence, or to describe and respond to all of the arguments of counsel. In these circumstances I must do what a computer cannot do, and that is to summarize. In this respect I have been brutal.

The Claim & The Territory: An Outline

The most striking thing that one notices in the territory away from the Skeena-Bulkley corridor is its emptiness. I generally accept the evidence of witnesses such as Dr. Steciw, Mrs. Peden and others that very few Indians are to be seen anywhere except in the large river corridors. As I have mentioned, the territory is a vast emptiness.

* * *

It would not be accurate to assume that even pre-contact existence in the territory was in the least bit idyllic. The plaintiffs' ancestors had no written language, no horses or wheeled vehicles, slavery and starvation was not uncommon, wars with neighboring peoples were common, and there is no doubt, to quote Hobbes, that aboriginal life in the territory was, at best, "nasty, brutish and short."

An Historical Overview

The evidence does not disclose the beginnings of the Gitksan and Wet'suwet'en people. Many of them believe God gave this land to them at the beginning of time. While I have every respect for their beliefs, there is no evidence to support such a theory and much good reason to doubt it.

* * *

The evidence suggests that the Indians of the territory were, by historical standards, a primitive people without any form of writing, horses, or wheeled wagons. ...The defendants... suggest the Gitksan and Wet'suwet'en civilizations, if they qualify for that description, fall within a much lower, even primitive order.

* * *

I am satisfied that the lay witnesses honestly believed everything they said was true and accurate. It was obvious to me, however, that they were recounting matters of faith which have become fact to them. If I do not accept their evidence it will seldom be because I think they are untruthful, but rather because I have a different view of what is fact and what is belief.

Some Comments on Evidence

Apart from urging almost total acceptance of all Gitksan and Wet'suwet'en cultural values, the anthropologists add little to the important questions that must be decided in this case. This is because, as already mentioned, I am able to make the required important findings about the history of these people, sufficient for this case, without this evidence.

The History of The Gitksan and Wet'suwet'en People

Who's "Nasty, brutish and short?"

Some of this evidence had a decided complexion of unreality about it, as if nothing had changed since before contact. This affects the credibility of statements which were often repeated that ancestors had been using these specific lands from the beginning of time, or similar expression. Aboriginal life, in my view, was far from stable and it stretches credulity to believe that remote ancestors considered themselves bound to specific lands.

* * *

I am unable to accept *adaawk, kungax,* and oral histories as reliable bases for detailed history, but they could confirm findings based on other admissable evidence.

The Creation of Aboriginal Interests

In my view it is part of the law of nations, which has become part of the common law, that discovery and occupation of the lands of this continent by European nations, or occupation and settlement, gave rise to a right of sovereignty. ...The events of the last 200 years are far more significant than any military conquest or treaties would have been. The reality of Crown ownership of the soil of all the lands of the province is not open to question and actual dominion for such a long period is far more pervasive than the outcome of a battle or a war could ever be. The law recognizes Crown ownership of the territory in a federal state now known as Canada pursuant to its Constitution and laws.

* * *

I am not able to conclude on the evidence that the plaintiffs' ancestors used the territory since "time immemorial" (the time when the memory of man "runneth not to the contrary"). "Time immemorial," as everyone knows, is a legal expression referring to the year 1189 (the beginning of the reign of Richard II), as specified in the **Statute of Westminster, 1275**.

* * *

I have concluded that the **Royal Proclamation, 1763** has never had any application or operation in British Columbia.

The Relevant Political History of British Columbia in the Pre-Colonial & Colonial Period

Being of a culture where everyone looked after himself or perished, the Indians knew how to survive (in most years). But they were not as industrious in the new economic climate as was thought necessary by the newcomers in the Colony. In addition, the Indians were a greatly weakened people by reason of foreign diseases which took a fearful toll, and by the ravages of alcohol. They became a conquered people, not by force of arms, for that was unnecessary, but by an invading culture and a relentless energy with which they would not, or could not compete.

...What seems clear, however, is that the source of Indian difficulty was not the loss of land for aboriginal purposes. So far as the evidence shows, they were largely left in their villages and aboriginal life was available to them long after the "Indian problem" was identified.

The Mask of the Injustice System, **by Kwakiutl photographer and artist, David Neel, was inspired by Chief Justice McEachern's decision.**

Photo: David Neel.

The Plaintiffs' Specific Claims For Aboriginal Interests

It became obvious during the course of the trial that what the Gitksan and Wet'suwet'en witnesses describe as law is really a most uncertain and highly flexible set of customs which are frequently not followed by the Indians themselves. I heard many instances of prominent Chiefs conducting themselves other than in accordance with these rules, such as logging or trappng on another Chief's territory, although there always seemed to be an aboriginal exception which made almost any departure from aboriginal rules permissable. In my judgment, these rules are so flexible and uncertain that they cannot be classified as laws.

* * *

I fully understand the plantiffs' wishful belief that their distinctive history entitles them to demand some form of constitutional independence from British Columbia. But neither this nor any Court has the jurisdiction to undo the establishment of the Colony, Confederation, or the constitutional arrangements which are now in place. Separate sovereignty or legislative authority, as a matter of law, is beyond the authority of any Court to award.

I also understand the reasons why some aboriginal persons have spoken in strident and exaggerated terms about aboriginal ownership and sovereignty, and why they have asserted exemption from the laws of Canada and the province.

They often refer to the fact that they were never conquered by military force. With respect, that is

not a relevant consideration at this late date, if it ever was. Similarly, the absence of treaties does not change the fact that Canadian and British Columbian sovereignty is a legal reality recognized by both the law of nations and by this Court.

The plaintiffs must understand that Canada and the provinces, as a matter of law, are sovereign, each in their own jurisdictions, which makes it impossible for aboriginal peoples unilaterally to achieve the independent or separate status some of them seek. In the language of the street, and in the contemplation of the law, the plaintiffs are subject to the same law and the same Constitution as everyone else.

...As to ownership, I have concluded that the

interest of the plaintiffs' ancestors, at the time of British sovereignty, except for village sites, was nothing more than the right to use the land for aboriginal purposes.

It follows, therefore, that the plaintiffs' claims for aboriginal jurisdiction or sovereignty over, and ownership of, the territory must be dismissed.

*   *   *

I am quite unable to say that there was much in the way of pre-contact social organization among the Gitksan or Wet'suwet'en simply because there is so little reliable evidence.

Extinguishment and Fiduciary Duties

In my judgment, intention sufficient to establish extinguishment must be examined broadly and need not be confined to a specific act or decision at a particular moment in colonial history. Instead, intention may more properly be discerned from a course of conduct over the whole of the colonial period.

The unanimous judicial decision of all the judges (in *Sparrow*) so long after these historical events to regard intention at a time of uncertain law and understanding as the governing factor in extin-

VANCOUVER SUN, JULY 13, 1991

A landmark ruling shocks anthropologists

By KEN MacQUEEN
Southam News

A RECENT LAND CLAIM ruling by the B.C. Supreme Court has so angered and disgusted many of Canada's leading anthropologists that they are considering legal action.

A committee of the Canadian Anthropology Society may try to intervene in the planned appeal of the massive Gitksan and Wet'suwet'en land claim, which was dismissed in March by Chief Justice Allan McEachern.

Anthropologists interviewed by Southam News slam the 394-page ruling on a number of counts. It gratuitously dismisses scientific evidence, is laced with ethnocentric bias and is rooted in the colonial belief that white society in inherently superior, they say.

The trial and ruling stretched over four years and is considered the longest, most expensive and potentially one of the most important land claims cases in Canadian history.

"He treats them something like wolves," anthropologist Michael Asch says of McEachern's assessment of the ancient Gitksan and Wet'suwet'en societies of northwestern B.C.

"The analogy would be closer to a wolf society than a human society," says Asch, a professor at the University of Alberta, whose professional expertise has been used in past legal proceedings.

Robin Ridington, an anthropologist from the University of British Columbia, says the judge has "really gone too far," by loading the ruling with colonial ideas of the superiority of western culture.

"There's just a bunch of horrible things there that if an Anthropology 100 student wrote anything like that in a paper, not only would you write a lot of red ink over it, you would say, 'Look, please come in and talk to me . . . you have real problems.'"

Ridington, who teaches and studies aboriginal cultures, sat as a spectator during some of the lengthy trial, which heard extensive evidence of the Indians' ancient and modern society from anthropologists and tribal elders.

He says McEachern dismissed that evidence out of hand, while adopting as his own federal and provincial government defence submissions that the Gitksan and Wet'suwet'en had a primitive, brutal society with few redeeming values.

"They (defence) just consciously laid on every bit of racist claptrap that they could think of, and he bought the whole package."

Ridington has written a 10-page analysis of the ruling. Among the criticisms of McEachern's rulings he and others raise:

● His dismissal of pre-European Indian culture: ". . . it would not be accurate to assume

---

Did the chief justice show white bias when he dismissed Canada's biggest native land claim?

---

that even pre-contact existence in the territory was in the least bit idyllic," McEachern wrote.

"The plaintiffs' ancestors had no written language, no horses or wheeled vehicles, slavery and starvation was not uncommon, wars with neighboring peoples were common and there is no doubt, to quote Hobbs [sic], that aboriginal life in the territory was, at best, 'nasty, brutish and short.'"

● His dismissal of a picture of an orderly clan system as "painted by the Indian witnesses and their anthropological experts."

Instead, he concludes that "many of the badges of civilization, as we of European culture understand the term, were indeed absent."

● His terminology. He refers to "our" native people. While Indians were "eking out an aboriginal life," the European contribution is described as "discovery, exploration, settlement and development."

● His dismissal of native oral history as "not literally true." And of the evidence of anthropologists, two of whom lived among the bands for several years. "It is always unfortunate when experts become too close to their clients, especially during litigation."

Antonia Mills, a University of Virginia anthropologist who gave six days of expert testimony during the trial, calls McEachern's "judgment and his language really reprehensible."

The dismissal of anthropological evidence in a land claims case is akin to dismissing psychiatric evidence in a criminal court, anthropologists say.

Anthropology, the study of human and societal development, "has been used in land claims hearings very steadily over the last several decades," says Harvey Feit, president of the 600-member anthropology society and a professor at McMaster University in Hamilton, Ont.

"It's a set of procedures for producing and understanding observations and information that is sharable with others, communicable with others and, in principle, would be similar to what other people, similarly trained, would produce."

Michael Asch says McEachern's ruling follows a line of European judicial logic that has, at various times, concluded that Christian societies had legal claims over infidels, that slaves were property, that women were not legal persons and that legal authority vests in the Canadian Crown.

Gitksan spokesman Don Ryan says that the elders are wounded by the court's dismissal of their lengthy testimony on oral history, legends and songs. They said: "This is the last time that the sacred boxes of our people will be opened for the white man to look at." ☐

ALLAN McEACHERN:

"treats natives like wolves"

---

guishment persuades me that intention in this context must relate not to a specific or precise state of mind on the part of historical actors, but rather to the consequences they intended for their actions. In other words, the question is not did the Crown through its officers specifically address the question of aboriginal rights, but rather did they clearly and plainly intend to create a legal regime from which is necessary to infer that aboriginal interests were in fact extinguished.

* * *

As aboriginal rights were capable of modernization, so should the obligations and benefits of this duty be flexible to meet changing conditions. Land that is conveyed away, but later returned to the Crown, becomes again usable by Indians. Crown lands that are leased or licensed, such as for clearcut logging to use an extreme example, become usable again after logging operations are completed or abandoned.

* * *

When I consider the effects of disease, alcohol and other insults upon the Indian community, it is apparent that interference with aboriginal uses of land, except for actual dispossessions, was not a principal cause of Indian misfortune.

. . .I cannot find lack of access to aboriginal land has seriously harmed the identity of these peoples.

Conclusions

(1) In my judgment the plaintiffs' aboriginal interests in the territory were lawfully extinguished by the Crown during the colonial period.

(2) It follows that non-reserve Crown lands, tit-

les and tenures granted by the Crown in the territory since the creation of the Colony of British Columbia in 1858 are unencumbered by any claim to aboriginal interests.

(3) The plaintiffs are entitled to a declaration that the Gitksan and Wet'suwet'en peoples are entitled, as against the Crown but subject to the general law, to use unoccupied, vacant Crown lands within the territory for aboriginal sustenance activities until it is required for an adverse purpose. I limit this declaration to the territory because that is the only land which is in issue in this action but I see no reason why it should not apply to the province generally.

Damages

I have already offered the comment that larger reserves should have been allotted, but I have also commented that the Indians did not always help their own cause. The evidence does not permit me to make an award in this matter. It is my view, as I have no jurisdiction to create reserves, that the plaintiffs' claims for larger reserves or compensation in their place is a matter for the Crown, and not for the Courts. There is no legal basis upon which I can assist the plaintiffs in this connection.

With regard to interference with aboriginal life, the evidence is similarly sparse.... Apart altogether from the strictly legal defences, there is insufficient evidence to conclude that the plaintiffs have established a cause of action for damages or compensation.

I am satisfied that it would not be proper to make any award of damages in this case and that claim is dismissed.

The Lands Subject to Aboriginal Rights at the Date of British Sovereignty

Although the Gitksan and Wet'suwet'en had well-established trails permitting visiting with other villages and people, as evidenced by the trail maps marked in evidence, there was little reason for the Gitksan to stray far from their villages or principal rivers in the Skeena, Kispiox and Babine River Valleys.

...The evidence raises serious doubts about the time-depth of particular Indian presence in distant territories, that is away from the villages. It is unlikely that the plaintiffs' ancestors, prior to the fur trade, would occupy territories so far from the villages, particularly in fierce Canadian winters.

This theory is well supported by a large number of reputable experts and casts doubts upon the plaintiff's positions that many of the far north and far south territories claimed by many Chiefs were used for as long as they allege.

* * *

It is impossible to infer a community reputation for an interest in land when a prominent, long life resident in the area like Mr. Shelford, a Member of the Legislature for many years, and a Cabinet Minister for a time, who acknowledges hearing about general land claims for a long time, has never heard until very recently of claims of ownership or jurisdiction, or claims to specific lands, including his own, by Chiefs whose families he has known personally for most of his life.

...There are far too many inconsistencies in the plaintiffs' evidence to permit me to conclude that individual chiefs or Houses have discrete aboriginal rights or interests in the various territories defined by the internal boundaries.

Abandonment of Aboriginal Rights

Aboriginal rights depend upon long time and, I think, regular if not continuous use of territory for aboriginal purposes. The difficulty is not with the principle, but rather in its application in particular cases. In this connection, I respectfully disagree with some academics who suggest that aboriginal rights can be ignored for long periods and then revived. It largely depends on how complete the abandonment is, and for how long the territory has been unused.

Canada argues that disuse for a generation, which is usually 20-25 years, is sufficient to constitute abandonment. ...Common sense dictates that abandoned rights are no longer valid and land must be used or lost.

* * *

I have no doubt aboriginal activities have fallen very much into disuse in many areas. This was admitted by several Indian witnesses who observed that many of their young people have very little interest in aboriginal pursuits. The aboriginal activities that are being pursued now may be indistinguishable in many cases from the wilderness activities enjoyed by many non-Indian citizens of the province.

Johnny David, Wet'suwet'en, 109 years old, on judgment day.
Photo: Steve Bosch, *Vancouver Sun.*

Notice of Appeal

Delgamuukw, on his own behalf and on behalf of all the members of the House of Delgamuukw, and all other Plaintiffs, hereby appeal to the Court of Appeal for British Columbia from the judgment of the Honorable Chief Justice, pronounced the 8th day of March 1991.

—April 2, 1991

Postscript

The Handle Of Life:
The Struggle Back On The Land

If we were concerned about the destruction of our territories before the Chiefs filed suit against the Province of B.C. in 1984, we were horrified by the sharp increase in logging, and the methods used, that took place from that point onward.

The ugly practices of clearcutting (cutting down all trees within a given block), and high-grading (taking only 15 to 50 percent of "marketable" trees from a clearcut), left vast chunks of the territories scraped raw. With every rainfall and spring run-off, the waters of the creeks and rivers would turn a deep, muddy brown from the topsoils of the clearcuts and the loosened earth of the hastily constructed logging roads.

It was obvious that a renewed effort to protect the land was necessary if we did not want to see a barren wasteland by the time *Delgamuukw vs. The Queen* had run its course through the Canadian justice system. The Gitksan and Wet'suwet'en people geared up for another round of direct action on the land.

In an effort to minimize our struggles on the land, the companies whose corporate interests were seen to be in jeopardy and supported by the provincial government, initiated a common line of attack and dismissal of our actions. The protests and resistance of the Gitksan and Wet'suwet'en, they claimed, should be dismissed as newly-invented, publicity-seeking stunts to bring attention to *Delgamuukw vs. The Queen*. We knew it to be otherwise. Ask any person from a given House, and you will be told of one or more of their ancestors who took part in some form of resistance against the encroachment and impositions of the European.

This chapter of our history tells how we took direct action to protect ourselves, our land and our resources from the time of earliest European contact. These specific actions are by no means the only ones we took to protect our interests, but they do offer an insight into the consistency and commitment of our people in addressing the injustices of the colonial powers.

In the early 1800s, when the first European fur-traders arrived, they were unable to infiltrate our trading and economic systems in the Northwest because they had nothing we needed or wanted that we couldn't get from our tribal neighbors. We resisted then.

When the government surveyors came to measure our reserves, we confiscated their equipment, pulled stakes from the ground and escorted them firmly out of the territory. We resisted then.

When miners negligently caused the burning of houses and poles in the village of Gitsegukla, the Chiefs and their House members protested their actions and the inactivity of the colonial government by blockading the Skeena River. When the influx of miners grew and began to occupy parts of the territories without the consent of the Houses, our people protested.

The list grew longer as the world progressed into the 20th century. Our families hid the children from missionaries and Indian agents so they would not be shipped out to residential schools; our Feasts went underground with the passing of the anti-Potlatch laws; we held secret meetings to discuss the "land question" when it became illegal for "Indians" to meet to discuss land issues; we hid family regalia to escape the burning barrels of the missionaries; Chiefs were arrested for halting road-building; women stoned federal Fisheries Officers sent to blow up a rock in Hagwilget canyon; young children suffered daily strappings from missionaries of Indian day schools for continuing to speak their own language in school.

As the forces, restrictions and impositions grew and spread throughout the territories, the Chiefs and House members necessarily grew more creative and aggressive in their resistance. We rebuilt and re-occupied fish camps to resist the restrictions of the Department of Fisheries. In Gitwangax, at the Anki Iss fish camp, women and children pelted well-armed officers with marshmallows as they attempted to break through the human blockade to seize a net from the river. In Kispiox, at the Gwin Oop fish camp, the people stepped aside and watched as a fishery officer snatched an empty cork-line from the river then, red-faced, beat a hasty retreat. Chiefs and House members, whose nets had been seized because of their refusal to accept permits for fishing at their traditional fishing sites, marched into the fisheries office and took back their nets.

On the territories, we blockaded logging roads and set up camps in an attempt to slow down the clearcutting of timber, to ensure proper standards were maintained to protect the environment from erosion and chemicals, and to ensure that standards of road building were being adhered to. We blockaded railroads to bring a halt to the hazardous spraying of chemicals along the rail lines that were polluting the spawning grounds, berry grounds and grazing areas. A well-coordinated blockade at the Babine River was successful in keeping Westar (the logging company) and the Province from opening up the untouched northern territories of the Gitksan to logging.

As much as the governments and big business want the general public to believe that our vocal and active protests are a newly created activity, the reality is that, historically and to the present, we have been active in our resistance to be silenced and to be made invisible.

The reality is that we have never given up, never sold, nor lost in battle, our ownership and jurisdiction to our territories. Our right and title is inherited from our ancestors who lived and governed themselves for thousands of years before Christopher Columbus emerged from his mother's womb and drew his first breath.

The reality is that *Delgamuukw vs. The Queen* is only one of many simultaneous activities undertaken by the Gitksan and Wet'suwet'en to protest the abuses of the Agents of the Crown since their first encroachment on to our territories.

The reality is that our societies, our cultures and our systems are alive and well. They have sustained us through more than 150 of the darkest, most destructive years that our people have ever known and will continue to sustain us as we reassume our right to be self-sufficient, self-reliant and self-governing.

What must be, will be.

—**Skanu'u (Ardythe Wilson)**

Marshmallow Wars—by Art Wilson
In the summer of 1986, a SWAT team of Ministry of Fisheries officers raided fishing nets in Kitsegukla. Figuring that the next likely raid would be at Kitwanga, people quickly built a smokehouse there. When the officers arrived, they were pelted with marshmallows.

**Hawaaw (Alice Wilson) at the Kispiox blockade against logging
on Gitksan Wet'suwet'en territories, 1988.**

Photo: Steve Bosch, *Vancouver Sun.*

Decadent—by Luu Goomix

"For us, the ownership of territory is a
marriage of the Chief and the land. Each
Chief has an ancestor who encountered
and acknowledged the life of the land.
From such encounters come power. The
land, the plants, the animals and the
people all have spirit—they must all be
shown respect. That is the basis
of our law."
—Delgam Uukw, May 11, 1987

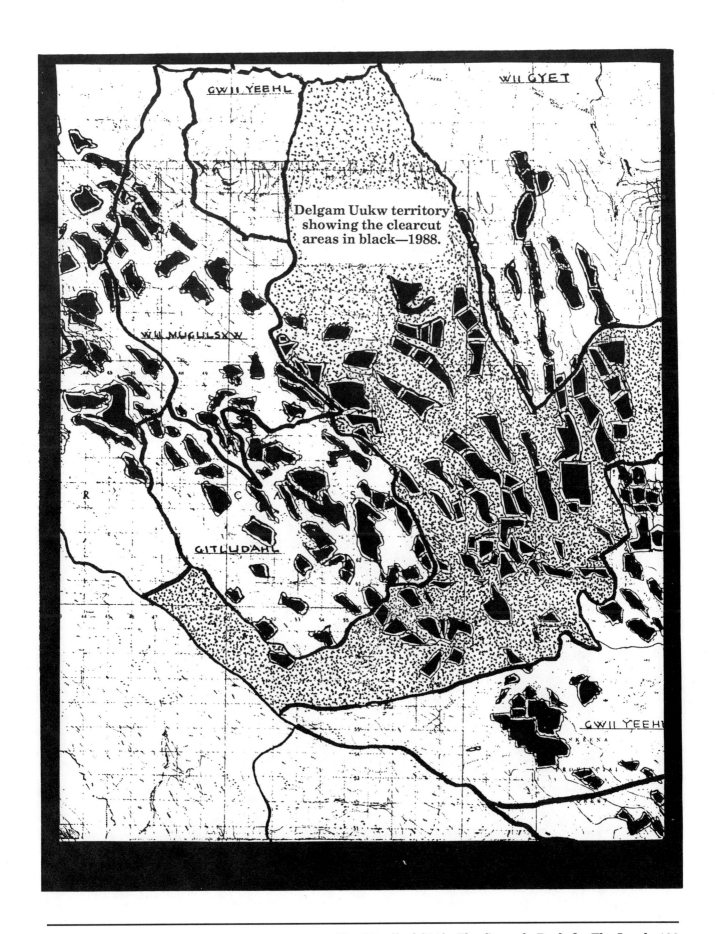

Delgam Uukw territory showing the clearcut areas in black—1988.

Seizure on Luulak's Land—Art Wilson

THE OFFICE OF GITKSAN
AND WETSUWETEN CHIEFS

                NOTICE OF SEIZURE

GITKSAN AND WETSUWETEN
TERRITORIES

THIS EQUIPMENT IS SEIZED
        AND CANNOT BE REMOVED.
        AS OF THIS DATE IT IS THE
        PROPERTY OF LUULAK.

BY ORDER OF: CHIEF LUULAK *Sandy Williams*
        DATE: *Feb 12 1988*

"Luulak confiscates illegal machinery on our territory,"—Bev Anderson.

Photo: Bev Anderson.

Opening of the House of Purification, Gitwangak,
August 1988.

The House of
Purification is a place
where people use
traditional and European
techniques to deal with
cases of alcohol and
drug abuse.

For more details about
the seizure on Luulak's
land (left), see page 212.

Witnesses to the opening of the House of Purification
in Gitwangak, Wilp si"satxw.

Photo: Bev Anderson.

Gitanmaax Radio has been operating a 2 watt FM system, without permits from the Canadian Radio & Tele-communications Commission, for over two years. It presently features young and old Gitksan Disk Jockeys, music programs, announcements and local news, and there are plans to encourage the Gitksan language and augment local forums and feasts.

Gitsegukla pole-moving, October 6, 1990.

Wii Mugulsx̲w (Art Wilson) on his (wounded) House territory, Kispiox.

Photo: Steve Bosch.

Summer 1990: First Nations throughout British Columbia mounted road blockades in support of the Mohawks at Oka, Québec, and to press for resolution of their outstanding claims to sovereignty.

An irate American ex-patriate living in the area of the reserve pulled his rifle on a young Wet'suwet'en man and screamed, "Get out of the way, you red bastard, or I'll shoot you." He was chased away. No charges were laid.

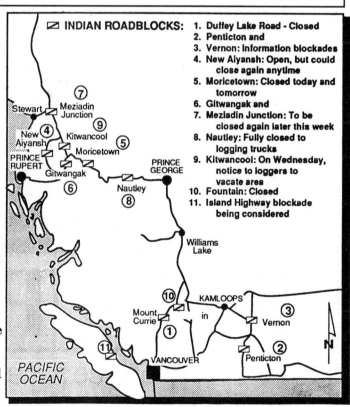

⊘ **INDIAN ROADBLOCKS:**
1. **Duffey Lake Road - Closed**
2. **Penticton and**
3. **Vernon: Information blockades**
4. **New Aiyansh: Open, but could close again anytime**
5. **Moricetown: Closed today and tomorrow**
6. **Gitwangak and**
7. **Meziadin Junction: To be closed again later this week**
8. **Nautley: Fully closed to logging trucks**
9. **Kitwancool: On Wednesday, notice to loggers to vacate area**
10. **Fountain: Closed**
11. **Island Highway blockade being considered**

Map courtesy: *The Vancouver Sun.*

Simgiigyet, Simgiigyet, where have you been?
We've been to Babine, to visit Sam Greene.

Simgiigyet, Simgiigyet, what did you see?
Dave Parker and Westar cutting a tree.

Simgiigyet, Simgiigyet, what did you do?
We set up a camp, and chased out those two!

Simgiigyet, Simgiigyet, what happened then?
They cried for an injunction to start cutting again.

Simgiigyet, Simgiigyet, what will you do?
Stay at Sam Greene and see this thing through.

Simgiigyet, Simgiigyet, can I give you a hand?
Certainly, friend, come help save our land.

—*Skanu'u (Ardythe Wilson)*

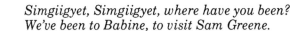

THE ROAD BUILDING WAS STOPPED AT THE FENCE THAT THE CHIEFS BUILT.

SURVEYORS TAPE OF ALL COLORS, TIED TOGETHER, COMPLETED THE SIGN FOR THE TURN-OFF TO THE CAMP.

Alfred Joesph, Robert Jackson, Josh Maclean, and 'Sam' the stray cat. Art Wilson carved the weeping face in a live tree.

Precedence—by Art Wilson

In 1988, Gitksan people decided at a meeting in Kispiox to allow no more logging and road construction by timber company, Westar, on traditional territory; Sam Greene Creek would be the limit. Camp was set up, and Westar applied for an injunction when surveyors were asked to leave. A precedent was set when the Chiefs won the case, arguing that the question of their aborignal ownership should be settled before logging be allowed to continue.

Eagle Clan Move

It is very important for us to demonstrate our ownership and jurisdiction of our territories through different political activities. We have demonstrated our authority in protecting our land, which is what we have done in the latter part of the '80s.

The '90s will be very different for us. We must take our direct action policies one step further. This we can do by intitating plans to use, and benefit economically from, our lands.

The Eagle Clan has already begun to do this very thing. A resource inventory is being taken on their land, which is an important step towards integrated resource management planning.

They are taking stock of the different species of trees in their forests, and what types of animals are using their lands. Areas where medicinal herbs grow are being mapped. Moose calving-areas are being protected to ensure their survival.

Each one of our House territories is following similar plans for integrated resource management.

We must plan a strategy of land use that will not harm our ecosystem. We cannot destroy our salmon resources as we log. We cannot develop mining activities at the expense of the wildlife. We cannot develop logging at the expense of the animals that also use the forests. This will be part of our main agenda for the '90s.

We cannot wait for the land claims court case to conclude. We cannot wait for judgment. The land is ours and we must act accordingly. It is interesting to note that while the land issue has been in court, the governments have been conducting business-as-usual. So it is important for us to do so also.

I urge all the people to defend their territories. I would advocate direct action. I would urge all the people to look to ways in which they could benefit from their land under their own authority.

—**Wii Seeks (Ralph Michell)**, *Gitksan Wet'suwet'en Bulletin*, 1990

The Corporation of the Village of Hazelton

P.O. BOX 40,   HAZELTON, B.C. V0J 1Y0   PH. 842-5991

On behalf of the residents of the Village of Hazelton I would like to wish the Gitksan and Wet'suwet'en Hereditary Chiefs and Headlines Theatre every success in their presentation of: **NO` XYA` (Our Footprints)**. This ambitious project is a clear indication of the Chiefs' commitment to explain issues surrounding Aboriginal rights and title to their neighbours and all Canadians.

It has long been a policy of this Municipality to support the Chiefs in their quest for fair adjudication of their Aboriginal land claim. We believe that the claim is just, and if successful would signal an exciting era of prosperity for the Upper Skeena region. Only when residents of rural regions such as ours control the powers of government and development will our full potential be realized.

Signed, Alice Maitland, Mayor, Hazelton BC, Canada (1987)

from NO`XYA` Canadian Tour program, 88

Run for Justice

Hazelton to Vancouver
Sept 29 to Oct 28
1988

This project was initiated and organized by Project North—Victoria.

Joshua McLean in his freshly-made bough hut shelter at Pine Nut blockade, Salmon River Road.

Below right: Jenny Naziel, Wet'suwet'en elder, making birch bark basket.

Left: Eric and Chester Macpherson at Kisgegaas Canyon fish camp.

Below: 'Waigyet harvesting Devil's Club.

Gitluudahl (Peter Muldoe) harvesting spruce noodles.

Photos: by Maht (Bev Anderson).

It may tick some people off but I support the slow down in the lumber industry, the Gitksan are asking for. We could stand with a real slow down.

2-mile/88

**Sam Greene blockade: Antgulilibix (Mary Johnson)
and Ron George.**

**Maas Gaak (Don Ryan) at
Marshmallow trial.**

**Above: Art Wilson completes a sign for the
Gwin'Oop fish camp.**

**Left: Studying maps of the territory at Pine
Nut blockade.**

Kathy Holland with freshly-harvested
Yellow Water Lily.

David Greene holds the finished product: dried
Yellow Water Lily.

All photographs by 'Maat (Bev Anderson).

'Waigyet prepares
salmon for
smoking in her
smokehouse.

Geel (Walter Harris) seen standing next to a 200-year old territorial marker on his House territory, 1989.

Photo: Dan Muldoe.